Wise Up!

Wise Up!

— Four Biblical Virtues for Navigating Life

ALYCE M. McKENZIE

CASCADE *Books* · Eugene, Oregon

WISE UP!
Four Biblical Virtues for Navigating Life

Cascade Books
An Imprint of Wipf and Stock Publishers
199 W. 8th Ave., Suite 3
Eugene, OR 97401

www.wipfandstock.com

PAPERBACK ISBN: 978-1-4982-0703-4
HARDCOVER ISBN: 978-1-4982-0705-8
EBOOK ISBN: 978-1-4982-0704-1

Cataloguing-in-Publication data:

Names: McKenzie, Alyce M.

Title: Wise up! : four biblical virtues for navigating life / Alyce M. McKenzie.

Description: Eugene, OR: Cascade Books, 2018 | Includes bibliographical references.

Identifiers: ISBN 978-1-4982-0703-4 (paperback) | ISBN 978-1-4982-0705-8 (hardcover) | ISBN 978-1-4982-0704-1 (ebook)

Subjects: LCSH: Wisdom—Biblical teaching. | Wisdom—Religious aspects—Christianity.

Classification: BV4211.3 M36 2018 (paperback) | BV4211 (ebook)

Manufactured in the U.S.A.   05/18/18

To Murry, my wise and wonderful husband,

with thanks for your love and support.

Contents

Preface

THIS BOOK IS FOR people who have bought the wrong things and would like to return them but don't quite know how. Its theme is quite straightforward. We have bought four things that we need to return. Reason for return: they don't fit our souls, they don't enhance our lives, they don't challenge injustices in our world, and they are destructive of our personal and communal peace and happiness. These four items are self-sufficiency, self-absorption, self-indulgence, and self-protection. We need to return them and exchange them for faith, compassion, self-discipline, and outspoken courage. These qualities are the four virtues of the wise life according to the Old and New Testaments. They are the Bible's four wisdom virtues. When we live by them, day by day, we live in a way that is pleasing to God. We live in a way that is shaped by God's wisdom. The specific scenarios of our daily lives are shaped by God's presence and God's guidance.

If you have scrolled down the screen of your Kindle store, or strolled down the aisles of a bookstore recently, the smell of coffee from the café stimulating your olfactory nerve, you have encountered an array of self-help books that offer "wisdom," advice about getting rid of negative patterns and adopting positive ones for health, wealth, and happiness. If you're standing before the shelf in a bookstore, you pick up, first one, then another brightly colored volume, turning it over to come face-to-face with the author, arms folded across their chest in that confident pose favored by book jacket photographers: chin lifted, big smile, bleached teeth. The author could be a politician, a fitness guru, a financial planner, a celebrity talk show host, an A-list movie star, a B-list teen idol, a C-list actor whose face we always recognize but whose name always slips our mind, or a D-list celebrity who pays the rent by appearing on game shows or joining the cast of one reality show after another. The author of a book on wisdom for living could be anybody, really. And why not? Why shouldn't anybody who wants to write a book about wisdom? Wisdom, after all, is not an exclusively religious phenomenon. It is the art of navigating the ins and outs of daily life. It is practical strategies for success in specific pursuits. There is a wisdom to cooking, getting physically fit, planning for a secure financial future, networking, and making a career comeback. There is a wisdom for just about every worthwhile pursuit in life. If a book offers practical advice on how to succeed in something, if it helps the reader shape a healthier, happier future, that's not a bad thing.

Self–help wisdom books, in their own ways, address an old question that Socrates posed centuries ago: "What is the best way to live?" Every culture and religion has its answers to that question, its own body of wisdom for living. Every person has his or her answer to the question: What is the best way to live? Every person has his or her own body of wisdom—lessons learned from life, goals worth pursuing. You need to read this book for the same reason I needed to write it: I experienced inner restlessness that I suspected was the result of my inner wisdom compass pointing me toward faith and my outer life being governed by fear. I was experiencing the painful condition called cognitive dissonance: defining wisdom in one way and living in another. I needed guidance in the art of exchanging fear for faith.

There is no better source of guidance on the exchange of fear for faith than the Bible. It depicts human fears with ragged honesty. It depicts the love and power of God continually and repeatedly to overcome them in our lives. It offers a pattern of exchange of fear for faith. You and I have both been practicing "the fear exchange" for years. I use the word *practicing* because I'm not sure we ever perfect the process, or reach a point at which we have no fears and it's all faith. The "fear exchange" is a work in progress for all of us.

Every now and then I encounter a person who says "I don't really have any fears." I resist the urge to applaud or bow and pay them homage. They would think I was mocking them. There's a chance that I would be. Because they often say it with just a hint of superiority for the rest of the poor human race that does have fears. That makes me wonder, "Have they really attained such an exalted spiritual state that they live in a constant, blissful condition of serenity and faith?" or "Are they just out of touch with reality?" I was talking with a colleague recently about my project to write a book on the relationship of faith and fear in everyday life. My colleague is a spiritual director and biblical scholar. His comment was, "To be completely without fear is to be psychotic. Like the main character in the movie *The Hurt Locker*. He dismantles bombs with no protective gear and no fear. To be utterly without fear is to be out of touch with reality."

I don't mean to imply that if you as a reader have no fears, you're psychotic. But I am saying that this book may not be relevant for you. This book is a book for people who, at least occasionally, experience anxiety. This is a book for people whose insides sometimes roil with anxiety. *Roil* is such a colorful and underused word. It means to "render muddy by stirring up the sediment." When I hear the word *roil*, I picture the Loch Ness monster swimming around the Loch swinging its monster tail. I imagine it has a pointy spike on the end. I've spent some time squinting at the photos, but they are too blurry to tell. Anyway, it's swinging it back and forth, stirring up the sediment.

Roiling with anxiety often happens at 3:27 AM, a time when many people wake up because of the glass of water they drank before bed and can't fall back asleep because of anxious thoughts. I have a friend who says when she wakes up at 3:27 AM, it's because God wants her to get up and pray. That's admirable, but most of us get up to go to the bathroom and lie back down to feel anxious.

This is a book for 3:27 AM, but it is not a self-help book that teaches you how to exchange fear for faith in yourself so that you can achieve greater health, wealth, and self-fulfillment. This is not a self-help book at all. It's a "God-help-us" book. It understands something self-help books often don't. That God, not our own ambitions or agendas, is the One whom we ought to allow to set our goals for this lifetime. That God, not our own willpower or resolve, is the One who empowers us to live joyful, peaceful, justice-seeking lives no matter what twists and turns our journey may take.

A person becomes wise, day by day, moment by moment, by responding to God's invitation to a life guided by God's wisdom, onto a path paved with wise choices. Wisdom is the only path to joy, a joy that does not depend on fortunate outward circumstances. Wisdom is the only path to peace, a peace that is sturdy enough to keep its sea legs when our life is buffeted by storms. When people disappoint us or we disappoint ourselves, sorrow and turmoil are not the only companions we have to choose from. When luck eludes us and health fails us, when an unwanted obligation is placed on our plate, joy and peace don't have to slink out the back exit. When we experience or observe injustice in our personal and communal lives, despair is not the only response open to us.

I'm not being pessimistic with such a litany, just realistic. Such times will come to our lives, if they haven't already. This book means to help us prepare for them by teaching us to come to the customer service counter and exchange self-sufficiency, self-absorption, self-indulgence, and self-protection for Scripture's far better gifts, the Bible's four wisdom virtues: faith in God, compassion for others, disciplined habits, and the courage to speak out and act out our convictions.

I feel qualified to write a book on wisdom for several reasons. The chief one is that living by the four virtues of the wise life comes down to a daily exchange of fear for faith. And I know a lot about fear. I've struggled with various fears for years. I also know enough about faith to know that it is vastly preferable to fear. I can't be the only person on the planet to struggle with fear. During the 1980s and '90s I served several churches in central and eastern Pennsylvania. I spent many hours counseling people about their fears and how their faith in God could address them. I spent even more hours turning my own fears over to God, taking them back again, and handing them over again, a seemingly endless process of purchase and return and repurchase and re-return. I found that the push and pull between fear and faith was a popular topic. It came up in conversations in hospital rooms, on the sidelines at soccer, baseball, and football games, at restaurants, in homeless shelters, you name it. I found that, while fear has many variations, it is a theme that spans generations, classes, gender orientations, and ethnicities.

When I was invited by Perkins School of Theology in 2000 to join their faculty as a professor of preaching, I hesitated. As a professor I would miss talking with people about their fears and their faith. So I thought. Until about a week into my new gig when I sat in my office with a young ministerial student as he shared his fears about whether his calling was real or imagined, whether he was adequate for the task, and how he would juggle the responsibilities of family, work, and church. That experience caused what had been a hunch to crystallize into a certainty: my own struggles with exchanging fear for faith could be a resource for helping others practice the same process.

I'm not an A, B, C, or even D-list celebrity, and I have never been on a reality show. I have spent the past twenty-five years studying the portions of the Bible known as "the wisdom literature," that deal in practical and specific terms with the question "What is the best way to live?" It has become clear to me that it is by allowing God's wisdom to guide our daily choices. When we do that, our life becomes a daily process of exchanging self-absorbed attitudes and actions for faith, compassion, self-discipline, and outspoken courage. This daily process is, at the same time, both a gift from God and a human response to that gift. It is what the Bible calls wisdom.

Introduction

ONE OF MY LEAST favorite tasks in life is returning things. The advent of online shopping has made the process much easier, though you still have to deal with printing out mailing labels, taping up the box, and driving to the UPS Store or post office. Sometimes I still like to buy things in actual stores. This gives me the opportunity to return things the old school way—in person. You know how that ordeal goes. You have to find the original packaging or bag and put the item back in it. You have to drive around for at least three weeks with the item in the back seat of your car or stare at it as it sits on the corner of the kitchen counter waiting for that perfect time to go by the store where you bought it. You have to get in line at the customer service counter, wondering why the people in line in front of you in line didn't have enough sense to pick out the right item the first time around.

When the clerk finally slides the small white card across the counter toward you, you have to confess "reason for return" in the space provided. The card offers a limited menu of reasons: wrong size, wrong color, defective. There is an "other" category, but they never give you enough room to give an honest answer. "Couldn't really afford it, but bought it on impulse because I was feeling bad about myself." "I knew they were a half size too small when I bought them, but I've always wished I had smaller feet." "My brother-in-law just bought one."

After baring your soul on paper, it's finally your turn to present your item for return, watching as the clerk scrutinizes its base, sides, and interior recesses to see if you've worn it, cooked with it, sawed down a tree with it, or done anything else with it that would render it *unreturnable*.

And then comes the crucial question that could make or break the whole transaction: "Do you have your receipt?" If the answer is no, the clerk shakes his/her head with mingled pity and contempt and informs you, "Then we'll have to do a store credit." If the answer is yes, here comes the part that almost makes all of what has gone before worthwhile. The clerk takes the unwanted item from you and either removes the charge from your credit card or, be still my heart, opens the register and hands you cash. And as you turn to walk out into a sunlit world, you feel lighter, freer, relieved of a burden . . . until the next time you buy something that doesn't fit, that you can't afford, or that you don't really need, and have to go through the whole grueling procedure all over again.

The moral of the story is "Stop buying things that don't enhance your life." At the very least, if you are going to keep buying things you are going to want to return, save your receipt. The theme of this book is quite straightforward. We have bought four things that we need to return. Reason for return: they don't fit our souls; they don't enhance our lives; they don't challenge injustices in our world; and they are destructive of our personal and communal peace and happiness. These four items are self-sufficiency, self-absorption, self-indulgence, and self-protection. We need to return them and exchange them for faith, compassion, self-discipline, and courage. These qualities are the four virtues of the wise life according to the Bible's wisdom literature, those portions of the Old and New Testaments that focus on navigating the ins and outs of daily life. They are the Bible's four wisdom virtues. I have labeled them the fear of the Lord, the listening heart, the cool spirit, and the subversive voice. When we live by these virtues, day by day, we live in a way that is pleasing to God. We spend our lives in a daily exchange of fear for faith, as, more and more, we allow our lives to be shaped by God's wisdom. The specific scenarios of our daily lives reflect the influence of God's presence and God's guidance.

The "wisdom literature" of the Bible refers to those portions that focus on practical strategies for navigating the twists and turns of daily living. Specifically, the term *wisdom literature* refers to three biblical books sandwiched between the end of the Israelites' salvation history and the beginning of the Prophets: Proverbs, Ecclesiastes, and Job. The words for wisdom (*hokmah* in Hebrew and *sophia* in Greek) show up in these books more than anywhere else in the Bible. These writings focus on observing patterns in daily life and, from those observations, offering guidelines for making practical, daily decisions. They view wisdom partly as a product of human effort (Proverbs 4:5–7) and partly as a gift from God (Proverb 2:6).

"Get wisdom; get insight: do not forget, nor turn away from the words of my mouth.

Do not forsake her, and she will keep you; love her, and she will guard you.

The beginning of wisdom is this: Get wisdom, and whatever else you get, get insight.

Prize her highly, and she will exalt you (Prov 4:5–7).

"For the Lord gives wisdom; from his mouth come knowledge and understanding" (Prov 2:6).

These three books aren't the only ones that focus on wisdom. So do the Song of Songs, Psalms 1, 32, 35, 37, 49, 112, and 128,[1] and the teachings of Jesus in the Synoptic Gospels. Jesus himself was a wisdom teacher. He used parables and proverbial sayings, the teaching genres of Israel's sages, to portray what the kingdom of God is like.

All of this begs the question "What exactly do we mean by the term *wisdom*?"

Wisdom is the answer to Socrates's question "How should one live?" It is an essential question of philosophy and world religions over the centuries.

A purely secular answer to this wisdom question is: "I should live my daily life so that I realize my potential and achieve my goals." That is not a bad answer, but there is a better one. It's the answer of biblical wisdom. "I should live in such a way that I am attentive to God's guidance and cooperate with it so that I contribute to God's good purposes on earth."

That's a noble goal, but I am easily distracted. Right now, for example, I'm trying to focus on writing this chapter but am fighting the temptation to check my email, tweet about the fact that I'm writing, or post some pictures from my weekend trip to Austin, Texas on Facebook. I find it difficult to submit to consistent disciplines. I need a personal trainer if I'm going to make acquiring wisdom from God my life's goal and inch toward it day by day. I need someone to encourage me, a daily plan, and a clearly spelled out end-game goal. That's why I was relieved to discover from my study of the Bible's wisdom literature that it offers all three of these things. Wisdom has three aspects in Scripture: It's proverbs to live by. It's a person to guide us in living by them. It is also a path paved under our feet when we live by those proverbial teachings.

Most people, when they think of wisdom in the Old Testament, think of the book of Proverbs, a collection of brief proverbial sayings. Wisdom in the Old Testament is also portrayed as the Person whose teachings we are to follow. In the book of Proverbs God's wisdom is personified as a wise woman, often called Woman Wisdom by scholars. In the New Testament, in the prologue to the Gospel of John, we encounter Jesus as the Word and Wisdom of God, the one whose teachings we are to allow to guide our lives.

Not only is wisdom a body of proverbs and a person in Scripture, but wisdom is also a path to walk along, a path paved by those teachings and guided by that Person. Woman Wisdom in Proverbs encourages the young to "walk in the way of the good," (2:20) rather than the "way (that) leads

---

1. Murphy, *The Tree of Life*, 103.

down to death" (2:18). Jesus assures his followers that he is "the Way, the truth, and the life" (John 14:6). Woman Wisdom's proverbs in the Old Testament and Jesus' teachings in the New Testament guide us in "the way" of life that results in our daily exchange of fear for faith. This gradual exchange is the lifelong task of the one who would live by wisdom.

Biblical wisdom is a jewel with three facets: proverbs, person, and path. This is true both with regard to wisdom in the Old Testament and to Jesus as "the Way" in the New Testament. God's light shines through all three facets to guide us as we learn to exchange the fear of any and everything for faith (the fear of the Lord) and we grow in compassion (listening heart), self-control (cool spirit), and courage (subversive voice).

Chapter 1, "Person, Path, and Proverbs," offers an overview of biblical wisdom as a body of wisdom teachings (proverbs), that invites us into relationship with a wise God (person) and that invites us to walk a way paved with faith, compassion, discipline, and courage (path). The next four chapters are devoted to introducing each of the four wisdom virtues in turn, encouraging us to exchange our poorly chosen purchases for these far better alternatives. Chapter 2, The Lead Sled Dog Virtue, presents the wisdom virtue the Bible calls "the fear of the Lord," which Proverbs repeatedly tells us is the beginning of wisdom (Prov 1:7, 9:10, 15:33, 31:30). The fear of the Lord is not the fear that God is about to zap us. It is, rather, the radical respect and awe we are to show to God and none other. The fear of the Lord is the wisdom literature's name for faith. It consists of equal parts trembling before God, trusting God, and taking directions from God. It is the lead sled dog of the four wisdom virtues. The other three follow its lead. If it is not in its place up front, they can't get into the harness. Chapter 2, Part One describes this virtue and Chapter 2, Part Two, entitled "Tremble, Trust, and Take Directions," coaches us on how to exchange fear for this wise and sturdy faith.

Chapter 3, Part One, called "The Listening Heart," describes the second wisdom virtue. The listening heart is an attitude of alertness to the needs and feelings of others beyond ourselves and to what God is calling us to discover and do in response to them. I derive the term "listening heart" from Solomon's prayer for wisdom in 1 Kings 3:9. God tells Solomon he can ask for anything. Solomon asks for a *lev shomea*, which can be translated a "discerning mind" or a "listening heart." Part Two of Chapter 3, entitled "Listen Up!" encourages us to come to the customer service desk and exchange self-absorption for a "listening heart."

Chapter 4, Part One, "The Cool Spirit," introduces the third wisdom virtue: what the Bible calls "a cool spirit." This is the impulse control that comes when we place our appetites and desires in the service of God for the good of the community. If that sounds like a boring, skippable chapter, think again. Consider the path of the person who lacks self-control. Think of what happens when a person has faith, compassion, and courage, but lacks control over themselves in a significant area of life. Examples abound when we look to history, literature, and current events, and perhaps, when we look in the mirror. I derive the term "cool spirit" from Proverbs 17:27 "One who spares words is knowledgeable; one who is cool in spirit has understanding." In Part Two of Chapter 4, "Cool Off!" we explore what it means to exchange a lack of discipline and self-control for "a cool spirit."

Chapter 5, Part One, "The Subversive Voice," is inspired by the strategies of Qohelet (Ecclesiastes), Job, and Jesus. Their teachings undercut the conventional wisdom of their day wherever it legitimized injustice and exclusion. No, says Job, suffering doesn't mean a person is sinful. No, says the author of Ecclesiastes, living by the principles of order and moderation does not guarantee a life of prosperity and renown. Jesus' wisdom teachings in the Gospels of Matthew, Mark, and Luke continue this undercutting of tradition. Ritual practices that have become externalized and meaningless do not please God. Holiness defined as exclusion of those who most need the forgiveness and community God offers is not God's definition of holiness. In the tradition of subversive sages, Qohelet (Ecclesiastes), and Job, Jesus undermined conventional wisdom through his short sayings and parables. And he paid the price. Chapter 5, Part Two, entitled "Speak Out!" is our coming to the customer service desk and exchanging self-protection for the courage to speak and act out our convictions, despite the cost.

I don't know where you were when you bought the wrong things. I do know that the divine customer service desk is closer than we think. I don't know how long ago you bought the wrong things. I do know that the divine exchange policy is more generous than any earthly store I've ever heard of. It is never too late to return unwanted items and exchange them for something far better.

So let's find the original packaging and maybe even our receipt and approach God with humble reverence. It's high time to begin the process of exchanging fear for faith.

Chapter 1

An Overview of Biblical Wisdom
"Wisdom as Proverbs, Person, and Path"

THE DINING ROOM TABLE was piled with folders and papers that Tuesday afternoon. A coffeepot sat in the middle with two cups steaming. One was for me. The other was for my friend and colleague Elaine Heath, now Dean of Duke Divinity School, who at that time taught evangelism at Perkins School of Theology. We sat at her table, afternoon sunshine filtering through the blinds, iPads in front of us, planning a course we were teaching together.

Darlene and Helen were back in Helen's sitting room. Helen is Elaine's elderly mother who, at that time, lived with Elaine and her husband Randy. Darlene was the health care worker who came every Tuesday to check on Helen.

"Dr. Heath," Darlene appeared at the door of the dining room, "you need to come talk to your mother. She has been sneaking down the hall to the bathroom without her walker and without her oxygen tank. When I scolded her about it, she said, "Darlene, I'm ninety-one years old. I've graduated from my walker and my oxygen tank!"

"That sounds like Mom!" said Elaine as she got up to go down the hall to adjust her mother's attitude.

We all know that, at age ninety-one, there is only one way to graduate from a need for oxygen and a walker. Just as at any age there is only one way to graduate from a need for wisdom. And I suspect that even death does not bring an end to our need to seek wisdom.

1

A Biblical Weather Map

I enjoy watching meteorologists report on the weather. They stand in front of their weather maps and reflect the weather that's coming in their faces, voices, and gestures. When reporting that the week will be in the mid-seventies with sunshine and light breezes, their faces beam with serenity. When reporting rain and wintry mixes their brows furrow slightly as they recommend umbrellas and defensive driving. When aggressive storms threaten or tornados tumble toward town, their eyes glitter and their faces flush in anticipation of danger. We should be grateful to them, both for their mundane advice about umbrellas, and for their potentially life-saving warnings about the approach of dangerous weather events. Sometimes paying attention to a weather report can mean the difference between life and death.

There is a reason I'm talking about meteorologists and weather maps. I'd like you to picture the Bible as a weather map and to imagine yourself as the meteorologist. Your job is to point people toward concentrations of wisdom in Scripture, the wisdom literature, in the Bible. Here is your teleprompter script: "We have heavy concentrations of concern with wisdom (*hokmah*) in three books sandwiched right here between the end of the salvation history and the beginning of Prophets: Proverbs, Job, and Ecclesiastes.

You also can see here on the map, concentrations of wisdom in several psalms, and, if you'll look over here in the New Testament, you see its occurrence in the short sayings and parables of Jesus in Matthew, Mark, and Luke. In this same area of the Bible, we can detect the presence of wisdom in the book of James, the opening to 1 Corinthians, and the prologue to the Gospel of John."

People Called Wise in the Hebrew Scriptures

All these texts on the biblical map have in common a concern with *hokmah* (wisdom) in Hebrew, *sophia* in Greek. Wisdom is a golden thread throughout the Hebrew Scriptures. You never know when it will gleam through the tapestry. Sometimes, in the Hebrew Bible, a particular person is described as being wise. Examples include Joseph (Gen 41:33), the wise woman of Tekoa (2 Sam 14:2), and the young King Solomon (1 Kgs 3:12). They are called wise in the sense that they have innate intelligence or shrewdness, administrative skill, interpersonal savvy, or good judgment.

Joseph, interpreting Pharaoh's dream about the fat and skinny cows and the fat and skinny ears of grain, gives this shrewd advice: "Let Pharaoh select a man who is discerning and wise, and set him over the land of Egypt."

And then, when Pharaoh selects him (Gen 41:39), I imagine he responds "Moi? Well, if you insist." When God tells young King Solomon he can have whatever he wants (1 Kgs 3:5), Solomon is smart enough to ask for "a wise and discerning mind," able to discern between good and evil for the governance of his people (1 Kgs 3:9). God responds, in effect, "Good answer!" and grants Solomon's request, plus a whole lot more. Just as his father David was credited with the authorship of the Psalms, so, over time, Solomon gets the credit for coining and collecting the book of Proverbs. While Solomon's wise advisors did coin many proverbs, the book of Proverbs is actually a collation of centuries of oral and written sayings put into their current form during the postexilic period, long after the reign of Solomon.

Another portrait in the biblical wisdom pantheon is that of the wise woman of Tekoa. She plays King David like a lyre, manipulating him into not destroying his son Absalom and all those who threw in their lot with him. Her feat is all the more impressive because we are told nothing about her physical appearance, and we are well aware of David's susceptibility to female beauty.

Wisdom as Proverbs, Person, and Path:

Wisdom as a Collection of Proverbs for Young and Old

I was talking to a colleague of mine recently. I told him I was going to be making a talk on the book of Proverbs and its relevance for our contemporary times. "Good luck," he said. "I think of the book of Proverbs as a bag full of fortune cookies. You just crack 'em open and pile up the little white slips of paper as you read your way through. There's not much to preach on there."

We got Chinese food last week. I'm the only person in the family who actually likes the taste of fortune cookies. So I couldn't resist the two remaining cookies lying on the plate.

I pulled out the little white slips, ate the cookies, then read the fortunes. One said "You will be a great philanthropist in your later years." The second said "You have a heart of gold." If that is all the book of Proverbs offered us, my colleague would be right!

But, as it happens, he couldn't be more wrong. Proverbs consists of thirty-one chapters of wisdom instruction and sayings, which fall into four major collections, at least one of which shows the influence of an Egyptian wisdom collection known as the Instruction of Amenemope, which dates from 1200 BCE (22:17—24:22).[1] They come from multiple settings throughout the centuries of Israel's history—field, court, wisdom school, and hearth. Chapters 1–9, which introduce the figure of Woman Wisdom, probably date from postexilic times (500–300 BCE) and have been added as an introduction to the collection. The rest of the book consists of sayings from earlier times collated during the turmoil of the postexilic period and placed on the lips of Woman Wisdom.

"Dr. McKenzie, will you write a letter of recommendation for me for a scholarship?" The young man making the request was named Brian, a twenty-something student in my Thursday morning preaching class several years ago. It was two weeks into the semester. I knew little about Brian except that he had shown up awake and on time, Starbucks coffee in hand, for two weeks in a row.

I told him, "If you can stop by my office after lunch, we can talk more about it."

So we sat in my office later that day as he filled me in on where he was from, what classes he was taking, and his evolving call to ministry Then I said, "So tell me, Brian, what would you say is your greatest strength?" He grinned and said, "I'm young, and I know everything."

"OK, so what would you say is your greatest weakness?" He grinned the same grin and said, "I'm young and I know everything."

The book of Proverbs was written for the Brians who really believe they know everything."

But even if you're well over twenty-five and this is not your first rodeo, the wisdom of Proverbs holds something for you. At the beginning of the collected sayings we call Proverbs, the sages who collected them state their purpose.

> To teach shrewdness to the simple (*peti*)
> Knowledge and prudence to the young—
> Let the wise also hear and gain in learning,
> And the discerning acquire skill (*tahbulot*) (Prov 1:4–5).

The linguistic background to the word *tahbulot* is "steering." Wisdom is described in Proverbs as the "art of steering" (*tahbulot*). This description of wisdom as a set of steering strategies is based on ancient Egyptian methods of navigating the Nile River, controlling the direction of the boat with a set of ropes. This is the source of our current day expression "learning the

---

1. Murphy, *The Tree of Life*, 23–24.

ropes." Israel joins her Near Eastern neighbors in understanding wisdom as skill in deciphering life.[2]

Some people are adept at discerning patterns of cause and effect in life and in choosing courses of action that lead to productive, peaceful lives. Proverbs would call them wise. They learn invaluable lessons from the specific scenarios of their lives. These lessons include the realization that they always have something to learn, no matter how advanced they are in their journey (1:5), that forgiveness is preferable to grudge-holding (16:9) and that, ultimately it is God's wisdom, not our own, that will prevail (21:30).

These people, as they grow in wisdom, make adjustments to their attitudes and actions. They are not the people who appear as guests on Dr. Phil, for whom the good doctor defines insanity as making the same choices over and over again expecting different results. I don't know if Dr. Phil realizes it, but he's giving a pretty good biblical definition of folly. Proverbs warns against repeatedly choosing courses of action that put self above community. Ironically, they often lead not only to community chaos, but also to self-destruction. Proverbs baldly states the truth: "There is a way that seems right to a person, but its end is the way to death" (Prov 14:12). Dr. Phil's question to his guests is a twenty-first–century version of the sages of Proverbs's implied question: "Howz that goin' for ya?"

Lots of people skip over the book of Proverbs because they see no unifying message in thirty-one chapters of short sayings. They share my colleague's view of the book as a handful of fortune cookies thrown in the bag with their takeout order. They're missing the thread that stitches the sayings together. Several years ago pastor and author Rick Warren published a tremendously popular book *The Purpose Driven Life*. Proverbs could aptly be called *The Purpose Driven Book*. It is driven by the determination of the older and wiser in the community to instruct the young and gullible in patterns of living that make for a harmonious personal and communal life.

Both my parents fulfilled this role as I was growing up. My mother daily quoted "To whom much is given, much is expected." I won't admit how old I was when I discovered, when reading Luke 12, that she is not the one who coined that saying! If I did you would think I didn't read my Bible very carefully until I was in college. While my mother was serving up the "you are privileged, better give back" proverb, my dad was pushing perseverance proverbs. That he would choose this theme makes sense in light of his challenging childhood. The youngest of ten children in Depression-era rural North Carolina, he had to work hard for everything he accomplished in life. Hence his top three sayings: "Your character is not tested when things

2. Bergant, *Israel's Wisdom Literature*, 81–82.

are going well, but in adversity"; "When the going gets tough, the tough get going"; and "Winners never quit and quitters never win." Now that I think about it, this proverbial brainwashing explains a lot of my current approach to life. I'm constantly aware of my privileged status in the world, and I can never give up on anything.

Nowadays I find myself offering proverbial wisdom to students about to graduate and begin serving churches. Recently I've heard myself saying things like, "Take a day off every week." "Get a hobby if you don't already have one." "Begin as you mean to go on." "Be open-minded but have a spine." "Being a people pleaser and a conflict avoider doesn't make for good leadership." "Nothing good ever comes from insecurity." Maybe the best thing about my advice is that it's free! Now if I could only learn to follow it myself!

What proverbial advice were you raised on? What do you offer to other people? We can all probably recall sayings or lessons from our parents. The older and wiser advise the young to live with discipline, moderation, and fair treatment of others. They point out that such lives have order and contribute to the community in a positive way. When it's written down, it's called "advice literature" and it usually appears in times of social turmoil as a means of reinforcing group identity.

A book as orderly as Proverbs had to have come out of a setting of social turmoil. A colleague who is retiring and cleaning out his office gave me a seven-CD "Modern Scholar" course on the history of Ancient Israel from the Patriarchs through the Romans. Since I have a twenty-five–mile commute to work, I've been listening to it for the last week on my way to and from work. Every day as I navigate the traffic on I-75 between my home in Allen, Texas and Dallas, a different foreign army is stomping into Jerusalem, burning the Temple and deporting the king, priests, and leaders. On Monday, it was the Assyrians. Nobody loved to deport people more that the Assyrians, who conquered the northern kingdom of Israel in 722 BCE. On Tuesday it was Nebuchadnezzar. Nebuchadnezzar was a master of cruelty! It was not enough that, in 586 BCE, in conquering the southern kingdom of Judah, he burned the Temple at Jerusalem. No, he had to kill poor Zedekiah's sons right in front of him, then put his eyes out so that was the last thing he saw before he had to walk to Babylon in chains. On Wednesday it was King Cyrus. In 539 BCE King Cyrus of Persia conquered Babylon and allowed the Jewish exiles to return to Jerusalem and rebuild their Temple. The books of Proverbs, Job, and Ecclesiastes all come from this extended postexilic period of turmoil and rebuilding.

They all offer different answers to the wisdom question "What is the best way to live?" Job, a figure who may well represent the whole suffering nation, expresses anger at unjust suffering. Ecclesiastes expresses melancholy resignation with a glimpse of gratitude for the pleasures of the present moment. Both books eventually arrive at faith in God's presence, though they leave certain questions unanswered. Job never answers the question "Why do the innocent suffer?" And Ecclesiastes, given the fact that he believes that both good fortune and bad come from God, never answers the question "How can we trust in such a God?" Proverbs offers practical, positive ways to live to regain group identity and make the best of a less-than-ideal situation. While Job and Ecclesiastes depict a concealing God who occasionally reveals, Proverbs portrays a revealing God who occasionally conceals. In Proverbs, the primary picture of God is as offering wise guidance for the one who diligently seeks the divine presence.

The tradition wants us to picture King Solomon (who died in 931 BCE) sitting down with his papyrus and quill, writing all thirty-one chapters in one fell swoop. My hunch is he was too busy accumulating wealth, building the Temple, and "socializing" with his wives to have been responsibility for such an extensive and impressive a collection. He may be the oral source of some of the sayings, but the book of Proverbs was written down in the postexilic period, long after Solomon, the product of centuries of observation of patterns of cause and effect in the varied situations of daily life. The sayings come from Israel's early days of field and farm, her later years in the king's courts, and her postexilic period, as parents and children gathered around hearth and home.

Proverbs' advice boils down to an answer to this question: "How can I (we) be my (our) own best friend rather than my (our) own worst enemy?" The answer comes in advice both about what not to do and what to do. Don't be immoderate in your habits, idolize wealth, and disrespect the poor. Do exercise restraint in speech and sexual behavior, work hard, and respect the poor.

Wisdom as a Person

The figure of Woman Wisdom, who makes her debut in Proverbs, is a hard worker. She shows up in Chapter 1, standing at the crossroads of daily life, calling those who pass by to choose her path of wisdom and life rather than that of folly and death (1:20f; 8:1f). She is present with God at creation in Chapter 8 (3:19–20; 8:22f). In Chapter 9 she gets her home and table ready to offer a feast of wisdom for the gullible young who are willing to "lay aside immaturity and live and walk in the way of insight." Chapter 31, an ode to a "strong woman," or a "woman of worth" (*eset hayil*) is commonly thought to be the description of the "total woman" of the Ancient Near East. It may be that more than an ideal human woman is being described here. This may be a description of Woman Wisdom and her household management. She invites us to join her household, promising both to care for us and to commission us to share her wisdom with others. Helping create the world, preaching in the town square, making dinner, throwing a house party to which we're invited—that's a long day. But, as jazz singer and songwriter, Peggy Lee sang back in 1963, in the title song of her album "I'm a Woman!," "She's a woman, w–o–m–a–n. I'm gonna say it again."

But what kind of woman?

Some say she is a preexilic goddess. Bernhard Lang argues that she is the goddess Astarte, a holdover from Israel's polytheistic days. He believes that the book of Proverbs, in the monotheistic climate of postexilic Judaism, has demoted her to being an employee of the One God of Israel.[3]

I think it is more likely that she is a postexilic personification, the personalizing of an abstract quality, in this case a characteristic of God: wisdom. Claudia Camp, in *Wisdom and the Feminine in the Book of Proverbs*, theorizes that she is the product of postexilic trauma dating from the early Persian period, the late sixth–fourth centuries BCE. Traditional male figures of authority and their institutions—king and court, priest and temple— were in shambles. Royalty and other powerful leaders had been deported and the Temple burned. But there was still the home and the hearth and the influence of parental teachings, by mothers as well as fathers. It is no coincidence, given this context, that a book arose that emphasized a particular aspect of God's character (wisdom) that was not reliant on cult or court. It is no coincidence that the language of covenant and chosenness gives way in Proverbs to the more universal focus on God the Creator's gift of wisdom and its (her) authority in instructing the young. With social structures in shambles, keeping the young on the straight and narrow, with habits of moderation in their speech and appetites was crucial to the stability of the community. Nor is it a coincidence that this aspect of the divine character (wisdom) was personified as a woman, a gender whose realm of influence had traditionally been the home, not the cult or the court.[4]

Woman Wisdom, then, is not an actual historical person; she is a metaphor for the divine presence and guidance that most likely developed during the post-exilic period when male authorities figures (king, priest) and male-run institutions (monarchy, priesthood) had been defeated and deported. In that situation, the locus of wisdom teaching shifted from school and court to hearth and home. Women and their teaching role in the home were seen

---

3. Lang, *Wisdom and the Book of Proverbs*.

4. Camp, *Wisdom and the Feminine in the Book of Proverbs*, chapter 4.

as an important source of stability. All that said, we shouldn't romanticize Woman Wisdom as a perfect, timeless female analogy for God. She shows the limitations of her historical context. She speaks exclusively to young men. Some of her themes and specific sayings are misogynist. Chapters five and six go into great detail about the wiles of loose women. Folly is personified as female in chapter seven. Specific verses bemoan quarrelsome wives (27:15) and warn the young against "giving their strength to women" (31:3).

She may not be perfect, but, warts and all, she is a welcome guide in the twists and turns of daily life. We all need a person to guide us from time to time. I've tried learning several new skills over the past few years. I have the entire boxed set of Rosetta Stone Latin America CDs. I have a guitar and the *Dictionary of Guitar Chords: Every chord you'll ever need, with over 550 chord diagrams.* I have the complete works of Bob Dylan with TABs. I have several yoga DVDs and an iPad app of yoga routines. I still find that in all these areas, there is nothing quite like a real teacher. I learned Spanish better when I attended a class at the local community college with a teacher and other people to talk to. I practice yoga more faithfully and effectively when I go my local gym on Monday nights at 8 PM and attend Anya's class with other people. And I just bought a month of guitar lessons at a local music school that were donated for our church's youth mission dinner/auction. Soon I'll be able to sit down with a real, live teacher.

We are fortunate to have the book of Proverbs. Its advice is quite helpful. But, as the sages of Israel realized, we need a real person, a real teacher, to guide us in putting them into practice in our daily lives. And so Proverbs personifies God's wisdom as a Wise Woman, standing at the crossroads of life inviting the young to abandon foolishness and enter upon her path (Prov 1:20ff).[5]

Wisdom's First Speech (Proverbs 1:20–33): "How long will you love being simple?"

The book of Proverbs contains two speeches by Woman Wisdom (1:20–33; 8:22–36) to her would-be followers. In the first speech she shows her awareness of the retailer's dictum, "Location is everything." She stands in the streets, the square, at the busiest corner, at the entrance of the city gates, calling the young to enter onto her "way" or path of life. This first speech emphasizes the perils of not entering upon her way, rather than the benefits of following her, which she highlights in Proverbs 3:13–18 and 8:32–36. She chooses this cautionary tactic in this first speech because the young

5. McKenzie, "The Appeal of Wisdom."

audience to whom she speaks has a history of ignoring her instruction (1:24–31).

She doesn't waste her energy threatening. She doesn't have to. The foolish will bring their own punishments down on their own heads—the consequences of their own foolish choices. She is a tough-love teacher with clear boundaries. She isn't going to lose any sleep when recalcitrant pupils receive their just deserts (v. 32). Instead, she will laugh when inevitable disaster descends (vv. 26–27) and/or will simply not be present (v. 28).[6] Her first speech is all in a minor key, weighted toward warning (1:20–32). We hear a lone, bright note of reassurance at the end: "Those who listen to me will be secure and will live at ease, without dread of disaster" (1:33).

Wisdom Second Speech (Proverbs 8:22–36) "My fruit is better than gold . . ."

Woman Wisdom's second speech, by contrast, is light on warning and heavy on reassurance (8:22–36). It contains nine verses about Wisdom's role in creation and her rejoicing in the world and the human race, three verses about the benefits of following her, and one concluding verse of warning about the consequences of those who do not listen and follow. ". . . Those who miss me injure themselves; all who hate me love death" (8:36).

Whether in a major or minor key, Wisdom continually calls out to potential followers (1:20–33; 8:22–36). She urges them to search diligently for wisdom, assured that in finding her, they have found the most valuable of treasures (Prov 3:13–18).

The active search for wisdom at times takes the form of a patient vigil. "Happy is the one who listens to me, watching daily at my gates, waiting beside my doors" (Prov 8:34). The search is also a gift. The gift is the presence, in every situation in our daily lives, of wisdom's gate, through which insights can come if we are open to them.

We are not only waiting at her door. She is also waiting at ours. In the Wisdom of Solomon, a wisdom writing from the second century before the birth of Jesus, we find this beautiful description of Wisdom's daily routine. "Wisdom hastens to make herself known to those who desire her. He who rises early to seek her will have no difficulty, for he will find her sitting at his gates. . . . She goes about seeking those worthy of her, and she graciously appears to them in their paths, and meets them in every thought" (Wis 6:13–16).

---

6. Clifford, *The Wisdom Literature*, 59.

Who is waiting at whose gates? Are we waiting at hers? Or is she waiting at ours? The answer is yes! As we prepare for a "wisdom stakeout," packing our cooler of snacks, blankets, and folding chairs to set up a vigil outside her door, we find that she is already waiting outside of ours.

Proverbs 31:10–31: "A woman of worth, who can find?"

This last portion of the book of Proverbs is often called "A Poem to a Woman of Worth," literally a "woman of strength" or "a woman of valor" (*eset hayil*, 31:10). The traditional interpretation of this poem is that it describes the ideal wife. This is the woman the wise young man should choose to enhance his future, the "good wife" celebrated in 12:4 as the "crown of her husband." It may be that we have here a portrait of what the ancients considered the perfect woman. This image of the feminine ideal was common across various Ancient Near Eastern cultures. She had dignity, and was also pious, energetic, thrifty, a capable manager, charitable, skilled at the loom, and a feast for the eyes.[7]

On the surface, this biblical super-wife seems like one more unattainable ideal for contemporary women. This understanding is what prompted a clergywoman friend to remark to me, "If anyone reads this text at my funeral, I'll haunt them! It describes a perfect woman, and everyone present will know it's not describing me!"

There are a number of clues that indicate that this poem describes Woman Wisdom herself rather than any earthly woman. No woman of ancient Israel held such a high place in family, society, or economy as the poem imagines. No woman held such authority or was granted such authority, even as an ideal. Women were not generally viewed as the source of their husbands' honor, rather the reverse. Add to this the uncanny resemblance between this woman and Woman Wisdom herself as we have encountered her in the first thirty chapters of Proverbs. Both are said to shed light on the way of those who follow her (compare 31:18b with 13:9). Both are said to be worth more than precious jewels (compare 31:10b with 3:15, 8:11;16:16; 18:19; 21:15). Both bring prosperity, protection, and honor upon those who trust in them (compare 31:11–12 with 4:6,8,9). Both Woman Wisdom and the woman of worth laugh at the future (compare 31:25 with 1:26). Both Woman Wisdom and the woman of worth, by both advice and example, teach us to fear the Lord. Throughout Proverbs we have been told that the fear of the Lord is the beginning of wisdom (1:7; 9:10; 15:33). In Proverbs the fear of the Lord refers to reverence for God as the source of moral

---

7. Gottlieb, "The Words of the Exceedingly Wise," 287.

knowledge and guidance. The woman of worth is described as "a woman who fears the Lord" (31:30).

The honor lavished on this woman by her husband and children does not come from her marriage to him, but from the wisdom inherent in her character. She possesses many of the traits of the wise person depicted in the collected sayings of Proverbs (Prov 10—29). She labors with discipline and diligence; she cares for the poor; she looks to tomorrow's needs with forethought; and she is strong and dignified. Her providential care for her household makes the future a carefree adventure. When she speaks, it is in words of wisdom.[8]

Recent scholarship agrees that the uncanny resemblance between the woman of worth and Woman Wisdom is no coincidence. The woman of worth is Woman Wisdom herself. This concluding poem of the book of Proverbs summarizes Wisdom's qualities and commends them to would-be followers. Rather than setting an impossible bar for human perfection, it points to Wisdom's provisions for humankind. Coming at the end of the book, it offers an invitation to readers to become members of the Household of Wisdom, honoring her presence in our lives and partaking of her benefits.

Wisdom as a Path: "The Way"

Wisdom in the book of Proverbs is often described as the Way (*derek*, Prov 4:11), as it also is in several Eastern faith systems. The Way is an apt title for wisdom, because wisdom paves a path under our feet for how to live in harmony with divine order, for how to live life as God intended us to live it. By no coincidence, in the early days of the church, Christians were described as "followers of the Way."

The "way" suggests an action of treading or trampling and calls to mind a path worn by constant use. Wisdom involves patterns of behavior, not just isolated acts. The purpose of this "way" is the formation of an interior disposition (2:1f; 3:1–5; 4:4, 21, 23; 6:21; 7:3).

What if we plugged the definition of "way" from Proverbs into Jesus' speech in John 14:6: "I am the Way, the Truth and the Life?" Here is how it would sound: "I am the path worn by constant use, that involves patterns of behavior, not just isolated acts" (John 14:6). We'll explore what those patterns are in Part Four when we turn to the proverbial wisdom of Jesus.

Proverbs 3:15 tells us that "Wisdom is more precious than jewels, and nothing you desire can compare with her." When the search for Wisdom is our motivation, our inner lives are shaped by her virtues, and our outer

8. McCreesh, "Wisdom as Wife."

lives pave a path of faith, compassion, self-control, and outspoken courage beneath our feet.

When I visited England some years ago, in almost every cathedral or graveyard I visited there were people with kits containing soft bristle brushes, masking tape, charcoal crayons, and butcher paper, there to make grave rubbings. They piqued my interest and so I found myself on the Association for Gravestone Studies website (yes, there really is such an association!) looking at a list of "Do's and Don'ts of Grave Rubbing." You should never rub a deteriorated gravestone. You should use a soft bristle brush to clean away lichen, never a stiff wire brush, putty knife, or nail file. You should use masking tape, never spray adhesive or duct tape. You should get permission whenever possible.

In reading this description, I realized that what I've been doing over the past twenty years is placing a big piece of butcher paper over the wisdom literature of the Bible. I've taped it down, and I've gotten out my charcoal crayons. I've done a grave rubbing. And the features of the wise life according to that literature have emerged gradually and come into relief. They are the four wisdom virtues that shape a life pleasing to God. They are an awestruck attitude (the fear of the Lord), a listening heart (compassion), a cool spirit (self-control), and a subversive voice (courage). They are the life that results when we live by the proverbs, listen to the person, and follow the path. We turn now to the premier virtue of the wise life according to Israel's sages—the fear of the Lord, the Bible's code word for faith.

Chapter 2

PART ONE—The Lead Sled Dog Virtue
The Fear of the Lord

An Awestruck Attitude: The Fear to End All Fears

AS WE DISCERN THE face of the wise person that comes through study of the Bible's wisdom literature, the feature that emerges first is the fear of the Lord. It is the premier wisdom virtue, the lead sled dog virtue that must be in the harness in order to pull the other three virtues along behind it. If you look up the word *fear* (*yireah*) in a Hebrew-English lexicon, you will find next to it three words: reverence, piety, and terror.[1] While, as we'll see, it involves trembling, it is by no means defined as a fear of imminent punishment from God. Rather, it is a radical respect for the Godness of God. It is radical trust in the faithfulness of God above all others. It is a radical reliance on the guidance of God above all others. The fear of the Lord, what I'm calling "an awestruck attitude," is at the core of the biblical portrayal of the wise life. It is the wisdom literature's name for faith. It is, according to Old Testament scholar Gerhard von Rad, the essential condition of wisdom.[2]

---

1. *A Reader's Hebrew–English Lexicon of the Old Testament.*
2. Rad, *Wisdom in Israel*, 67.

What the Fear of the Lord is Not:
The Fear of Imminent Punishment

A few years ago I sat in the passenger seat of my daughter Rebecca's Honda Civic. The back seat was loaded high with clothes from Old Navy, bins from the Container Store, and college dorm accessories from Bed, Bath, and Beyond. We were on our way to Southern Methodist University in Dallas, Texas to move her into her freshman college dorm room. It was only a twenty-five–mile drive from Allen, Texas where we live, but there are actual miles and there are emotional miles, when your baby girl is going off to college.

As we sat at a stop light, I noticed that the car in front of us bore two bumper stickers. The one on the right side demanded, "Where will you spend eternity?" The one on the left said, "The fear of the Lord is the beginning of wisdom."

"I've always hated that saying," Rebecca said, pointing to the one on the left. "I'm about to start college. I'm already afraid of everything. And now I'm supposed to be afraid of God too?!"

That's how most people think of the fear of the Lord. "Be afraid because God's gonna getcha." One more fear to add to your others. The fact is that, as we have seen, while there are three strands of meaning of the fear of the Lord in Scripture (trembling, trust, and taking directions), none of them boils down to the fear of imminent punishment. No matter how many preachers have tried to motivate people by the fear of hell, no matter how instinctive it is to assume when something bad happens to us or others that it is God's punishment, the fear of the Lord is not the fear of imminent punishment.

What the Fear of the Lord is Not:
The Fear of Someone or Something Other than God

Biblical Examples

Neither is the fear of the Lord to be confused with our garden variety personal and social fears, as legitimate as they may be. There are numerous examples in the Bible of people filled with fear of things and people rather than the fear of the Lord. The fear of someone or something other than God is the root cause of many biblical people's negative actions. For others, it is the reason they hang back from taking positive actions God wants them to take. Cain had a fear of being one-upped by his brother Abel, which contributed to the first murder in the human community. Sarah's jealous fear of Hagar and her son Ishmael led her to pressure Abraham to send them out into the wilderness of Beersheba. There they would have died, were it not for God's intervention, telling Hagar not to be afraid, for God would care for her and her child (Gen 21:8–21).

Moses had a fear of public speaking and a fear of Pharaoh (Exod 4:10). If God had not lost patience with his excuses he would never have led anybody out of anywhere. Pharaoh had a fear of losing his free labor force. That led him repeatedly to try to foil God's plan for the liberation of the Israelites. One summer when I taught Vacation Bible School, we watched a cartoon film of the Exodus. It showed the Egyptian soldiers and their horses being overcome by the waves and drowning. One girl raised her hand after it was over. "That's not fair. They were just doing what Pharaoh made them do. Their death was his fault." I couldn't argue with that!

Pharaoh's fear of the loss of power and wealth led to the death of his own soldiers and their horses. At the same time, he himself lacked the "fear of the Lord." As Moses says to him after the seventh plague, "As for you and your officials, I know that you do not yet fear the Lord God" (Exod 9:30). God asks Pharaoh before the eighth plague, the plague of locusts: "How long will you refuse to humble yourself before me? Let my people go, so that they may worship me" (Exod 10: 3).

Saul had a fear of David's rising popularity (1 Sam 18:12). It led him to wage a war on David that resulted in many deaths. The prophet Elijah had a pretty good reason to fear Queen Jezebel (1 Kgs 19:3). She had, after all, put out a hit on him. She had sent a messenger to him informing him that she had arranged to have him killed within the next twenty-four hours (1 Kgs 19:2). I would have fled into the wilderness too! So God staged an intervention. Locating Elijah sitting under a broom tree, he asked him this key question: "What are you doing here, Elijah?" God then motivated Elijah to get up and get going to complete his mission.

In the New Testament King Herod was afraid of a baby. While the infant slept in the manger, Herod, robbed of sleep, was pacing the length of his palace. Legend has it that his fear of the loss of his power led him to put many children to death in what is referred to as "the slaughter of the innocents" (Matt 2:16f). Peter had a fear of losing Jesus and wanted no part of Jesus' prediction of future betrayal and death, even though it ended in resurrection. He stopped listening when he heard the words "be killed" (Matt 16:21–23). His fear led him to try to hold Jesus back from fulfilling his identity and mission. Judas had a fear that Jesus was an underachiever, a popular, charismatic leader unwilling, due to his strange stubborn streak, to put his gifts to proper military use. It led him to betray Jesus. The Pharisees feared Jesus' popularity and the loss of their own position and prestige. Their fears led some of them to manipulate events to bring about his trial and crucifixion. Pilate feared the anger both of the people and of the Jewish religious leaders. It led him to hand Jesus over to be crucified. Fear of everything and everyone but God never leads to anything good in the Bible.

There is a causal relationship between the lack of the fear of the Lord and the fear of something or someone other than God. And it's not a good relationship! To fear anything less than God while, at the same time, lacking the fear of the Lord is a lethal combination. When the fear of something less than God competes with and seeks to overpower the fear of the Lord, that is called idolatry, the worship of a false god. That is the definition of spiritual enslavement. Says Jesus, "Do not fear those who kill the body but cannot kill the soul; rather fear him who can destroy both soul and body in hell" (Matt 10: 28).

The Fear of Something or Someone Other than God: Contemporary Examples

In my introduction to preaching classes at Perkins, I hand out an index card the first day of class and ask students to write on it name, email, phone, denomination, current appointment, amount of preaching experience, what they hope to learn from the class, and their greatest fear. I started this practice when I taught preaching at Princeton Seminary in the nineties. I quickly learned that I needed to make question about fear more specific: "What is your greatest fear about the class?" I got home one evening and, after I had put the kids to bed, started going through the cards. Under the greatest fear question, some students had written things like, standing in front of a group, being evaluated by my peers, misinterpreting God's Word, and being boring. I nodded approvingly as I read each one. The class was designed to address those fears. But then, near the bottom of the stack, next to greatest fear, somebody had written "aging." Someone else had written "death." And one poor soul, in a spurt of honesty, had written, "Life in general, mostly dogs."

I remember the time I was on a 6 PM flight from Memphis to Dallas. I had given several lectures at Memphis Theological Seminary. I had preached at their midweek chapel service. I was physically and mentally fatigued. It was a small American Eagle plane, the kind that has two seats on the right and one on the left and no first class. I had somehow gotten the best seat in the house! I was sitting in the first row on the right, in an aisle seat, the row that faces into a carpeted wall. I glanced over at the man to my right in the window seat. He was a strapping guy, late thirties with a pony tail. He looked like a younger version of Robert de Niro. He was holding a gigantic cup of coffee and had his eyes closed. I thought, "Good, no need to exert myself to make conversation for the next few hours." We took off, and I got my mystery novel out to escape for a couple of hours. "Is that a good book?" he asked. "I've heard that's a good book. Is it a good book?" I glanced over to where my seatmate, now wide awake, was peering at the cover of my book with bright-eyed interest.

I answered him, and that led to our chatting for over an hour about mystery authors, movies, and places we had traveled. He had a rapid-fire speaking style, jumping quickly from topic to topic. While I did my best to shake off my fatigue and match his energy level, at several points, I considered confiscating that cup of coffee he still held in both hands. It was a smooth flight until we got near Dallas and began to experience turbulence. I always appreciate a little turbulence on a long flight. It breaks up the monotony.

But my conversation partner fell suddenly silent. He turned pale beneath his tan, and a sheen of sweat appeared on his forehead. He suddenly stomped his cowboy booted foot against the carpeted wall in front of us. He then continued the stomping at fifteen-second intervals. I know because, after the second one, I started counting. Then he began talking again, in staccato bursts of speech. "I'm not afraid of snakes, heights, or public speaking. I'm fine with the takeoff and the landing. But turbulence really freaks me out."

"Let's hope it doesn't last long," I said. He continued his foot stomping punctuated with commentary. "We're in a cigar-shaped tube, thousands of miles above the ground, completely at the mercy of wind and weather. There is the constant possibility of mechanical failure or human error. We couldn't possibly be in a more vulnerable situation. Turbulence is a metaphor for the essential helplessness of the human condition."

Well, when he put it that way, I began to turn pale under my tan, and I don't even have a tan. I briefly considered joining him in the foot-stomping thing, but refrained out of consideration for the already on-edge flight attendant. She didn't need two of us.

There is a fear for everyone. It's not like trick-or-treating as a child where the adult handing out the candy holds out the bowl and says "Only one per person." You can have more than one fear! You can empty the whole bowl of fears into your pillowcase if you want to and lug it home. Many people have done exactly that.

These fears are not just personal fears. They coalesce into what theologian Scott Bader-Saye has labeled a "culture of fear." We live with fear of terrorist attack, economic disaster, and being left behind as other world economies outperform us. In our current political climate, we live with the legitimate fear that our nation's racial, economic, political, and religious divisions may fracture our most deeply held common convictions. Fear used to be an appropriate response to a specific threat, like a pop-up ad on a website. It has become the screen saver backdrop to our culture.[3]

In a culture of fear, rather than see God's hand at work in some overarching story of salvation in the world, we are more likely to see randomness, chaos, and threat. And is it any wonder when almost every week brings news of a suicide bombing or some other form of terrorist attack, both here and around the world? Never have we more urgently needed this piece of good news: that the Bible nowhere says that the fear of terrorist attack and economic disaster is the beginning of wisdom. Scripture strongly asserts that only one fear is the beginning of wisdom. Instead of being fearful, we are called to be fear (of the Lord) full, to live with an "awestruck attitude." Other fears don't need to be cultivated. They spring up like weeds that would choke the wholesome harvest of our lives. There is one and only one fear we are to spend our lives cultivating, the fear of the Lord, an "awestruck attitude."

What the Fear of the Lord Is: An Awestruck Attitude

The fear of the Lord, that intriguing mix of attraction and appropriate terror, is what I'm calling "an Awestruck Attitude." It's Mr. Beaver's insight about Aslan, the lion, the King of Narnia in *The Chronicles of Narnia*, that Aslan is "not safe, but he's good."[4] The fear of the Lord, the "awestruck attitude," consists of three responses to three aspects of God's character as revealed to us in Scripture: Trembling, Trust, and Taking Directions. It is a radical respect for the Godness of God in all three aspects. An awestruck attitude means that we kneel in homage, that we stand boldly to face the challenges each day brings, and that we set our steps on the way of wisdom that leads to life.

"The fear of the Lord is the beginning (*reshit*) of knowledge" (Prov 1:7) It is the first step or first principle (*tehilla*) of wisdom (9:10). Injunctions to fear the Lord pepper the Proverbs collection (1:7; 9:10; 15:33; 31:30). The postexilic collectors of the sayings in the book of Proverbs woke up every morning asking themselves the question: "How can we instill the fear of the Lord in the young?" That's why they emblazoned it on a banner that they

3. Bader-Saye, *Following Jesus in a Culture of Fear.*
4. Lewis, *The Lion, the Witch and the Wardrobe*, chapter 7.

draped over the whole collection: "The fear of the Lord is the beginning of knowledge" (Prov 1:7).

They didn't emblazon any of the following mottos on that opening banner:

The fear of failure is the beginning of wisdom.

The fear of rejection is the beginning of wisdom.

The fear of my children moving to another state is the beginning of wisdom.

The fear of death of a beloved partner is the beginning of wisdom.

The fear of declining membership is the beginning of wisdom.

The fear of picking the wrong career is the beginning of wisdom.

The fear of not even having a career is the beginning of wisdom.

The fear of dying alone is the beginning of wisdom.

The fear of the death of my pet is the beginning of wisdom.

The fear of a return of my cancer is the beginning of wisdom.

The fear of losing my child is the beginning of wisdom.

The fear of losing my job is the beginning of wisdom.

The fear of other people's opinions of me is the beginning of wisdom.

The fear of my supervisor is the beginning of wisdom.

The fear of aging and death is the beginning of wisdom.

The fear of people of other faiths, races, sexual orientations, and religions is the beginning of wisdom.

Life entails loss and pain. The landscape of our lives includes areas over which we have no control. These fears are understandable and legitimate. But none of them is the beginning of knowledge. Since we have a habit of assuming we have only ourselves to rely on, no wonder myriad fears flood our souls and cloud our minds. But none of them is the first step toward wisdom. That distinction belongs to one fear and one alone: the fear of the Lord, the fear to end all fears.

The wise life is a process of coming to the customer service desk each day and making this fundamental exchange: of everyday, garden-variety fears for the fear of the Lord, in other words, for faith. This exchange of fear for faith is not a one-time occurrence; it is not an accomplishment we can ever check off the list as "been there, done that." It is more a habit, a skill. And, as with any other skill, with practice, we can get better at it. When we daily exchange the false assumption that we have only ourselves to rely on for faith in God (the fear of the Lord), something amazing happens. We open the floodgates of faith: it energizes us to exchange our other three bad purchases: self-absorption, self-indulgence, and self-protection. As we repeatedly practice the skill of letting lesser fears be overpowered by the fear of the Lord (faith), we are more and more able to live by the other three virtues of the wise life: a listening heart, a cool spirit, and a subversive, courageous voice.

Exchanging the fear of everything but God for the fear of the Lord that is the beginning of wisdom is a physiological and not just an emotional or spiritual experience. The knot of fear in the pit of our stomach dissolves by the power of our God who banishes all lesser fears. "The fear of others lays a snare, but the one who trusts in the Lord rests secure" (Prov 29:25). "The fear of the Lord is a fountain of life, so that one may avoid the snares of death" (Prov 14:27). When the knot reties itself, as it has an annoying habit of doing on a daily basis, we practice invoking the power of God the giver of grace and wisdom to loosen it again.

The Fear of the Lord: A Three-Stranded Braid

The fear of the Lord as a human response to God takes three forms in the Hebrew Bible. Since God is God and not a human being, we tremble before God (Exod 19:16; Isa 6:4–5). Since God has promised to be faithful to God's covenant people, we trust God and pledge that our loyalty in return (Deut 10:20). Since God has given us the gift of wisdom to guide our daily lives, we take directions from God rather than our own faulty instincts (Prov 1:7; 3:5–7). Each of these human postures is in response to the character of God. They are responses to the gracious initiative of God the giver of Wisdom.

Strand One: Trembling before the Holy: Isaiah 6

Most people think that the fear of the Lord means cringing in fear of imminent divine punishment. There is an undeniable element of what Old Testament scholar Ellen Davis calls "ordinary fright" involved in the fear of the Lord. But there is also awe and attraction.

First let's face into the fright factor. We certainly detect a tremor of terror in Isaiah's response to his close encounter with the divine in Isaiah 6:6. As the temple trembles beneath his feet and visions of the exalted Lord on his throne and six-winged seraphim with burning coals fill his eyes, he suddenly recognizes, as never before, the gap between human and divine.

His instinctive response is to cry out, "Woe is me! . . . For I am a man of unclean lips, and I live among a people of unclean lips; yet my eyes have seen the King, the Lord of hosts!" (6:5). Says Davis,

> To experience the full measure of God's power and *not* to feel some stirring of fear would indicate a profound state of spiritual numbness . . . . A sickly lack of fear in the face of God's power is exactly the condition described in the book of Exodus as Pharaoh's "hardheartedness" (see Exodus 8:15, 32; 9:7) . . . . Moses diagnoses the spiritual condition that ultimately brings ruin on the whole land of Egypt: "But as for you and your officials, I know that you do not yet fear the LORD God" (Exod 9:30).[5]

Fear is our basic human response to an overwhelming force. The Israelites are said to have experienced fear (or terror) in the face of the thunder and lightning of their earthshaking encounter with the Lord at Sinai. And with good reason. Trembling was the appropriate response to God's revelation through Moses and God's formidable, holy otherness (Exod 19:16).

Such fear is not altogether misplaced. But along with the terror, there is an attraction or fascination.[6] The fear of the Lord that is trembling at the recognition that we are human and God is God results in "awe and regard, a kind of wariness, probably the sort that would mean watching your step in God's presence."[7] It is Job's response to his encounter with God in chapter 39 of the book of Job. After thirty-eight long chapters of Job's "Why me's?" and his friends' finger-pointing, God has apparently had enough. God speaks to Job out of the whirlwind, asking "Where were you when I laid the foundation of the earth?" God continues this line of questioning for three challenging chapters. This is how I hear God's message to Job: "You need to understand that the fear of the Lord is the beginning of knowledge, the first step to wisdom. And part of that fear means appropriate trembling in the presence of the One who is God while you are not."

Job gets it. He responds in chapter forty-two: "I had heard of you by the hearing of the ear, but now my eye sees you" (42:5). Job acknowledges his humanity in the face of the almost overwhelming divinity of God. His immediate impulse is then to confess and repent, and he does so in terms that sound a lot like Isaiah's "Woe is me!"

Says Job, "Therefore I despise myself and repent in dust and ashes" (Job 42:6).

---

5. Davis, *Proverbs, Ecclesiastes, and the Song of Songs*, 28.

6. Melchert, *Wise Teaching*, 37.

7. Holmer, *Making Christian Sense*, 55.

When we encounter God this dramatically, we recognize, in an anguished flash of insight, all within us that is not of God. And we recognize that all that is not of God must go.

For Job, the fear of the Lord as trembling is the beginning of his restored life.

In the book of Ecclesiastes, the author doesn't talk about the fear of the Lord as the beginning of anything. Rather, the author repeatedly encourages readers to "fear God," to experience appropriate awe in the face of the divine, recognizing the gulf between the human and the divine. Fearing God is as much an end as it is a beginning. It's a "know your place" kind of insight that brings an end to needless questions about why things are the way they are and naïve hopes that living wisely guarantees a fortunate life.[8]

"Never be rash with your mouth, nor let your heart be quick to utter a word before God, for God is in heaven, and you are on earth; therefore let your words be few" (Eccl 5:2).

Elements of the fear of the Lord as trembling make their way into the book of Proverbs in its portrayal of Woman Wisdom. She is not a warm and fuzzy character. While she delights in helping create the world and human beings (8:30–31) and provides diligently for her household (31:10–31), she has no patience with those who choose the path of folly that leads to death. While she draws near to those who need wisdom and offers it to them in the midst of their daily lives, she distances herself from those who refuse that gift.

"Because I have called and you refused . . . when distress and anguish come upon you . . . you will call upon me, but I will not answer; you will seek me diligently, but will not find me . . . . Because you hated knowledge and did not choose the fear of the Lord" (Prov 1:29).

In the British television series *Rumpole of the Bailey*, the main character is an aging barrister named Horace Rumpole. He is both very eccentric and very effective at his job, and respected in the public realm. One of his eccentricities is secretly to refer to his wife Hilda, before whom he trembles at home, as "She Who Must Be Obeyed."

This name is a good fit for Woman Wisdom in the book of Proverbs. If you don't listen to her, if you don't step onto the path of life that she provides, if you don't embrace the virtue of the fear of the Lord she offers you, better start trembling!

But if you do, your prospects brighten considerably. The virtue of the fear of the Lord brings a peace and security to the one who cultivates it. It is the fear to end all fears. To fear the Lord is to experience blessedness

---

8. McKenzie, *Preaching Proverbs,* 48.

(Prov 28:14) and security (Prov 19:23). Trembling is only the beginning. Trembling, that terror-stricken attraction to God we call awe, is intended to lead to trusting and taking directions from God rather than relying on our own so-called wisdom (Prov 3:5).

Strand Two: Trust: Deuteronomy 10:20

If the fear of God were just trembling at God's transcendence, it would be paralysis. If we spent all our time trembling prostrate before the throne of God, we wouldn't accomplish the purposes God has for our lives. Trembling isn't the only response God wants from us.

William Muehl, who for years taught Christian Methods at Yale Divinity School, once preached a sermon on the parable of the Pharisee and the Tax Collector from Luke's gospel (Luke 18:10–14a).[9] In his sermon, Muehl points out that the tax collector makes a good beginning in the life of discipleship in his prayer, "Lord have mercy on me a sinner." But, Muehl wonders, what if we came back a week, a month, or a year later and found him still in his corner beating his breast? He wouldn't have made much progress in the life of faith. He wouldn't be a good model of discipleship for us.

The fear of the Lord is not just a life of perpetual trembling; it is also the sturdy trust in God that gives us the courage to face the challenging times and tasks that lie ahead. The fear of the Lord as trust is the conviction that God will hold up God's end of the relationship God has formed with us.

> Although heaven and the heaven of heavens belong to the Lord
> your God, the earth with all that is in it, yet the Lord set his heart
> in love on your ancestors alone and chose you, their descendants
> after them, out of all the people, as it is today (Deut 10:14–15).

To trust God is to return the favor to God. God has been loyal to us. To trust God is to be loyal to God. The book of Deuteronomy describes the covenant loyalty we need to cultivate in relationship to God. "You shall fear the Lord your God; him alone you shall worship; to him you shall hold fast, and by his name you shall swear" (10:20). Proverbs 3:5–7 gives the same command to the wisdom student. "Trust in the Lord with your whole heart . . . fear the Lord, and turn away from evil." To fear the Lord is to choose God as the object of the loyalty of our heart. And that doesn't just involve our emotions. For the Hebrews, the heart was not just the seat of the emotions, but also of understanding and will. It is the seat of character and of decision making.

9. Muehl, *All the Damned Angels*, 25–31.

Trembling leads to a trust in God's presence and faithfulness. We come to the realization that we need not tremble before any earthly person, circumstance, or power. Because we are filled with the "fear of the Lord," we need fear nothing and no one else. The fear of the Lord as trust brings security and a strange kind of freedom. When we embrace the fear of the Lord we can relinquish lesser fears. "The fear of others lays a snare, but the one who trusts in the Lord is secure" (Prov 29:25).

People in the Bible discover and rely on this trust. God promises Jacob in his dream at Bethel, "Know that I am with you and will keep you wherever you go, and will bring you back to this land; for I will not leave you until I have done what I have promised you" (Gen 28:15). Moses reminds Joshua of God's faithfulness as Joshua becomes his successor in leading the people into the promised land. "It is the Lord who goes before you. He will be with you; he will not fail you or forsake you. Do not fear or be dismayed" (Deut 31:8). The Lord reminds Joshua of this promise in Joshua 1:9 in almost identical words. "Be strong and courageous; do not be frightened or dismayed, for the Lord your God is with you wherever you go."

The same promise sounds through the psalms and the prophets. "With the Lord on my side I do not fear. What can mortals do to me?" (Psalm 118:6).

All these passages attest to the same truth: The Lord is the source of our confidence as we face an uncertain future. The only One before whom we need to tremble is with us. With trust in God we face the future without fear.

God is our refuge and strength,
a very present help in trouble.
Therefore we will not fear, though the earth should change,
though the mountains should shake in the heart of the sea;
though its waters roar and foam,
though the mountains tremble with its tumult (Ps 46:1–3).

Strand Three: The Fear of the Lord as Taking Directions: Proverbs 3:5–7

In Proverbs the fear of the Lord is mentioned repeatedly. The emphasis is not on the otherness of God that is too overwhelming for us to look upon. It is on acknowledging that God, not our own insight, is the source of moral guidance for the community. That is why the fear of the Lord is the beginning of knowledge (1:7; 9:10). Because we must start at the source.

To fear the Lord in Proverbs means to take directions from God and God alone. Proverbs lays out a road map for what happens in a person's life when he/she trembles and trusts. That person gets in the daily habit of taking directions from God. We all know how easy and dangerous it is to confuse our own inner desires with the voice of God. One of the hallmarks of a fool is that he or she does not recognize that there is any distinction between the two! The opening of the Proverbs collection contrasts the attitude of the fear of the Lord that is the beginning of knowledge (1:7a) with the attitude of fools who "despise wisdom and instruction" (1:7b). A synonym for fool throughout the collection is the one who is "wise in their own eyes." Proverbs 3:5–7 puts it well:

> Trust in the Lord with all your heart,
> and do not rely on your own insight.
> In all your ways acknowledge him,
> and he will make straight your paths.
> Do not be wise in your own eyes;
> fear the Lord, and turn away from evil.
> It will be a healing for your flesh
> and a refreshment for your body.

Straight paths don't mean a life free from adversity, but a life free from anxiety. It is possible to live life directed by God and moving toward God and to walk a way paved with inward security and peace. Our circumstances may twist and turn. We may encounter thorns and dark valleys, but an inner path unfurls beneath our feet. It is a path of wisdom along which we walk with God and toward God amid the most tumultuous of external circumstances.

The path paved by the fear of the Lord is a path of trembling, trust, and taking directions from God. There is only one way to experience the benefits of walking this path. That is to walk this path. Only in walking it do we feel and live our way into its daily joys. Only in trembling, trusting, and taking directions, do we live into the truth that "the fear of the Lord is a fountain of life" (Prov 14:27; 10:27; 1:7; 9:10 and 15:16). Only in trembling, trusting, and taking directions do we experience the truth that "the fear of the Lord banishes sin" (3:7; 8:13; 16:6). Only in trembling, trusting, and taking directions do we live into the fact that "the fear of the Lord banishes other fears" (14:26; 19:23; 29:25).

The Fear of the Lord: Knowing to Whom to Entrust our Lesser Fears

I was asked to lead a women's retreat at Lantana Lodge on Ray Roberts Lake near my home in Texas. Before I left for the retreat, I happened to have a conversation with a pastor of my acquaintance named Gayle.

"What is the topic of the retreat?" she asked me.

"Exchanging fear for faith," I told her.

Her face seemed to fall. "What? Don't you like the topic?" I asked.

"Well, I just hope you won't boil it all down to 'Simply have faith and don't be afraid anymore.' There is a lot to fear in life. And being told it should be a simple matter to stop would make me feel inadequate on top of being afraid. I hope the retreat shows some respect for their fears and helps them cope with them."

I appreciated her caution and remembered it as I stood before the group that night. The retreat was attended by about thirty women from St. Andrew Presbyterian church in Denton, Texas. They were seated at round tables in the big conference room. The setting sun over the lake outside shed a reddish golden glow over the room. I gave them these instructions for our opening exercise: "Share your top three fears with the other people at your table." When it came time to share them with the larger group, the fears expressed were things like "getting older," losing my job," "the death of my child," "the death of my spouse," "my parent becoming completely dependent on me," and "the return of my cancer."

Some of the women in attendance had had their worst fears come true and lived to tell about the toll they had taken, yet how they had survived and, in some cases, even thrived.

This was several years ago, and if I were speaking to them today, the recent spate of violent events at home and around the world would be fresh on their minds. The sense that the world is spinning out of control and is a dangerous place has built in the years since I led this retreat. It is naïve and misleading to minimize legitimate fears for the future of our communities and the safety of our children and grandchildren.

As I looked out over their faces, I heeded Gayle's warning. I did not tell them that if they had faith they wouldn't have these fears. I didn't tell them that their fears were unfounded, unnecessary, or unnatural. Instead I said this: "Faith is not the absence of our natural fears. In Mark 4:35–41, when Jesus stills the storm, he doesn't rebuke his disciples for being afraid, but for doubting that his presence was more than a match for the chaotic forces around them. Faith is an ongoing, daily, repeated process of entrusting our fears of everything and everyone other than God to God. Faith is entrusting our legitimate fears to God who in the Old Testament shows us that God's faithfulness is even stronger and more persistent than our fears. Faith is entrusting our legitimate fears to God, whose Son modeled what it meant to tremble, trust, and take directions from God and in whose crucifixion and resurrection we discern that God's love is stronger than death. Faith is entrusting our legitimate fears to God, whose hands hold us even in death and in whose arms we can live forever."

In Part Two of this chapter we'll explore the dynamics of how we do just that—how we tremble, trust, and take directions from God amid the uncertain, complicated, and demanding lives we lead.

Chapter 2

PART Two—Learning to Tremble, Trust, and Take Directions

IN PART ONE OF chapter two I introduced the premier, the lead sled dog virtue of biblical wisdom—the fear of the Lord, what I'm calling "an awestruck attitude." It is, not fear of imminent punishment at God's hands. It is not the fear of anyone or anything less that God. It is an appropriate response to God's transcendence, faithfulness, and wisdom: trembling, trusting, and taking directions. In the presence of God who is holy and transcendent, the appropriate response is to tremble. In the presence of God our faithful covenant partner, the appropriate response is to trust. In the presence of God who is our wise and reliable guide to the twists and turns of daily life, the appropriate response is to take directions: to ask for the wisdom to discern and to follow divine guidance.

Learning to fear the Lord takes practice and daily repetition. In this second part of chapter two we are going to practice returning the fear of everything but God and exchanging it for the fear of the Lord. Because, as we have seen, there is a difference between being fearful and being fear (of the Lord) full. There is a difference between being anxious and being awestruck.

Learning to Tremble

Who is awestruck in Scripture?

- Moses trembles at the burning bush (Exod 3:6).
- Isaiah trembles when he sees a vision of God in the Temple (Isa 6:5).

- The Israelites tremble in the face of the thunder and lightning of their earthshaking encounter with the Lord at Sinai (Exod 19:16).

- Job trembles when God finally speaks to him out of the whirlwind and he learns his place.

- The disciples tremble and cry out in fear in the boat when the ghostly figure walks toward them on the water (Matt 14:26).

- The soldiers at the tomb "shook and became like dead men" when the angel appeared in Matthew's gospel, and rolled the stone away from the tomb (Matt 28:4).

- Peter, James, and John on the Mount of Transfiguration were "terrified" when Jesus dazzled and God spoke from a cloud (Mark 9:6; Luke 9:34).

Such fear is a completely appropriate response when a human being encounters God. These biblical people didn't have to remember to tremble. Their experience was so overwhelming that it was an instinctive reaction.

The winds of a hurricane, the waves of a tsunami or the rumbling of an earthquake and their aftermath can cause us to quake before the sometimes destructive power of natural forces and even to question the goodness of God, in much the same way Job did. Some would say the appropriate response to God in such circumstances is anger and distrust. But to hear Job tell it, the appropriate response to the mysteries of life, including innocent suffering, is trembling, humility, and trust in a partially mysterious, transcendent God.

Biblical theophanies are meant to inspire not terror, but trust. I don't know about you, but such dramatic theophanies are not a daily occurrence in my life. But that is no excuse for me to forget how to tremble, to forget that God is God and I am not. Fortunately, this holy God speaks to us in small ways as well as through angelic visitors and mountaintop bedazzlements. Consider the experience of Elijah the prophet at Horeb. God has just made the followers of Ba'al and their prophets tremble with displays of divine power (1 Kgs 18:20–40). God has just brought the drought to an end in dramatic fashion (1 Kgs 18:41–46). There is no doubt this is a God before whom both Elijah and the prophets of Ba'al ought to tremble.

But when Queen Jezebel puts out a hit on Elijah, this prophet of God trembles before her instead of God. He hides out in a cave near Horeb. God tells Elijah to

> "Go out and stand on the mountain before the Lord, for the Lord is about to pass by." Now there was a great wind, so strong

that it was splitting mountains and breaking rocks in pieces before the Lord, but the Lord was not in the wind; and after the wind an earthquake, but the Lord was not in the earthquake; and after the earthquake a fire, but the Lord was not in the fire, and after the fire a sound of sheer silence. When Elijah heard it, he wrapped his face in his mantle and went out and stood at the entrance of the cave. Then there came a voice to him that said, "What are you doing here, Elijah?" (1 Kgs 19:11–13).

God then sends Elijah back to work, to fulfill the mission God has for him.

We contemporary people need to remember to tremble. We need to be reminded that ours is a God who is not under our human control, who is formidable and powerful and not to be domesticated. We need these accounts of biblical people's dramatic encounters with God to remind us of the Godness of God. There is comfort, though, in standing side by side with Elijah in front of his cave. We realize that, though our daily lives may not contain dramatic displays of divine wind, earthquake, and fire, God is present to us in the sound of sheer silence. It is a silence that can drown out even Queen Jezebel's death threats and bring our idolatrous fears to their knees, bowing before God, filled with the fear of the Lord, the fear to end all fears.

Jesus reminds us of God's power and warns us not to tremble before anyone or anything less than God. "Do not fear those who kill the body but cannot kill the soul; rather fear him who can destroy both soul and body in hell" (Matt 10:28). While trembling at God's majesty, we also need to remember God's mercy. In the same breath that he warns his followers to tremble before God's power, Jesus teaches us that we are valued by God to such an extent that God has all the hairs on our heads counted (Matt 10:29). The fear of the Lord means remembering that we are limited human beings valued by God beyond measure. It means remembering that God can accomplish marvelous things, in and through our limitations. As the Apostle Paul says, "When I am weak, then I am strong." The fear of the Lord doesn't just involve being in awe of God's limitless majesty. It is also awe before God's limitless mercy, perseverance, and ingenuity.

We often tremble before the power of tragedy and the pervasiveness of human imperfection and sin. How often do we tremble with awe at the good God can do through tragic circumstances and human imperfections? We cultivate this practice of trembling before God when we remember that, even with our limitations and sins, we are forgiven and loved beyond human reason by an infinitely merciful God. We practice submitting our failings, sins, and limitations to God, confident that God can burn away the dross and use even our weaknesses and past failures to accomplish greater things that we can predict or imagine. Cultivating an "awestruck attitude" means practicing several sorts of trembling: trembling in awe at God's majesty and transcendence, but also before God's mercy and faithfulness. We cultivate the habit of trembling in anticipation of the marvelous things God has yet to do through us. It's a good idea to cultivate our respect for the Godness of God in daily periods of prayer, because times of testing await us all.

For some years, I have served on the Board of Ordained ministry for the North Texas Annual Conference of the United Methodist Church. Candidates for deacon and elders orders come before the board to be examined on their theological knowledge, their calling and commitment, and their understanding of preaching and the sacraments. They move from one interview to the next, each one half an hour long. By the time they get to the preaching and the sacraments group, they are trembling. I've learned to recognize the tell-tale signs. The foot going back and forth. The anxious light in the eyes. The pearls of sweat on the brow. The nervous laugh. We ask them a series of questions like "What Scriptures inform your understanding of infant baptism? Why is baptism a non-repeatable sacrament and the Lord's Supper a repeatable sacrament? What are the three most important qualities in an effective sermon?"

At our last session, after several interviews, I noticed that one of our colleagues had not asked any questions. She had just sat there calmly, breathing deeply, a serene expression on her face. "Why are you so quiet?" I asked her. "I'm praying for each candidate while you ask them questions," she said. "I'm praying that their fear of us might be replaced by the fear of the Lord."

Learning to Trust

I once read a daily devotional by a man who confessed that he tended to wake up in the middle of the night and worry. He described the experience as a "fear parade" marching down the Main Street of his mind. Each fear had its own float.

His devotional inspired me to think in terms of a "fear exchange." Why not visualize another parade, a "faith parade," consisting of several scriptural promises we tend to forget in times of stress?

Here comes Proverbs 29:25 down the Main Street of my mind.

"The fear of others lays a snare, but the one who fears the Lord rests secure."

Here comes Proverbs 3:5, 6.

"Trust in the Lord with your whole heart. And do not rely on your own insight. In all your ways acknowledge God and God will make straight your paths.

Now Psalm 118:5 passes by.

"Out of my distress I called on the Lord; the Lord answered me and set me in a broad place. With the Lord on my side, I do not fear. What can mortals do to me?"

Along comes Philippians 4:6, 7: "Do not worry about anything, but in everything, with prayer and supplication with thanksgiving let your requests be made known to God. And the peace of God which surpasses all understanding will guard your hearts and your minds in Christ Jesus."

The best time to cultivate the awestruck attitude is in the wee hours of the night. A faith parade is a better use of mental and spiritual energy than a fear parade. We set the faith parade in motion by remembering what we already know. As we lie staring at the ceiling above our bed, we remember that we need to tremble before no one and nothing else but God. We remember that God is a trustworthy covenant partner. We put the fear of the Lord up against our lesser fears and see which one vanquishes the other. We expect and experience a fear smackdown!

My friend Dale was taking care of his then two-year-old daughter Katie one afternoon. His wife and his mother were the other caregivers for Katie. They split the privilege evenly. The women were out food shopping. Dale was taking the bath and dinner shift. He bathed Katie carefully and changed her into her footie pajamas. He put her in her play area in the family room and went into the kitchen to make dinner. He opened the oven to put the casserole in and realized he'd forgotten the French fried onions. He ducked into the pantry closet just off the kitchen to get them and heard a yowl and came back into the kitchen to find Katie with her hands on the oven rack. He rushed her to the ER, called mom and grandma, and they all met around the table where Katie lay as the doctor put ointment and bandages on her hands that would heal in a few weeks with no permanent damage. Her eyes were closed and her lips were moving as they watched. "What's she saying?" Dale's wife Deb asked. He leaned closer and heard her saying in a whisper, over and over again, "Mommy, Daddy, Grandma. Mommy, Daddy, Grandma. Mommy, Daddy, Grandma."

In times of distress, we call upon the ones we trust. Upon what or whom do you call, when you are afraid? Whom do you trust above all others? We cultivate the awestruck attitude, the fear of the Lord as trust, by turning to God, not just in times of crisis, but in between crises. We hold fast to the One, the only One before whom we tremble, trusting that, with that One at our side, we can face whatever life holds.

Don't Be Afraid, Because the God You Fear is With You

I've always been intrigued by paradoxes. So my interest is piqued when we are told repeatedly in Scripture to not be afraid, because the God we fear is with us. That's strangely comforting, isn't it?! As Deuteronomy tells us, "You shall fear the Lord your God; him alone you shall worship; to him you shall hold fast, and by his name you shall swear" (Deut 10:20).

Over and over again, God or an emissary of God in the Old Testament tells people on the brink of challenges, "Do not be afraid." Why? Because the God before whom they tremble will be with them to give them courage and strength to meet and overcome every challenge.

Through the prophet Isaiah God commands the "people who live in Zion," "Do not be afraid of the Assyrians" (Isa 10:24). God assures them that God will vanquish their enemies. On the victory day, these words will be on the people's lips:

> Surely God is my salvation; I will trust, and will not be afraid,
> for the Lord God is my strength and my might; he has become
> my salvation (Isa 12:2).

In response to the prophet Jeremiah's protest that he is too young and inexperienced to be a prophet, God says, "Do not be afraid of them, for I am with you to deliver you" (Jer 1:8).

On the brink of the promised land, the Israelites were "grumbling in their tents," afraid of the Amorites they would have to battle. Moses offers them this combination of comfort and chastisement.

> "Have no dread or fear of them. The Lord your God, who goes
> before you, is the one who will fight for you, just as he did for
> you in Egypt before your very eyes, and in the wilderness, where
> you saw how the Lord your God carried you, just as one carries
> a child, all the way that you traveled until you reached this place.
> But in spite of this, you have no trust in the Lord your God, who
> goes before you on the way to seek out a place for you to camp,
> in fire by night, and in the cloud by day, to show you the route
> you should take" (Deuteronomy 1:30–33).

The prophet Nehemiah instructs the people to be bold in facing their opponents:

> Do not be afraid of them. "Remember the Lord who is great and
> awesome" (Neh 4:14).

Ezekiel, in his "vision of the scroll," heard a voice enjoining him to courage:

"And you, O mortal, do not be afraid of them, and do not be
afraid of their words, though briars and thorns surround you
and you live among scorpions; do not be afraid of their words,
and do not be dismayed at their looks, for they are a rebellious
house" (Ezek 2:6).

The Psalms, the prayer book of Israel, are filled with moving testimony that,
when we rely on the Lord, we need not be afraid.

I lie down and sleep;
I wake again, for the Lord sustains me.
I am not afraid of ten thousands of people
who have set themselves against me all around (Ps 3:5, 6).

The Lord is my light and my salvation;
whom shall I fear?
The Lord is the stronghold of my life;
of whom shall I be afraid? (Ps 27:1).

My enemies trample on me all day long,
For many fight against me.
O Most High, when I am afraid,
I put my trust in you.
In God, whose word I praise,
in God I trust; I am not afraid;
what can flesh do to me? (Ps 56: 2–4).

Then he led out his people like sheep,
and guided them in the wilderness like a flock.
He led them in safety, so that they were not afraid;
but the sea overwhelmed their enemies (Ps 78:53).

For the righteous will never be moved;
They will be remembered forever.
They are not afraid of evil tidings;
Their hearts are firm, secure in the Lord.
Their hearts are steady, they will not be afraid (Ps 112:6–8).

Out of my distress I called on the Lord;
the Lord answered me and set me in a broad place.
With the Lord on my side, I do not fear.
What can mortals do to me? (Ps 118:5).

Jesus commands his followers "Therefore I tell you, do not worry . . ." (Matt
6:35) and continues with a challenging yet comforting question. "Can any
of you by worrying add a single hour to your span of life? . . . Strive first for

the kingdom of God and his righteousness and all these things will be given to you as well" (Matt 6:27, 33).

In the fourteenth chapter of John's gospel, Jesus says,

> "Peace I leave with you; my peace I give to you. I do not give to you as the world gives. Do not let your hearts be troubled, and do not let them be afraid" (John 14:25–27).

Paul instructs the Philippians,

> "Do not worry about anything, but in everything by prayer and supplication with thanksgiving let you requests be made known to God. And the peace of God, which surpasses all understanding, will guard your hearts and your minds in Christ Jesus (Phil 4:6, 7).

If we imagine each inspiring text as a float, clearly the faith parade wins out over the fear parade. Praying these texts and internalizing them so they are a part of us will help us activate the faith parade in the anxious hours of the night.

Learning to Take Directions

When the fear of the Lord as trembling and as trust come together, we become people who take our directions from God. In Proverbs fear of the Lord is the beginning of wisdom (1:7; 9:10). It is acknowledging *God* as the source of all moral insights that guide the community. In Proverbs wisdom means taking directions and walking along a path of peace that had formerly been paved with anxiety.

When we acknowledge God's supreme guidance over our decisions, we cultivate the muscle memory needed to walk a path, the path of wisdom. It is the way of life, light, and wisdom. It is to be chosen in preference to the way of death, darkness, and folly.

When our fear of the Lord results in our taking directions from God and no one else, we know where wisdom starts (with the fear of the Lord), where it leads (a deeper understanding of the fear of the Lord; Prov 2:1–5), and what paves the path in the middle (the fear of the Lord). The first three chapters of the book of Proverbs describe the fear of the Lord in these three ways:

1. The fear of the Lord is the first step in the life of wisdom (1:7).

2. The fear of the Lord is a virtue that characterizes the wise person and the path paved by that virtue.

"Do not be wise in your own eyes; fear the Lord, and turn away from evil. It will be healing for your flesh and a refreshment for your body" (Prov 3:7, 8).

Proverbs says of the person who lives by wisdom, "Then you will walk on your way and your foot will not stumble" (3:23).

3. The fear of the Lord is the goal, destination, and reward for the life spent seeking wisdom.

"If you seek it (wisdom) like silver, and search for it as for hidden treasures—then you will understand the fear of the Lord and find the knowledge of God" (Prov 2:4, 5).

The author of Proverbs expresses the substance of the fear of the Lord as trusting in God that results in our taking directions from God and God alone. We are to trust in God rather than our own insights (Proverbs 3:5–6).

There is a Chinese proverb that says, "He who deliberates fully before taking the first step will spend his whole life standing on one foot." There is a Korean proverb that often appears on inspirational posters that says "A journey of a thousand miles begins with a single step."

The fear of the Lord, radical respect for and trust in God, is that single step. We often hear about the need to take a leap of faith. Proverbs asks for an action that is much more modest, but that requires frequent repetition. Built on the conviction that the fear of the Lord is the beginning of wisdom, the sages encourage us to take just one small step of trembling and trust. And follow that with another, and follow that with another.

Psalm 1, in language very similar to Jeremiah 17:5–8, advises us to take directions from God rather than ourselves.

> Happy are those who do not follow the advice of the wicked
> or take the path that sinners tread,
> or sit in the seat of scoffers;
> but their delight is in the law of the Lord,
> and on his law they meditate day and night.
> They are like trees
> planted by streams of water,
> which yield their fruit in its season,
> and their leaves do not wither.
> In all that they do, they prosper.
>
> The wicked are not so,
> But are like chaff which the wind drives away.
> Therefore the wicked will not stand in the judgment,

Nor sinners in the congregation of the righteous;
For the Lord watches over the way of the righteous,
But the way of the wicked will perish (Ps 1:1–6).

The book of Proverbs sees as its purpose to set forth in the starkest of terms the two options—trust God (fear the Lord) and take directions from God that lead to life, or trust yourself and chart your own path to spiritual death. The stakes of choosing to take directions from God rather than from ourselves are higher than we might suppose.

The good news is that God's Wisdom is close by and available for consultation all along the way. It's possible to consult with the Wisdom of God before, rather than after, we decide on courses of action. It is a matter of discerning the difference between the inner ping of divine direction from the desire for self-promotion. It is a process of spiritual maturation in which we begin to trust our inner impulses because they are becoming more in line with the will and wisdom of God. This habit of taking directions from God proceeds from our prior habits of trembling with awe before God's majesty and trusting in God's faithfulness. It's more a cyclical process than a linear one, a cycle of Wisdom. Tremble, trust, take directions, tremble, trust, take directions. It's a cycle of the fear of the Lord, the Bible's code word for faith. Proverbs promises that living by wisdom will have a steadying effect.

My child, do not let these escape from your sight;
keep sound wisdom and prudence,
and they will be life for your soul
and adornment for your neck.
Then you will walk on your way securely
and your foot will not stumble (Prov 3:21–23).

Our biblical portrait gallery offers us some models of people who took directions from God, but also some cautionary tales.

Some people began well, but their faith fizzled out and self-assertion flooded back into their inner lives. Solomon was one who feared the Lord as a young man, at least enough to ask for a *lev shomea*, which could be rendered in English either "a discerning mind" or a "listening heart" (1 Kgs 3:9). With that request he was asking for the wisdom to take directions from God. But Solomon is said to have turned to other gods later in his life. The division of the kingdom after his death was a result (1 Kgs 11:9–13).

As the folk poem says so well:

King David and King Solomon lived very wicked lives.
With way too many concubines and far too many wives.
So when old age came creeping on, they both were filled with qualms.

So Solomon wrote the Proverbs, and David wrote the Psalms.

By contrast, Mary, in the Gospel of Luke, is portrayed as one who cultivated the virtue of the fear of the Lord from start to finish (Luke 1:26–38). I would suspect that she began with a bit of trembling before Gabriel. But then she trusted God's strange message. And finally, she allowed God to direct her actions to the very end. "Here I am, the servant of the Lord; let it be with me according to your word" (Luke 1:38).

Jacob, Saul, and Lot seem to be examples of people who largely trusted in and took directions from their own insights and agendas rather than the wisdom of God. Abraham, Noah, Joseph, Daniel, Moses, Joseph, and Mary are presented as people who largely trusted in and took directions from God and not from their own insights and agenda.

Most of us are not either God-trusters or self-trusters, but live our lives pushed and pulled between the two poles. Human nature being the complex mire that it is, each of us struggles in the tension between trusting God and self-assertion. David is an obvious example of the struggle between the two. Jacob, the heel-grabbing opportunist, had moments of trust and even Mary, the model of faith, perhaps had moments of uncertainty.

The recognition we all have that we are imperfect, flawed humans comes into sharp relief when we are confronted by the presence of God. Notice the common reaction of people in the New Testament when they realize they are in the presence of the divine. When Zechariah saw an angel of the Lord, standing at the right side of the altar of incense, "he was terrified and fear overwhelmed him" (Luke 1:2). When the shepherds noticed that an angel of the Lord was standing before them, "they were terrified" (Luke 2:9). Perhaps an exception is Mary, who, though nonplussed, was remarkably composed. Peter, stunned by the miraculous catch of fish, "fell down at Jesus' knees, saying, 'Go away from me, Lord, for I am a sinful man'" (Luke 5:8). The citizens of Gerasene reacted with fear to finding the demon-possessed man quiet and in a sane frame of mind. "They asked Jesus to leave them, for they were seized with great fear" (Luke 8:37). Mark and Luke recount that the disciples were terrified when Jesus was transfigured and a cloud overshadowed them on the Mount of Transfiguration (Mark 9:2–8, Luke 9:28–36). Matthew recounts that when they heard the voice from the cloud identifying Jesus as God's Son, "they fell to the ground and were overcome by fear" (Matt 17:1–9). When two men in dazzling clothes stood beside the women at the empty tomb, "they were terrified and bowed their faces to the ground" (Luke 24:5).

What is Jesus' or the angelic messenger's response to human terror? It is most often, "Take heart, Do not be afraid." There is no getting around the fact that God is a demanding God and that Jesus' way of discipleship is narrow and hard. At the same time, over and over again, we find that the drawing near of the awesome, transcendent God in the person of Jesus means not punishment or destruction, but healing, wisdom, and salvation.

We mentioned several biblical people whose lives were characterized by trust in God. But I can think of only one person who perfectly embodied the trembling, trust, and taking directions from God that make up the fear of the Lord: Jesus, God's Son. Jesus trusted God with his life and with his death and is alive again. And how is one who has faith in God through Christ to respond to this incredible outcome? With trust. The fear of the Lord in the New Testament takes the form of trust in Christ. It is followed by the disciple's following Jesus along the way. "I am the Way, the truth and the Life," says Jesus (John 14:6). Early Christians were called "followers of the Way." As we follow Jesus throughout our earthly lives, we have the confidence that "Wisdom in person," is by our side to guide us in living out the wisdom teachings he offered when he walked the earth.

A pastor I met recently told me the following story, one that comes from the days before smartphones with built-in GPS were a commonplace.

A funeral procession was making its way from Vidor, Texas to Franklin for a late afternoon committal service. The funeral director gave the hearse driver some vague, scrawled directions on the back of a funeral bulletin and sent him off to lead the procession. The hearse was in the front, the family in the next several cars. They left Vidor midafternoon, and went north on 69, then west on 190, then at Huntsville, turned north on 45 but when the turnoff came to go left on 79 at Buffalo to go southeast toward Franklin, the hearse missed it and kept going on 45 north toward Corsicana. The deceased man's daughter in the second car felt like something wasn't right, but couldn't find her Garmin, though she frantically looked all through the car.

Meanwhile the preacher doing the committal was waiting by the grave with his cell phone trying to contact anybody to find out what the holdup was. He finally got the hearse driver and said, "Hey, we're running out of daylight. Where are you?"

Finally around dusk, the procession rolled up at the graveside. The preacher and a cemetery worker directed the cars to circle the grave and keep their headlights on so they could see to lower the body into the grave.

The family began clambering out of their cars, stretching their stiffened joints and pulling on sweaters and jackets against the chill in the air. The man's daughter realized she'd left her jacket in the trunk. When she opened the trunk, she heard a frantic, robotic female voice repeating "U Turn as soon as possible! U turn as soon as possible!"

There comes a time when we tire of driving around in a state of perpetual disorientation with our smartphone in the trunk. The wisdom seeker has the choice to put the Wisdom of God in the driver's seat of his or her life and see where it leads. The fear of the Lord, when all is said and done, comes down to an exchange of garden-variety fears for faith, a bone-deep trust in the God before whom we tremble, in whom we trust, and from whom we take directions.

In the next chapter we will turn to the second wisdom virtue, the Listening Heart.

Questions for Reflection on The Fear of the Lord

1. How did you understand the fear of the Lord before reading this chapter?

2. What are some of your greatest fears? For yourself, your friends and family? Our nation and world?

3. Before what or whom do you tremble in life?

4. What or whom do you trust most in life?

5. From whom do you take directions?

6. What experiences in your life have challenged your faith?

7. What experiences have strengthened your faith?

8. How would you like to grow in faith in the days ahead?

Chapter 3

PART ONE—The Second Wisdom Virtue
The Listening Heart

"Give your servant therefore a listening heart to govern your people, able to discern between good and evil" (1 Kgs 3:9).

Solomon's "Right Answer"!

SEVERAL YEARS AGO A friend of mine was appointed as senior pastor of a sizeable church. This was a new responsibility for him. He had been an associate pastor on a large church staff prior to this new role. He told me "Alyce, I feel like a little boy going into work carrying Daddy's briefcase." I imagine this is how the young King Solomon felt when it came time to fill King David's shoes. In the story of the young king's dream at Gibeon, God invites him to make a request: "Ask what I should give you" (1 Kgs 3:5). Solomon expresses his gratitude, acknowledges his insecurities, and then gets around to answering God's question. "Ask what I should give you." Solomon asks for a *lev shomea*, which the NRSV renders *"an understanding mind"* (1 Kgs 3:9), but which could just as well be rendered a *"listening heart."*[1]

The Hebrew understanding of the concept of heart did not reduce it to the seat of emotions. They did not place mind or intellect in one Tupperware container and heart or emotions in another. *Lev* referred to the seat of decision making, not just feelings. The book of Proverbs, as we've seen, contains sayings from centuries of Israel's history, collected and ascribed to Solomon.

1. Murphy, *The Tree of Life*, 2.

Reflecting this, the multiple appearances of the word *lev* in Proverbs, are sometimes translated as *mind* and sometimes as *heart*. In this collection, the heart (*lev*) is like a jewel with many facets. It is the seat of understanding and therefore the faculty whereby a person grasps wisdom. The heart is referred to as the seat of reflection in several proverbs (6:18; 15:28; 16:9; 19:21; 24:2). Elsewhere, the heart is equated with memory (6:21; 7:3) and with wisdom (15:21; 19:8).[2] The heart is also regarded as the seat of emotions: joy (15:30), sorrow (14:10, 13), pride (16:5; 18:12; 21:4), obstinance (17:20; 28:14), or malice (26:23). The heart is viewed as the seat of character, either bad or good (11:20; 12:8). The heart can also refer to the disposition (25:20) and the inner person (3:5).

When Solomon asks for a *lev shomea* he is asking for the quality that will enable him to be a good ruler. He is asking for the "listening heart" or the "hearing mind" that will enable him to "judge" (*shaphat*) the people and to discern (*havin*) the difference between good and evil (1 Kgs 3: 9a). God, in granting the request, refers to it as a request for "discernment to hear justice" (*havin lishmoa' mishpat*, 3:11b).[3]

Mountaintop spiritual experiences don't last forever. Sooner or later, some conflict, catastrophe, or chore always calls us back down to earth. Solomon's reception of the gift of a "listening heart" comes not a moment too soon. As soon as his feet hit level ground, two women approach him, both of whom claim the rights to one baby. There are no witnesses (1 Kgs 3:18b), and both stories are equally plausible (vv. 22–23). Solomon resolves the problem by making a proposal: Divide the baby in half. The proposal succeeds because it brings the character or the heart of each woman to light.[4]

As this incident shows, God has given Solomon the gift of the *lev shomea*. But Solomon, and anyone else who would become wise, must cultivate the gift. One does that by attending, first to God, but also to other people. The Hebrew verb for "hear" or "listen" (*shama*) refers to more than physical hearing. It means responsive obedience to God. The central prayer of the Jewish prayer book, the *Shema*, which begins with Deuteronomy 6:4, is "Hear, (or 'Listen') O Israel, the Lord Your God, the Lord is One." It continues in verse 5, "And you shall love the Lord Your God with all your heart, and with all your soul and with all your might." These are the first words taught to Jewish children, the prayer parents pray with them before they fall asleep, and the last earthly words spoken by devout Jews.

2. Oesterley, *The Book of Proverbs*.

3. Moberly, "Solomon and Job," 4.

4. Ibid, 4–5.

The habit of hearing or listening with our heart/mind (*lev shomea*), responsive obedience to God, is especially important when we encounter difficult situations. Judaism teaches that if we are to be fully attentive to people, we must first be fully attentive to the will of God as expressed in the judgments (*mishpatim*) of Torah.[5] As Christians we cultivate the habit of attentiveness to the will of God as expressed in the teachings of Jesus. When, in Matthew 22:34–40, a lawyer asks Jesus, "What is the greatest commandment?" Jesus responds with a collation of Deuteronomy 6:5 with Leviticus 19:18. The greatest commandment involves listening with our hearts to God and to neighbor.

This attentiveness, to both God and other people, is an active rather than a passive pursuit. It involves an intense alertness. To cultivate a "listening heart" is to commit to a lifelong attentiveness to all of life, one's own experiences, those of others, and the created order. It is to regard all of these as arenas for God's wisdom and guidance.

Prominent in the opening chapters of Proverbs are the calls to the disciple of wisdom for openness and attention: "Hear . . . turn . . . receive . . . be attentive . . . cry out for insight . . . seek . . . incline your ear . . . receive . . . keep your heart with vigilance . . . let not your heart turn aside . . . listen . . . watch . . . wait . . . ." So valuable is the quality of attention that it is thought of as a gift from the Creator's hand.

"A listening ear and a seeing eye,
The Lord indeed has made them both" (Prov 20:12).

The habit of attentiveness encourages one to seek wisdom in one's present circumstances.

"The discerning person looks to wisdom, but the eyes of a fool to the ends of the earth" (Prov 17:24).

In this present moment, nothing in God's creation is too small or obscure to warrant profound attention. The sage's attentiveness brings with it a profound sense of wonder.

"Three things are too wonderful for me;
Four I do not understand:
The way of an eagle in the sky,
The way of a snake on a rock,
The way of a ship on the high seas,
And the way of a man with a girl" (30:18–19).

5. Ibid.

The sage enters the world of the ant, the badger, the locust, and the lizard, with a fine attentiveness to the lessons they may hold (30:24–28).[6]

Attentiveness to the wisdom to be gained in the here and now leads, doesn't end, in reflection. It leads to action.

"Those who are generous [or who have a 'generous eye'] are blessed, for they share their bread with the poor" (Prov 22:9).

Macrina Wiederkehr is a Catholic nun, a member of Scholastica Monastery in Fort Smith, Arkansas. In her book *A Tree Full of Angels: Seeing the Holy in the Ordinary* she uses the metaphor of harvesting crumbs for this habit of attentiveness by which wisdom grows from day to day. Her metaphor expresses the habit of looking for the sacred in the ordinary that impels the life of living with a listening heart.

> There is a yearning deep in the human heart—so deep it is an ache within. An ache for God! . . . The ache in our heart needs to be fed . . . . Crumbs are those small things that the world would toss aside, seeing little value in them. However, to the one who lives under the eye of God, they are far from valueless . . . . Everything in life can be nourishing. Everything can bless us, but we've got to be there for the blessing to occur. Being present with quality is a decision we are invited to make each day . . . .
>
> Due to the reality of our terribly distracted, cluttered, and noisy existence, the decision for real presence is not easy. If we can make this decision and live it, it will be a kind of salvation for us. It can save us from many kinds of death: the death of apathy, . . . selfishness . . . meaninglessness. There is nothing so healing in all the world as real presence. Our real presence can feed the ache for God in others.[7]

Macrina Wiederkehr invites her readers to see the holy in the ordinary, to harvest angels out of the crumbs. She believes we live in a world of theophanies. "Holiness comes wrapped in the ordinary. There are burning bushes all around us. Every tree is full of angels. Hidden beauty is waiting in every crumb. Life wants to lead you from crumbs to angels, but this can happen only if you are willing to unwrap the ordinary by staying with it long enough to harvest its treasure." She says that it's time to harvest

- a spider web, wearing the morning's dew
- a mistake, reflected upon and learned from

6. Eaton, *The Contemplative Face of Old Testament Wisdom*, 41–42.

7. Weiderkehr, *A Tree Full of Angels*, xii–xiii.

- reconciliation after a quarrel
- an autumn tree letting go of her leaves
- a spring tree putting leaves on again
- a wound, embraced and understood.[8]

Frank Davis, an elderly man from the Pawnee tribe, offers another metaphor for the life of attentiveness to wisdom in a story about his mother's wisdom advice to him.

> My mother was a good woman. I thought she was the wisest person in the whole world. So one day—when I was just a little feller, maybe six or seven—I asked her how I could become wise like her. She just laughed and laughed and said I was awfully young to be asking such questions. But, she said, since I asked, she would tell me. "Life is like a path," she said, smiling down at me, "and we all have to walk the path . . . . As we walk down that path we'll find experiences like little scraps of paper in front of us along the way. We must pick up those pieces of scrap paper and put them in our pockets. Every single scrap of paper we come to should be put into that pocket. Then, one day, we will have enough scraps of papers to put together and see what they say. Maybe we'll have enough to make some sense . . . . Take them to heart and then put them back in your pocket and go on, because there will be more pieces to pick up. Keep walking and every now and then take them out and make some sense of them. That's how we become wise, or at least wiser than we were."[9]

The Listening Heart and the Fear of the Lord

The listening heart flows from the fear of the Lord. We have seen that the fear of the Lord, the Bible's code word for faith, is a matter of trembling, trust, and taking directions from God and God alone. The common denominator of those directions is that we be radically attentive to those around us.

The listening heart is the total person attuned to what God is doing in the world, with special focus on the needs of people God has placed in our path. Listening to our anxieties, fears, and self-centered agendas drains our mental focus and emotional energy so that there is nothing left with

8. Ibid., xiii.
9. Wall and Arden, *Wisdomkeepers*, 100–1.

which to listen to others. The wise person who is cultivating the gift of the *lev shomea* exchanges a life of self-absorption for a life of attentiveness to the hearts and minds of those around her and the ways God would have her use her gifts as she interacts with them. Self-help wisdom advises us to cultivate people for the ways they can advance our agendas and goals. Biblical wisdom advises us to cultivate the virtue of the listening heart. Why? Because it will direct us in how to use our gifts for the good of the community.

"Work is love made visible," wrote the Lebanese poet Kahlil Gibran.[10] In the same way, the listening heart is the fear of the Lord made visible. The listening heart is the fear of the Lord expressing itself as a reverent, humble attentiveness to all of life as the arena of God's revelation. If we have faith, the book of James reminds us, we will have works. In the same way, if we fear the Lord, we will live life with a listening heart. Wisdom scholar Kathleen Farmer points out that to be "wise," as the authors of Proverbs, Ecclesiastes, and Job use the term, means "both to reflect on one's own observations and to pay attention to the observations of others, to sift through and weigh one's own experiences over against the testimony of others."[11]

"Be Attentive!" The Listening Heart in the Book of Proverbs

Proverbs puts a hand on the shoulder of the reader and points her toward the fields of inner life, interrelationships, and the natural world. It spreads before her a rich array of insights that can be harvested from these fields.

Repeatedly throughout Proverbs, the young are enjoined to listen and hear the wisdom that is continually being offered to them by both mother and father (1:5, 8).

The parental teachings are compared to a "fair garland for your head and a pendant for your neck" (1:9) The wise youth will "bind them upon his heart always; and tie them around his neck. When he walks, they will lead him; when he lies down, they will watch over him. When he awakes, they will talk with him. "For the commandment is a lamp and the teaching a light and the reproofs of discipline are the way of life" (6:21–23).

"Keep my teachings as the apple of your eye; bind them on your fingers, write them on the tablet of your heart. Say to wisdom, 'You are my sister,' and call insight your intimate friend" (7:2–4).

If one does not listen to Wisdom, it is not because she has been inaccessible! The eloquent Wisdom discourses in chapter 1:20–33 and in chapter

10. Gibran, *The Prophet*, 14
11. Farmer, "The Wisdom Books," 129.

8 depict Wisdom as here, now, and available. We have a choice, of course. We can refuse to listen to Wisdom and come to ruin (5:13; 8:35–36). We can actively go against Wisdom's teachings, listen to words from lying lips, and become malicious fools (7: 24–27; 17:4). Or we can make a better choice. We can listen to Wisdom and find life (1:33; 3:13–18).

The book of Proverbs is the harvest of the sages' exercise of their listening hearts as they paid attention to their inner lives, their observations of others' behavior and their interactions with them and the world of nature.

General Observations

"When pride comes, then comes disgrace" (11:2).

"Where there is no guidance a nation falls" (11:14).

"The timid become destitute, but the aggressive gain riches" (11:16).

"Those who are kind reward themselves, but the cruel do themselves harm" (11:17).

"Some give freely, yet grow all the richer; others withhold what is due, and only suffer want" (11:24).

Observations on the Inner Life

"Anxiety weighs down the human heart, but a good word cheers it up" (12:25).

"Hope deferred makes the heart sick, but a desire fulfilled is a tree of life" (13:12).

"The heart knows its own bitterness, and no stranger shares its joy" (14:10).

"Like a city breached, without walls, is one who lacks self-control" (25:28).

Observations on Human Behavior and Relationships

"Like a dog that returns to its vomit is a fool who reverts to his folly" (26:11).

"A soft answer turns away wrath, but a harsh words stirs up anger" (15:1).

"One who forgives an affront fosters friendship, but one who dwells on disputes will alienate a friend" (17:9).

"Let your foot be seldom in your neighbor's house, otherwise the neighbor will become weary of you and hate you" (25:17).

"Like somebody who takes a passing dog by the ears is one who meddles in the quarrel of another" (26:17).

"Better is open rebuke than hidden love" (27:5).

Observations About Wealth and Poverty

"The poor are disliked even by their neighbors, but the rich have many friends" (14:20)

(19:4,7).

"A ruler that oppresses the poor is a beating rain that leaves no food" (28:3).

"A slack hand causes poverty, but the hand of the diligent makes rich" (10:4).

"Do not rob the poor because they are poor, or crush the afflicted at the gate; for the Lord pleads their cause and despoils of life those who despoil them" (22:22).

"Those who oppress the poor insult their Maker, but those who are kind to the needy honor him" (14:31).

Observations About Relating to Rulers

"When you sit down to eat with a ruler, observe carefully what is before you, and put a knife to your throat if you have a big appetite" (23:1,2).

"Do not desire the ruler's delicacies, for they are deceptive food" (23:3).

"Do not put yourself forward in the king's presence or stand in the place of the great; for it is better to be told, "Come up here," than to be put lower in the presence of a noble" (25:6, 7).

These observations come from many realms of experience: field and farm, king's court, and home and hearth. The sages of Proverbs were the Sherlock Holmes of wisdom, mastering the art of inductive reasoning, noticing very small things, that add up to patterns that ultimately yield guidelines for everyday living.

The Listening Heart in Job

There are several sayings in Proverbs that acknowledge that human knowledge is limited, that human life is unpredictable, and that the best-laid plans can falter and fail. Scholars call them the "limit" proverbs (16:1,2,9;19:21; 20:24; 21:30–31).[12] Old Testament wisdom scholar John Collins reminds us that the collaters of Proverbs, though upbeat, kept in mind this central truth: that "No degree of mastery of the rules and maxims of wisdom can confer absolute certainty. Life retains a mysterious and incalculable element, and it is precisely in this incalculable area that Yahweh is encountered."[13]

That said, it is fair to say that they preferred to focus on what they could discern and control. The sages who collected the sayings in Proverbs were, on the whole, an upbeat bunch. If they were to write their job description, I imagine they would say something like this: "Our job is to promote wisdom as the means to crafting an orderly, prosperous life. We understand that human beings can't predict the future and that we can't understand all the mysteries of God. But we don't choose to focus on those things. We'll leave that to the sages of Job and Ecclesiastes." The sages of Proverbs are like authors of positive human interest stories. The sages of Job and Ecclesiastes are more like investigative reporters, shining their spotlight on scenes of pain and injustice.

Picture all these sages sitting in an auditorium listening to a piece of music. The sages of Proverbs listen for the major key themes, the accessibility of Wisdom and the chance to use it to shape an orderly life. The sages of Job and Ecclesiastes listen for the minor key themes, those situations that showcase the unpredictability of life and our inability to guarantee positive outcomes by wise living. Job, his mind a haze of shock over his own sudden sufferings, sees one thing with crystal clarity: the traditional notion that outward suffering is a result of inward sin is bankrupt. His friends are so focused on defending that notion that they are oblivious to the anguish of their friend on the ash heap. Twentieth-century American satirist Dorothy Parker's wisecracking question could well apply to Job's friends: "With friends like these, who needs enemies?"

I recently began experiencing floaters in my right eye. I went to the eye doctor, who examined both eyes carefully. He concluded, "You don't have

12. Murphy, "Wisdom Theses," 198.

13. Collins, "Proverbial Wisdom and the Yahwist Vision," 10.

a retinal detachment but you may have one on the way." He wrote his cell phone number on the back of his business card and handed it to me. "Call me if you experience a dark curtain descending over your vision or if you lose your peripheral vision. Because that's a sure sign of trouble."

I heard in his words a metaphor for our spiritual lives. If we lose our peripheral vision in spiritual terms, we lose the willingness to face into what biblical scholar John Collins has baptized "the incalculable area" of life. We only want to see examples of conventional wisdom's "do good, get good" formula. We stare straight ahead, and we do not see the people who have lived wisely and still suffered misfortune. Or we see them, but blame them for their own adversity. If we ourselves are suffering adversity, this kind of cause-effect theology leads us to seek to assign blame somewhere. We blame ourselves, others, or God. Job's friends choose to blame him. "What did you do, Job, that this misfortune has befallen you?" ask Job's friends. At a social level, nations scapegoat whole groups of people as a way of explaining economic downturns, military defeats, or social chaos.

Sometimes our blinders are blown off our eyes by circumstances beyond our control. Just when our lives are sailing on smooth waters and we think we have everything figured out, we experience an unexpected misfortune. It causes us to come face-to-face with our inability to control an unpredictable life. It presents us with a choice—to meet the event with anger and bitterness or to meet it with a listening heart, attentive to what God may be saying to us through it, attentive to how we are connected to others who suffer in similar ways. Such occasions can become sacred spaces, wisdom crucibles, in which, through our own experience of suffering we become sensitized to that of others.

Amy Oestreicher, actress and artist, speaking out of experiences of illness and abuse, refers to them as potentially sacred detours and to those who can see the opportunities in them, as "detourists."

She says, "A detourist travels along detours—simple enough. But in addition, a detourist embraces those unexpected routes as opportunities for growth, change, and self-fulfillment. I am living proof *that a detour can lead to* unexpected blessings. Resilience takes work—especially when nothing seems to go our way. The good part is that *everyone* has had an unexpected detour one time or another, and the best teachers are the *stories* we hear."[14]

Social change happens over time when injustice and misfortune make it past our blinders. When individuals meet personal misfortune with a listening heart they can become change agents for entire societies. Organizations are launched when a child has become ill with a rare disease, a loved

14. Oestreicher, "What's a Detourist?"

one has been killed by a drunk driver, a town near an industrial plant has discovered a higher than average incidence of cancer, or a person has been the victim of violence because of their race, religion, sexual orientation, or line of work. Both the Black Lives Matter and the Back the Blue movements came out of individuals who experienced violence or death at the hands of others, whether young black men at the hands of white police officers or police officers at the hands of retaliatory snipers. As these individual instances stack up, we can't help but discern in them larger patterns of racism and violence in our society.

A good example of a contemporary person who exercised the listening heart is Leigh Anne Tuohy, the Memphis, Tennessee woman who, with her family, adopted Michael Oher into her home. Michael was a sixteen-year-old boy who had experienced multiple foster homes and periods of homelessness and trauma. With the Tuohys' care and support he became an All American football player and first round NFL draft pick in 2004, eventually playing for the Baltimore Ravens. Author Michael Lewis wrote the book *The Blindside* about the relationship between Oher and the Tuohy family that was made into an Oscar-nominated film in 2009 starring Sandra Bullock as Leigh Anne Tuohy. In a scene from the film, Tuohy and several friends are having lunch ($18 salads in an upscale Memphis restaurant). One of them says to her "You are changing that boy's life." She replies "No, he's changing mine."

To cultivate the virtue of the listening heart we must take off the blinders and notice the pain of others. Our attentiveness calls us out of our cocoons into community. Our peripheral vision restored, we act and speak for justice for the people and situations conventional wisdom has largely factored out.

Several years ago I was working on a book on the sage, or wisdom seeker, as a model for our Christian identity. I interviewed a number of pastors and laypeople from various backgrounds around the United States. I asked them the question "What does being a sage look like to you?" More than one person said it meant facing into the sufferings and struggles of life rather than numbing ourselves to them. One pastor expressed this truth especially well:

> Life is the anvil on which we hammer out our new growth. We can choose to learn something and grow, or we can choose not to. I have seen people die young but take years to bury! To learn and to grow we must not ignore our own or others' pain. Experience continually moves us out of each stage and each comfort zone into the next.

The more experiences we open ourselves to, the more in-
tensely we will struggle. Job's friends did not want to open themselves to the emotional impact of his situation. They didn't want
to have to struggle along with him. They didn't want to factor
his pain into their theology, didn't want to widen their life-lens
to take it in.[15]

The sages responsible for the book of Job were attentive to human suffering, but also to the suffering of Earth. They depict Job's listening heart
as moving him beyond the cocoon of his own discomfort into a sense of
community with the world of nature, with the sufferings of Earth, animals,
and plants.

The mistake he makes is in blaming God for them. He looks up from
where he sits on his dunghill scraping his sores, surveys the landscape
around him, and sees the animals and the plants, and he blames God for
their suffering too.

Ask the animals and they will teach you;
the birds of the air, and they will tell you;
ask the plants of the earth, and they will teach you;
and the fish of the sea will declare to you.
Who among all these does not know that the hand of the Lord has
   done this?
In his hand is the life of every living thing
and the breath of every human being (Job 12:7–10).

Job views Earth as he views himself, as a victim of divine injustice. So
he presumes to speak on Earth's behalf as well as his own. He refuses to rest
until he can confront the God who exercises such harsh power to destroy
the innocent and sustain the wicked.

By the end of the book, Job comes to realize that he has drawn the
wrong conclusions from his attentiveness to Earth's sufferings. At first he
sees in the natural world signs of God's unjust treatment, and he depicts
God as a capricious, interfering force. But then, in chapters 38—42, God
speaks out of the whirlwind informing Job that he has radically misunder-
stood what he has seen and heard.

Job has drawn the wrong conclusions from the evidence. Reading the
book of Job, sometimes it seems as if Job plays the role of Dr. Watson and
the reader plays the role of Sherlock Holmes. In chapter 1 of the Sherlock
Holmes tale *The Hound of the Baskervilles*, Holmes makes a comment
to Watson that captures the general tone of their interactions in all their

15. McKenzie, *Hear and Be Wise*, 69.

adventures. "I am afraid, my dear Watson, that most of your conclusion were erroneous . . . but noting your fallacies I was occasionally guided toward the truth."[16]

Near the end of Job, God notes Job's fallacies or misinterpretations and guides him toward the truth. Job undergoes an attitude shift from resentment to reverent obedience to a Creator God whose creation is full of forceful beauty and whose ways exceeds our human knowledge. This God confronts Job with a vision of a world whose inhabitants, from the least to the greatest, are mysteriously interconnected. Job, who relied on what he heard and listened to "with his ears," now looks at Earth and says to God "my eye sees you." He is listening with his heart.[17]

Not only does Job's listening heart sensitize him to the sufferings of Earth; it also opens his eyes to the sufferings of the Earth's poor. Job undergoes a second change of perspective. The Job described in the Prologue was "blameless and upright," an aristocratic figure, comfortable and safe within the confines of his estate, offering charity and prayers for the poor. His experience of suffering leaves him sick, naked, and vulnerable, feeling a kinship with those from whom he had formerly been able to distance himself. Liberation theologian Gustavo Gutierrez calls Job chapter 24:1–12 "the most radical and cruel description of the wretchedness of the poor found in the Bible." Job portrays the condition of the very poor, lacking the necessities of physical life, exploited by their employers and subjected to capricious, repeated violence. Job cries out on their behalf. Gutierrez observes that here the language of Job more closely resembles the language of the prophets than any of the other Old Testament wisdom writings.[18]

> They go about naked, without clothing;
> though hungry, they carry the sheaves;
> between their terraces they press out oil;
> they tread the wine presses, but suffer thirst.
> From the city the dying groan,
> and the throat of the wounded cries for help;
> yet God pays no attention to their prayer.

The book of Job was most likely the result of a school of wisdom, whose members were trying to make sense of the suffering of the postexilic nation of Israel. In Chapters 38—41 the poetic genius(es) responsible for the book of Job portray God taking Job to school, drawing his attention to the stunning beauty and complexity of creation. The author of Job has

16. Doyle, *The Hound of the Baskervilles*, 1.

17. Sinnott, "Job," 90–91.

18. Gutierrez, *On Job*, 32.

watched the dawn with wonder. He has noticed how, when daylight grows from the east, lines and forms stand out in the distance, like clay responds to a seal (38:12–14). Light and dark, snow, hail, rain, lightning, ice, and constellations: the poet of Job has considered them all with deep reverence (38:16–38). He has reflected on the wonders of animal life: the birth of the young, the free running of the wild ass, the strength of the wild ox, the migrations of the birds. To all these the poet-sage listens with his heart. In return, they speak to him of the mystery of creation and the Creator. In them, his listening heart meets that mystery of our Creator God.[19]

The listening heart's attentiveness promises that, as we continually exercise it, we will continually encounter God—sometimes where we could never have imagined we would encounter God. And the God we encounter may have little resemblance to the "do good, get good" God we have been raised to expect. We encounter this God in the sufferings of nature and the poor, with whom we are compelled by our own sufferings to identify. We encounter this God in the artistry of a sunrise and the amazing array of plant and animal life. In being attentive to the complexity and beauty of God's creation, the listening heart discovers both an anguish and a glory that can too easily escape our notice.

The Listening Heart in Qohelet

The name *Ecclesiastes* is the Latin transliteration of the Greek *ekklesiastes,* which is a translation of the Hebrew *Koheleth.* Koheleth means "Gatherer," but is traditionally translated as "Teacher" or "Preacher." It is the pseudonym used by the author(s) of the book. The name Qohelet is used to refer to the group of sages responsible for collating and perhaps coining the sayings of the book of Ecclesiastes. For convenience's sake, I'll use singular pronouns to refer to Qohelet throughout this work.

The name Qohelet probably comes from the Hebrew verb *qahal,* "to gather." Whether it refers to his gathering students or gathering proverbs is anyone's guess. Maybe both. Qohelet's wisdom is the product of the exercise of his listening heart in his particular time and place. He lived in Palestine in the fifth century BCE, when the nation was under the domination of the Persians. The capricious rulers played favorites, doling out land and jobs as it struck their fancy. The people living under their thumb became competitive and insecure. Prospects for freedom from this social and political domination seemed remote.

19. Eaton, *The Contemplative Face of Old Testament Wisdom,* 42.

Qohelet's book reflects the reality that daily life in his time, with the manual labor it entailed, was a dangerous venture rife with risks. Digging a pit put one in danger of falling into it (10:8a). Breaking through a wall put one at risk of being bitten by a hidden snake (10:8b). In this risky environment, many people felt hopeless. They speculated about the end times and looked to God to intervene in a dramatic way. But Qohelet rejects that avenue to hope, observing that "there is nothing new under the sun" (1:9). He puts his energies into figuring out how to deal with an extended present in which all is not as he thinks it should be and as he had hoped it would be. He trains his listening heart, as did the sages of Proverbs and Job, on the various realms of inner life, human behavior, and the natural world. He notices both the pleasures of life and scenes one has to ignore to maintain a relentlessly upbeat attitude. His book reveals both the pleasure and the pain of attentiveness.

His insights remind me of the website called Despair.com. The site offers calendars, stationery, and Post-it Notes that feature sarcastic, cynical sayings. It also features a series of posters called "demotivators." The originators of the site got the idea by noticing the motivational posters about self-esteem, learning from your mistakes, setting goals, and teamwork that hang on the walls of many corporate offices. These often feature scenes from nature and smiling people working together. I'm not knocking them. But the demotivator website is. And I think Qohelet, the name given to the person or group responsible for the book of Ecclesiastes, would feel quite comfortable decorating his walls with demotivator posters.

One "demotivator" poster features a huge grizzly bear about to catch a salmon in its paws with the caption, "Sometimes a journey of a thousand miles ends very badly." Another shows a man in a kayak about to go over a monster waterfall with the caption, "Believe in yourself. Because the rest of us think you're an idiot." Yet another features an ocean liner sinking with the caption, "It could be that the purpose of your life is only to serve as a warning to others."

The author of the book of Ecclesiastes, as we shall see, is by no means a complete pessimist. Still, his habit of training his listening heart on shadows as well as sunshine would make him a good candidate for the demotivators' design team!

Qohelet, in his pursuit of wisdom, first trains his listening heart on his own inner responses to a life of intentional self-indulgence. He concludes that drinking, building elaborately landscaped custom homes, having many possessions (that includes people as well as gold bouillon), and having multiple sexual partners does not pave a path to happiness (2:1–11).

He develops the outlook that "All is vanity." It becomes a refrain throughout the Book. The Hebrew word often translated "vanity" is *hebel*. It is sometimes rendered in English as *vapor,* and it refers to the quality of being fleeting rather than lasting. Qohelet uses *hebel* to describe human existence and experience. He uses *hebel* to speak of the fleeting quality of life (6:12; 7:15; 9:9), of something that is of little consequence (5:7;6:4, 11), of joy (2:1), of human accomplishments (2:11; 4:4), and of youth and the prime of life (11:10). He does not, however, use *hebel* to describe God or the cosmos in general.[20]

Wisdom scholar Michael V. Fox, in his book *Qohelet and His Contradictions,* believes that Qohelet experiences life as a series of disappointments with the promises of optimistic conventional wisdom. *Hebel* is the word he uses to describe those realities and situations that disappoint his positive assumptions about God and the benefits of seeking divine wisdom.[21] Qohelet's listening heart results in his constant attentiveness to *hebel*. We all experience occasional disappointments of our expectations, from mild to severe. In between, we seek to regain our balance and sense of purpose in life. But Qohelet's experience of disappointment is habitual, chronic, and long-term. Everywhere he turns he sees contradictions of conventional wisdom's promise that if we live wisely our lives will go well. His response is a permanent sense of futility. He lives with a constant inner question: "What's the point?"

As I read the through the book of Ecclesiastes I imagine walking through a gallery in which are hung lots of demotivational posters. We could take the captions straight out of his book! The gallery would be a visual record of things Qohelet notices when he trains his listening heart on life with him and around him. He notices that everyone dies, the wise as well as the fool. "There is no enduring remembrance of the wise or of fools, seeing that in the days to come, all will have been long forgotten. How can the wise die just like fools?" (1:16).

He notices that one's hard-earned wealth, at one's death, sometimes goes to slacker relatives who did nothing to assist in its accumulation. "Sometimes one who has toiled with wisdom and knowledge and skill must leave all to be enjoyed by another who did not toil for it" (2:21). He notices that, contrary to prevailing wisdom, wise actions do not always lead to good fortune, nor do evil ones lead to misfortune. "There is a vanity that takes place on earth, that there are righteous people who are treated according to the conduct of the wicked, and there are wicked people who are treated

20. McKenzie, *Preaching Proverbs,* 258.

21. Fox, *Qohelet and His Contradictions,* 32.

according to the conduct of the righteous" (8:14). He observes, "I have seen slaves on horseback, and princes walking on foot like slaves" (10:7).

He notices that each stage of life has its joys and its sorrows, and he concludes that everything has its set, preplanned time (3:1–8). He notices the cyclical quality of nature. "The sun rises and the sun goes down, and hurries to the place where it rises. The wind blows to the south and goes around to the north; round and round goes the wind, and on its circuits the wind returns. All streams run to the sea, but the sea is not full" (1:5–7).

When we come to Ecclesiastes 3 in Qohelet's poster gallery most of us assume that it is a lovely visual litany of "there is a time for this . . . and there is a time for that." We may picture the gallery walls filled with bright posters depicting planting, healing, building up, laughing, dancing, embracing, loving, and peace. But Qohelet's gallery also includes visuals of killing (3:4a), "breaking down"(3:3b), tearing (3:7), hating (3:8b), and war (8:b).

While verses from this passage are hung on walls and embroidered on pillows, they are not the potpourri of pleasantries most of us assume. They are more illustrations of Qohelet's conviction that human life exists in a predetermined pattern and there is no point in trying to resist that fact. We live at the mercy of powers we can't control and are foolish to try to oppose them. That's why I shuddered when the pastor began to read this passage at my dad's funeral. My dad, a publisher, novelist, and entrepreneur, came from a hardscrabble upbringing in the Depression-era South. He put a high premium on free will, convinced that life offers choices and opportunities. He believed that it's up to us to respond to those opportunities and, when necessary, to create them for ourselves. The goal for him was to do something with our lives to improve the world and leave a lasting legacy. Not a good match-up with the theology of Qohelet! The preacher who read Ecclesiastes 3 in soothing tones at my dad's funeral service should have done some exegesis first!

Continuing through his poster gallery, Qohelet's listening heart causes him to notice and include depictions of the rich oppressing the poor. Coming from a middle class, privileged social position, he does not feel motivated to do anything about it, but at least he has the decency to shed some tears over it and perhaps to lose some sleep. "Look, the tears of the oppressed, with no one to comfort them!" (4:1). He notices that envy motivates many human actions. "Then I saw that all toil and all skill in work come from one person's envy of another" (4:4). He notices that wealth creates, not contentment, but a craving for more wealth. "The lover of money will not be satisfied with money; nor the lover of wealth, with gain" (5:10). On a slightly more positive note, he notices the importance of sticking together, in human relationships as well as nature: "A threefold cord is not quickly broken" (4:12).

His listening heart doesn't allow him to ignore the unpredictable quality of life. "The race is not to the swift, nor the battle to the strong, nor bread to the wise, nor riches to the intelligent, nor favor to the skillful; but time and chance happen to them all" (9:11).

Nor can he help but notice the reality that misfortune can strike quickly. "Like fish taken in a cruel net, and like birds caught in a snare, so mortals are snared at a time of calamity, when it suddenly falls upon them" (9:12).

He acknowledges that a wise person can have a good influence (9:13–17). But he can't help but add a Debbie Downer dose of reality: "One bungler destroys much good" (9:18b).

He notices that "Dead flies make the perfumers' ointment give off a foul odor." He compares this with the fact that "A little folly outweighs wisdom and honor" (10:1).

He is alert to the dimmed vision, the trembling limbs, the bent back, the worn teeth, the deafness, the weakening sexual powers, and the white hair of the elderly (12:1–8).

What portrait of Qohelet himself emerges from our gallery tour? Is Qohelet simply the Debbie Downer of the Bible, our source for Ancient Near Eastern snark and sarcasm?

If Qohelet had only noticed the negatives in life we could dismiss him as a pessimist. But he was an equal-opportunity listener—he gave the upside of life as much of a chance as he did the down. He believed that wisdom was a guide to life. "The wise have eyes in their head, but fools walk in darkness" (2:14). He pointed out that toil holds inherent enjoyment. "There is nothing better for mortals than to eat and drink and find enjoyment in their toil" (2:22). He commented that wisdom is better than might (9:16).

Yet, because he was such a keen observer of all of life, each of his positive affirmations is paired with its pessimistic twin. Wisdom is a guide to life, but "The same fate befalls all of them" (2:14). Toil holds enjoyment (8:15) but it is ultimately futile and injustice is rampant (8:14). "Wisdom is better than might; yet the poor man's wisdom is despised and his words are not heeded" (9:16). In these times of terrorist attacks and mass shootings, "One bungler destroys much good," plays and replays in my mind, and I am heartened by the fact that an unflinching observer like Qohelet manages to discern any hope at all in his dire surroundings.

It is clear that Qohelet can't listen to the positives in life without also hearing and observing the negatives. By the same token, he can't observe the negatives without being mindful of the positives. The reason is because, in his view, both justice and injustice, pleasure and pain, joy and sorrow are from the hand of God. Qohelet believes that the pleasures of toil, eating and drinking, and human relationships are gifts from God (2:24; 5:18–20; 7:14;

8:15). At the same time, he asserts that all the deeds of both the righteous and the wicked are in the hand of God. He adds "Whether it is love or hate one does not know" (9:1).

The optimistic sages of Proverbs assure us that the one who seeks wisdom will find the knowledge of God (Prov 2: 5). Qohelet insists that, although we yearn to know God, God remains hidden, as do the mysteries of what lies beyond this life (Eccl 3:9–11; 5:2b; 8:16,17; 9:7–10).

His God is distant and inscrutable, responsible for enjoyment and injustice alike, to be revered but not challenged. So he gives this advice, which was certainly not the approach taken by Job! "For God is in heaven, and you upon earth; therefore let your words be few" (5:2b).

Qohelet's ultimate conclusion is that the pursuit of wisdom is another example of *hebel*, vapor. "In much wisdom is much vexation, and those who increase knowledge increase sorrow" (Eccl 1:18). Qohelet's trust in conventional wisdom's optimistic wall posters that basically promise "Do good, get good" has been undermined by his close observation of life and all the situations that give a lie to it.

I disagree theologically with Qohelet as I place his book in the context of the entire canon of Old and New Testament, my experience of God, and that of the United Methodist ecclesial tradition from which I come. I don't believe that God is wholly distant and inscrutable, I don't believe that God is the author of good and bad alike. And I don't believe that this life is all there is.

Nor do I believe that Qohelet's wisdom dead ends in demotivation. What stands out about his book for me is not its pessimism, but its realistic grasp of the joy that can be ours in the midst of an often unjust and unpredictable world. That for me is the fruit of his exercise of the wisdom virtue of the listening heart. I respect him for the way his wisdom honors the complexity of life. It promises no warm and fuzzy deity, no fairy-tale endings, no permanent bliss. God is distant, and yet gift-giving. Wisdom cannot free us from death, and yet is worth pursuing. Pleasure is fragile and fleeting, yet real and gratifying. Joy is only in the present but is thereby doubly precious. Qohelet's listening heart yields some positive advice for living—live in the present, with awe for a mysterious God, grateful for the gift of life, enjoying the pleasures of your little corner of the world. Realize that life is precarious, and value its preciousness all the more. Qohelet's unflinching exercise of his listening heart, noticing the pain with the joy, leads him to exchange what could have been a perpetual posture of fear to positive affirmation of faith in the generosity and presence of God.

The Listening Heart in Other World Religions

The biblical virtue of the listening heart comes into even sharper focus when we view it through the lens of a broader cultural, religious perspective. All the major religions commend three interrelated types of active listening to their followers. They are to be attentive to signs of the divine presence that is a pervasive force in the universe. They are to listen to their inward lives as at least one realm where the divine reality is present and communicative. They are to listen to the sufferings of others as a prelude to a helping response.

All major religions concur that a divine force pervades the world beyond the terrain of one's inner life. The Abrahamic religions (Judaism, Islam, and Christianity) insist on a distinction between Creator and creatures, while Eastern religions generally affirm their essential oneness. Various spiritual disciplines are a means of remaining alert to that presence amid the demands of daily life.

In the second place, a variety of religions commend attentiveness to the inner life, because of the influence it exerts on the actions of the individual and his or her outward circumstances. The goal of this attentiveness is to overcome the ego's greedy grip on the life of the individual. The ego-driven life is characterized by materialism, destructive addictions, and spiritual tumult that prevent human life from being and becoming a full expression of divine life.

Hinduism has its psychophysical yogic disciplines. Buddhism has its emphasis on "right mindfulness," the seventh step in its "eightfold path." The term refers to a rigorous, continuous self-examination aimed at keeping the mind in control of the senses and impulses rather than being driven by them.[22]

Islam has its discipline of prayer five times a day focusing on the praise and gratitude that are due to the Creator from the creature.

The third habit of attentiveness commended by many religions focuses on the sufferings of human life, not just one's own, but also those of others. One's religious life is, at least to some degree, to be directed toward the alleviation of others' suffering. Islam's third pillar is charity, whereby the comfortable should share with the unfortunate.[23] Confucius considered benevolence to be the virtue of virtues and emphasized concern for one's parents and respect for the aged. Buddhism commends the four noble virtues

---

22. Smith, *The Illustrated World's Religions,* 75
23. Ibid., 162.

of loving-kindness, compassion, equanimity, and joy in the happiness and well-being of others.[24]

All the religions mentioned have in common the use of imagery, metaphors, legends, anecdotes, and pithy sayings to convey religious truths, both in relation to the individual's meditative life and to his or her interactions with others. The use of these vivid vehicles is evidence of the sages' attentiveness to daily life around them.

Jesus' Listening Heart

Recent scholarship has pointed out that Jesus, in addition to being a prophet and healer, was also a sage, a wisdom teacher who both modeled and encouraged the listening heart. The miracles and healings of Jesus, as depicted in all four Gospels, are meant to lead people to faith, repentance, and discipleship. But they do not cause them by spontaneous combustion. Those whose faith is inspired by miracles and healings are those who have been listening to his teaching. Following the feeding of the four thousand in Mark's gospel (8:14–21), Jesus chastises his disciples. They can give him precise statistics about how much bread was left over, but they have missed the event's s upiritual significance. Jesus asks them a rhetorical question, "Do you have eyes and fail to see? Do you have ears and fail to hear?" (Mark 8:18).

Both Jesus' parables and his short, proverbial saying reveal his habit of attentive listening to life around him. Like the sages of Proverbs, Jesus observed and learned from the created world. His many analogies and similes between aspects of the kingdom of God and the everyday world make this clear. He heard the sound of seeds hitting the earth and saw a woman ransacking her home, searching for a coin. He saw a house sinking because it was built on sand, and heard someone knocking on a friend's door late one night, begging for bread. He noticed foxes crawling into their holes, birds settling in their nests, and trees barren of fruit. He noticed someone trying to get a speck out of his eye, reeds blowing in the wind, the beauty of lilies, and the behavior of vultures.

Jesus was not the first religious teacher to use parables. Within his own tradition other rabbis used them, but primarily to illustrate the known: existing scriptural passages. Jesus used them, with an infusion of oddity and paradox, to illustrate the unknown: the inbreaking reality of the kingdom of God, already but not yet. Jesus' parables incorporate his hyper-attentiveness to detail. He took circumstances and characters he observed in everyday life and wove them into scenes that, at first glance, seem quite unremarkable.

24. Ibid, 82.

Until the listener (or reader) discovers that they contain a strange twist. Things don't go the way they do in the everyday life scenarios familiar to his listeners. People don't act the way they normally do in the real world. A vineyard owner pays those who worked the least hours as much as those who worked the most hours. At the last minute, the leading lights of the community renege on attending a banquet to which they've already RSVP'd and the host fills the banquet halls with people from alleys, bus stations, and homeless shelters. It is through the strange twist in the story that Jesus cracks open our window on the world and shows us a glimpse of the kingdom of God, already but not yet. Through Jesus' short stories (parables), our minds are teased into questioning our own habitual behavior and our assumptions about God's behavior. We are led to consider how the kingdom of God is different from the kingdoms of this world. New Testament scholar C. H. Dodd offered the definitive definition of a parable as Jesus used the genre. A parable is a "metaphor or simile drawn from nature or common life, arresting the hearer by its vividness or strangeness, and leaving the mind in sufficient doubt about its precise application to tease it into active thought."[25]

Jesus' listening heart shaped, not only his parables, but his short sayings, proverbial in form. Several of them sound like they could have come right off the pages of the book of Proverbs in their expression of conventional wisdom. "A city built on a hill cannot be hid" (Matt 5:14). "Today's trouble is enough for today"(Matt 6:34). "Where your treasure is there will your heart be also"(Matt 6:21).

Jesus' short sayings also include a number of unconventional wisdom sayings. These sayings challenged traditional, status quo–preserving wisdom. They questioned the religious and social conventions of his day. A prime example is, "It is not what goes into the mouth that defiles, but what comes out" (Matt 15:11; Mark 7:15). This saying undermined the ritual purity laws of religious practice of his day. Yet another example is "Whoever would save his life must lose it" (Matt 16:25; Mark 8:35; Luke 9:24). This saying challenged the choice of safety and prosperity as the ultimate goals of one's life. We will explore Jesus' edgy sayings more fully when we discuss his subversive voice in Chapter Five.

Clearly Jesus' listening heart shaped his parables and proverbial teachings. It also shaped his encounters with troubled, often fearful people. He habitually perceived their hidden motives, identified the sources of their fears and invited them to exchange them for faith.

---

25. Dodd, *Parables of the Kingdom*, 5.

Jesus was uncannily perceptive in listening to hidden human motives After he healed the paralytic lowered through the roof, Jesus discerned the inner objections of the scribes and asked, "Why do you raise such questions in your hearts?" (Mark 2:8); Following his healing of the man with a withered hand in the synagogue on the Sabbath, Jesus discerned the inward anger of his adversaries. Says Mark, "He was grieved at their hardness of heart" (Mark 3:5).

Sometimes the hidden motive is desire for greatness. On the way to Capernaum Jesus perceives the conversation going on among his disciples and, on arriving at the house, asks, "Why do you argue over who is greatest?" (Mark 9:33). The same scenario is described in Luke 9:46. "Jesus, aware of their inner thoughts, took a little child and put it by his side, and said to them . . . the least among all of you is the greatest."

Sometimes the hidden motive is love of material things. Jesus discerns the inward spiritual condition of the rich man who comes to him and asks him about the requirements for entry into eternal life. "Jesus, looking at him, loved him and said, 'You lack one thing; go, sell what you own, and give the money to the poor, and you will have treasure in heaven; then come, follow me" (Mark 10:21–22).

Sometimes the hidden motive is arrogance in relation to others. In Luke's version of the woman anointing Jesus, Simon the Pharisee, whose home was the site of the dinner, raised objections in his own mind. Luke tells us that Jesus discerned those thoughts and addressed them. "Simon, I have something to say to you." He then tells a brief parable about the forgiveness of debts. It seems clear that Jesus intends for Simon to apply the parable to himself and his colleagues in their presuming to judge this woman's standing before God (Luke 7:39–42).

Jesus not only listened with his heart to the hidden motivations in others' hearts. He also was attuned to their faith. He noticed the faith of the four friends lowering the paralytic through the roof. "When Jesus saw their faith, he said to the paralytic, 'Son, your sins are forgiven'" (Mark 2:5). He commended the centurion for his faith with these words: "Nowhere in Israel have I found such faith" (Luke 7:9). He offered healing words of encouragement to the woman who had suffered for twelve years with a hemorrhage, "Daughter, your faith has made you well. Go in peace" (Luke 8:48).

In addition to training his listening heart on people's hidden motives and faith, Jesus listened to their fears. Telltale phrases express his attentiveness to the pain and fear of others. "Moved with pity" (Mark 1:41), "I have compassion for the crowd" (Mark 8:2), "Do not weep" (Luke 7:13).

Jesus listened to people's fears and countered them in both his teachings and in face-to-face encounters. "Do not fear those who kill the body but cannot kill the soul; rather, fear him who can destroy both body and soul in hell. But even the hairs on your head are counted, so do not be afraid" (Matt 10:31; Luke 12:4ff). In Matthew 14:26 Jesus walks toward the disciples on the water. When they cry out in fear, he says "Take heart, it is I. Do not be afraid." In Matthew's version of the transfiguration, when the disciples heard the voice of God from the cloud, "they fell to the ground and were overcome by fear, but Jesus came and touched them, saying, "Get up and do not be afraid" (Matt 17:6,7). Mark and Luke do not emphasize Jesus' reassurance of the disciples in their fear (Mark 9:2–8; Luke 9:28–36). To the disciples after his resurrection, the Matthean Jesus said, "Do not be afraid; go and tell my brothers to go to Galilee. There they will see me" (Matt 28:10).

Jesus comforts the leader of the synagogue whose daughter was believed dead with these words: "Do not fear; only believe and she will be saved" (Mark 5:36). He teaches his disciples "Do not be afraid, little flock, for it is your Father's good pleasure to give you the kingdom" (Luke 12:32). When Peter realizes a divine force is at work in the miraculous catch of fish and says to Jesus "Go away from me, Lord, for I am a sinful man," Jesus replies, "Do not be afraid; from now on you will be catching people" (Luke 5:10).

When the book of Proverbs repeatedly enjoins us to "fear the Lord," we have seen that it is not advising us to fear imminent punishment at the hands of God. Rather, fear of the Lord is a code word for faith, for a three-stranded braid composed of awe before the divine (Isa 6), covenant faithfulness that puts no other loyalty above God (Deut 10:20), and confidence in God for moral direction (Prov 3:3–5). The fear of the Lord in the New Testament takes the form of acknowledgement of Jesus' sonship and authority. We have seen in the Old Testament that trembling with awe before God's transcendence is a crucial component of the fear of the Lord. It remains an appropriate posture when the human encounters the transcendent in the New Testament. Examples include the earthquake at the death of Jesus and the subsequent terror of the guards (Matt 27:51–54), the exalted humble one of Philippians 2, the exalted Lamb in Revelation 5, and the pitiful showing of the principalities and powers in Romans 8, whose best efforts to separate us from the love of God are doomed to fail.

But the Gospel writers do not emphasize trembling in awe at God's transcendence in their portrayal of people's response to Jesus' ministry. When the divine draws near through the presence of Jesus, it is primarily to energize and embolden people's faith, not to cause them to tremble with awe.

The sages of proverbs talked a good deal about proper speech. Jesus has more to say about the importance of listening. "Those who have ears to hear, let them hear" (Mark 4:9; Matt 11:15). Those who want to be his disciples, then and now, are to listen to his words and also to observe his life. When we do so, we realize that his life and teachings grew out of the habit of intense listening. As a sage with a listening heart, Jesus lived in a state of hyperattentiveness to God at work in his inner life, Scriptures, and life around him. In like manner, we are to listen for where God is speaking to us in our inner lives, Scriptures, and life around us through Jesus' life and teachings. Who better to guide us in living with a listening heart?

In Part Two of this chapter we will explore how to cultivate the virtue of the listening heart in our daily lives. In that process, the example of the sages of the Old Testament and Jesus enlighten us. And the presence of Jesus the crucified and risen sage, with us in the person of the Holy Spirit, guides and emboldens us.

Chapter 3

Part Two—Listen Up!
Cultivating the Listening Heart

A closer look at the heart that we are cultivating

The heart is "the authority within."

To the ancient Hebrews the heart was the seat of character and decision-making as well as emotions. When we are told to love God with all our heart (Deut 6:5), we are being told to keep all our emotions and all our thoughts working for God. The Hebrew alphabet was originally pictorgraphic. Each letter of the alphabet originated in a picture of a daily object or concept. In the case of *lev* (heart) the *lamek* ("l") depicts a shepherd's staff and indicates control or authority over someone or group. The letter *bet* at the end of *lev* originated in a picture of a house. Hence *lev* or heart means "the authority within." To live with a listening heart is to live so that God directs the exercise of the heart, the authority within. The first picture in this Hebrew word is a shepherd staff and represents authority as the shepherd has authority over his flock. The second letter is the picture of the floor plan of the nomadic tent and represents the idea of being inside as the family resides within the tent. When combined they mean "the authority within."

The Heart is the Wellspring of Speech Both Good and Bad.

"Like the glaze covering an earthen vessel are smooth lips with an evil heart" (Prov 26:23).

"What comes out of the mouth proceeds from the heart and this is what defiles" (Matt 15:19)

"The mouths of the righteous utter wisdom, and their tongues speak justice. The law of their God is in their hearts; their steps do not slip" (Ps 37:30–31).

The Heart is the Wellspring of Actions Both Good and Bad.

"This people honors me with their lips
But their hearts are far from me" (Matt 15:7–8).

"Where your treasure is, there will your heart be also" (Matthew 6:21; Luke 12:34).

"No good tree bears bad fruit, nor again does a bad tree bear good fruit; for each tree is known by its own fruit. Figs are not gathered from thorns, nor are grapes picked from a bramble bush. The good person out of the good treasure of the heart produces good, and the evil person out of evil treasure produces evil; for it is out of the abundance of the heart that the mouth speaks" (Luke 6:43–45).

The Heart is the Seat of the Will and the Intentions

Hear oh Israel, the Lord is our God, the Lord alone.
    You shall love the Lord your God with all your heart, and with all your soul, and with all your might. Keep these words that I am commanding you today in your heart." Recite them to your children. And talk about them when you are at home and when you are away, when you lie down and when you rise. Bind them as a sign on your hand, fix them as an emblem on your forehead, and write them on the doorposts of your house and on your gates (Deut 6:4–5).

You shall put these words of mine in your heart and soul, and you shall bind them as a sign on your hand, and fix them as an emblem on your forehead. Teach them to your children, talking about them when you are at home and when you are away, when you lie down and when you rise (Deut 11:18).

A scribe asks Jesus "Which commandment is the first of all?" Jesus replies "Hear, O Israel, the Lord our God the Lord is One. You shall love the Lord your God with all your heart, and soul and mind and strength. The second is this: you shall love your neighbor as yourself. There is no other commandment greater than these." The scribe responded to the effect that he agreed and understood. Then Jesus said "You are not far from the kingdom of God" (Mark 12:28–34).

The heart is known by God and cleansed by God.

All deeds are right in the sight of the doer
But the Lord weighs the heart (Ps 51:7).

You desire truth in the inward being;
Therefore teach me wisdom in my secret heart.
Create in me a clean heart, O God,
And a new and right spirit within me" (Prov 21:2).

"I will give them one heart, and put a new spirit within them. I will remove the heart of stone from their flesh and give them a heart of flesh so that they may follow my statutes and keep my ordinances and obey them (Ezek 11:19–20).

"Blessed are the pure in heart for they will see God" (Matt 5:8).

"Likewise the Spirit helps us in our weakness, for we do not know how to pray as we ought, but that very Spirit intercedes with sighs too deep for words. And God who searches the heart, knows what is the mind of the Spirit, because the Spirit intercedes for the saints according to the will of God" (Rom 8:26).

The heart is the seat of trust, joy and thanksgiving.

"Trust in the Lord with your whole heart . . ." (Prov 3:5).

"I will give thanks to the Lord with my whole heart.
I will tell of all your wonderful deeds" (Ps 91:5).

"I have trusted in your steadfast love;
My heart shall rejoice in your salvation" (Ps 13:5).

"If we had forgotten the name of our God,
Or spread out our hands to a strange god,
Would not God discover this?

For he knows the secretes of the heart" (Ps 42:21).

"My flesh and my heart may fail, but God is the strength of my heart and my portion forever" (Ps 73:26).

"I commune with my heart in the night; I meditate and search my spirit" (Ps 77:6).

The heart comes in several varieties

There is the endangered heart of Cain. In Genesis 4:7 God warns Cain, "Sin is lurking at your door. You must master it." Cain doesn't heed God's warning and, in the very next verse, says to his brother "Come, Abel, let's go into the fields."

Other types of hearts appear throughout Scripture.

- The hardened heart (Pharaoh in the book of Exodus)
- The heart of stone, the heart of flesh (Ezek 11:19)
- The tender heart (Deut 10:15)
- The circumcised heart (Deut 10:16)
- The brave heart (Ps 27:3)
- The stubborn heart (Isa 4:12)
- The trusting heart (Prov 3:5)
- The whole heart (Luke 10:27). The lawyer stands up to test Jesus and Jesus replies: "You shall love the Lord your God with all your heart, and with all your soul and with all your strength, and with all your mind, and your neighbor as yourself."

Cultivating The Listening Heart: The Role of Prayer

What kind of heart do you want to have? What is your "authority within"? I would like a heart that is tender, brave, and wholly entrusted to God. I would like to live with a listening heart. Such a heart doesn't happen overnight. It must be cultivated. The way to cultivate such a heart is by the daily practice of allowing God to direct our thoughts, emotions, and actions. On this path, day by day, we come to understand more deeply that the fear of the Lord is the wellspring of all other virtues, the listening heart included (Prov 2:1–5).

There are three types of prayer that are especially effective in cultivating the listening heart. They are the examination of consciousness, contemplation, and biblical meditation or spiritual reading. The examination of consciousness involves a nightly review of the day for moments when God's grace has been in evidence and a review of our responses to those moments. It involves identifying times and places where we were not as open to God's guidance and resolving to try again with a new day.[1]

Contemplation is wordless resting in the presence of God, actively listening, having cleared away mental distractions through breathing, visual focus on some object of inspiration such as an icon, candle flame, or flower, or through the repetition of a brief mantra. It is a form of listening to God that replaces our usual habit of doing all the talking in our relationship with God.

Biblical meditation takes two forms. One is the meditative repetition of a word or phrase from a biblical text. Another is prayerful entry into biblical narratives using methods devised by St. Ignatius of Loyola, a sixteenth-century Spanish priest who founded the Society of Jesus (Jesuits).[2] He composed the Spiritual Exercises as a retreat handbook. They are a set of meditations on Scripture passages, prayers, and imaginative mental exercises meant to allow Christians to learn how to see God's grace active in their everyday lives.

Cultivating the Listening Heart: The Art of Paying Attention

A few months ago our daughter Rebecca and her husband Dallas invited us to dinner on a Friday night. It had been a long week. I was somewhat tired, but eager to spend time with our family. The four of us were sitting around their table enjoying our daughter Rebecca's delicious cooking, when, in the middle of the pork chops, our son-in-law Dallas said, "Would you like to see the whiteboard Rebecca has made for me in our home office? It covers an entire wall and she has put a green wooden frame around it." At the time Dallas was a PhD student writing a dissertation on Dietrich Bonhoeffer. I felt an immediate surge of excitement and even envy. What writer wouldn't covet a wall-sized whiteboard? Even better, one with a frame around it! I noticed nothing strange in his interruption of our meal, but said immediately, "Yes, I'd love to see it!" My husband Murry and I, Dallas and Rebecca, trooped into their home office. As I stood admiring the huge, green-framed idea board, there were several things I didn't notice. I didn't notice the balloons all over the floor. I didn't notice the little yellow onesie pinned to the board. I didn't notice the words in the middle of the board that said "Baby

1. Thompson, *Soul Feast,* 92–94.
2. Ibid., 17–30. Nouwen, *In the Name of Jesus,* 62.

Gingles, November 20, 2013!" It's amazing what it's possible not to notice when we're tired and focused on something that is not the main thing!

But when we cultivate the listening heart, we exchange habits of distraction and self-preoccupation with attentiveness to the revelatory glimmers of God's redemptive work in everyday life. Wisdom's second virtue, the listening heart, offers us directions for where to look and what to look for. Each wisdom book offers a slightly different variation on the theme: "Pay attention!" "Listen up!" This chapter is instructions in "listening up" from the biblical wisdom we've been exploring: Qohelet, Job, Proverbs, and Jesus' proverbial sayings.

We need instruction and reminders because cultivating the listening heart is a discipline we must continually nurture. It is much easier for us not to pay attention. "For lack of attention," writes the English mystic Evelyn Underhill, "a thousand forms of loveliness elude us every day."[3] The sages of Scripture would have agreed.

The rabbis of the first three centuries of the common era emphasized attention. Their ethical teachings have been collected in a work called *Pirke Avot* (*Sayings of the Fathers*). This collection of ethical sayings emphasized attention. "Live without hesitation. Dwell not on outcome or reward. Act with full attention"[4]

One of the great English spiritual writers, William Law (1686–1761), observed that "All the world preaches to an attentive mind, and if you have but ears to hear, almost everything you meet teaches you some lesson of wisdom."[5]

Barbara Brown Taylor, a gifted contemporary preacher and teacher, in her book *The Preaching Life*, calls on us to become "detectives of divinity," emphasizing that "the extraordinary is hidden in the ordinary."[6] Thomas Troeger, poet, hymn writer, and teacher of preaching, challenges us to "train our eyes to trace the play of heaven's light upon earth's shadowed surface," and to "tune our ears to hear the overtones of graces that sound in human speech." He observes that "it takes discipline to see and to hear the visions and voices of God in our life."[7] Mystic theologian Howard Thurman insisted that Christians ought to be "apostles of sensitiveness."[8]

3. Brussat and Brussat, *Spiritual Literacy*, 52.
4. Shapiro, *Wisdom of the Jewish Sages*, 4.
5. Eaton, *The Contemplative Face of Old Testament Wisdom*, 42.
6. Taylor, *The Preaching Life*, 50.
7. Troeger, *Creating Fresh Images for Preaching*, 12.
8. Thurman, *Deep is the Hunger*, ix.

Listen Up! Proverbs Style

How do the wisdom portions of Scripture guide us in cultivating a listening heart? They each model paying attention to inner life and outer circumstances—both relationships and the natural world. Their notions of what to listen to and to what end differ. Here is a preview to guide your journey through the Bible's listening heart.

Proverbs teaches us how to notice patterns of cause and effect in which wise living leads to good results on a journey to greater knowledge of Divine wisdom toward the goal of community harmony (*shalom*).

Qohelet teaches us to notice deviations from the do good, get good patterns of Proverbs, with the result that we let go of unrealistic expectations and enjoy the precious, if precarious, gifts of our transcendent God in our current circumstances.

Job teaches us to notice that we are human and not God, to accept what we cannot know given the limits of our human understanding and to maintain faith in God in the midst of undeserved adversity.

Jesus teaches us to listen and look for injustice, to participate in the inbreaking kingdom of a demanding and yet gracious God who assures us that, despite all appearances to the contrary, righteousness and justice will prevail without fail.

So there is our preview of coming attractions. Let's begin our training in cultivating our listening heart by consulting with the biblical sages responsible for the book of Proverbs. They insist, first and foremost, that we pay attention to the God's trustworthy guidance at the core of our lives, discernible in our inner lives, our relationships and in the world of nature that surrounds us. And, just as we are attentive to signs of wisdom in all these arenas, we are to be on the lookout for signs of folly, the rejection of wisdom's guidance. I have coined the term "knack for noticing," for this habit of paying attention to our inner lives (inscape), our surroundings (landscape), and insights from our biblical heritage (textscape).

Proverbs encourages us to be on the alert for examples of wise living yielding positive results. Characteristics of wise living in Proverbs include self-restraint, hard work, honesty, forgiveness, generosity of spirit, honoring the poor, wise speech, and a humble attitude. Such attentiveness might yield the following scenarios. At an airport you observe a restaurant owner serving a free meal to a homeless person at a back table. You note the glance of kindness and gratitude that flashes between them. "Whoever is kind to the poor lends to the Lord, and will be repaid in full" (Prov 19:17).

At a social reception at a professional meeting, you see a colleague new to the group standing at the edge of the room, obviously feeling awkward.

You approach her and engage her in conversation, and ease her discomfort at entering a new social situation. Later in your career, that person is asked to write a letter recommending you for a promotion. "Those who are kind reward themselves, but the cruel do themselves harm" (Prov 11:17).

The sage's listening heart is attentive, not only to signs of wisdom but to folly as well. He or she is to be on high alert for signs of the consequences of foolish behavior: overindulgence, anger, hardheartedness, dishonesty, disrespect for the poor, and prideful self-promotion. A given week could yield a rich harvest of cautionary tales. A teenager loses her keys. Her mother chews her out about it, calling her irresponsible and asking how she ever expects to accomplish anything in the adult world when she is so disorganized. The next day, the mother loses her own keys. "Pride goes before destruction, a haughty spirit before a fall" (Prov 16:18).

A government official builds his career on "family values," condemning in political and religious terms all those whose lifestyles deviate from his views. He is discovered at an hourly rate motel with an underage girl. "The Lord detests lying lips, but he delights in those who are trustworthy" (Prov 12:22). "Keep your heart with all vigilance. For from it flow the springs of life" (Prov 4:23). "A false witness will not go unpunished, and a liar will not escape" (Prov 19:5).

A pastor is visiting a local shelter for abused women and children. She observes an exhausted mother snap at her seven-year-old son, "One more word and I'm leaving you here and never coming back." The pastor, observing the combined rage and anguish on the young boy's face, realizes that she is seeing a future batterer in the making. "A gentle answer turns away wrath, but a harsh word stirs up anger" (Prov 15:1).

You hear of the high incidence of cancer and the destruction to plant and animal life in a low-income area affected by nearby factories dumping chemicals into the river. A local activist is interviewed and makes the comment that "If this were in an affluent white area, the government would have cleaned this up long before now." "Wealth brings many friends, but the poor are left friendless" (Prov 19:4).

There is a reason that Proverbs encourages us to be attentive to the realms of the human heart, human interactions, and the world of nature. Why? Because it is there that evidence of the advisability of living wisely and the destructiveness of foolish choices are to be found. We see within us and around us tangible evidence of the truth of Proverbs' practical wisdom.

Listen Up! Ecclesiastes Style

Like the sages of Proverbs, Qohelet, the name given to the sage(s) responsible for the book of Ecclesiastes exercises his listening heart in scanning his inner and outer worlds for guidance on how to live wisely each day. He rejects the expectation that if we live wisely everything will turn out well for us and our loved ones. At the same time, his listening heart notices some positive value to wise living. He reminds us the benefit to be had in friendship. Perhaps you hear a story of a friend who goes along to the clinic with another friend, to keep her company while she waits for serious medical test results. The two friends have lunch together in the hospital cafeteria and express how much each values their friendship, all the more poignantly in light of life's uncertainties. "Two are better than one, because they have a good reward for their toil. For it they fall, one will lift up the other" (Eccl 4:9, 10).

Qohelet also notices that there is enjoyment to be found in our daily work. So imagine that this week, despite the things you dislike about your job, perhaps including aspects of your boss's personality (!) and the tedium of repetitive tasks, you have a day when you find joy in your work. A customer comes back to your station and expresses appreciation for your job well done. Or maybe you solve a problem and feel a sense of satisfaction, regardless of outward affirmation. On a day like that, we might hear the voice of the old sage in our ear, encouraging us to find joy in that experience, as fleeting as it may be. "There is nothing better for mortals than to eat and drink, and find enjoyment in their toil" (Eccl 2:24). (See also Ecclesiastes 5:18–20).

Qohelet's listening heart, as we have seen, results in a series of reflections on the absurdity of life and the futility of seeking wisdom. He piles up example after example of situations that contradict Proverbs "do good, get good" perspective.

Qohelet highlights those situations in which the poor are oppressed and mistreated. While we get the feeling he would rather not notice such scenes, he cannot seem to help himself. "Look, the tears of the oppressed — with no one to comfort them!" (4:1b). His wisdom reminds me of the big bad wolf from the story of the "Three Little Pigs," huffing and puffing on a house made of straw. It forces us to discern the flimsiness of conventional wisdom's assurance that wise choices will insure personal, social, and financial success. Qohelet won't allow the rich to assume that their neighbors' poverty is a sign of foolish living. If we are to listen up like Qohelet, we will notice statistics on the high percentage of children in our county who have no health insurance or adequate nutrition. We will pay attention to the story about a group of illegal immigrants who suffocated when left by their traffickers in a crowded truck in the desert heat.

Activating the listening heart in our lives today means taking a step beyond Qohelet's social passivism and determinism that would have us lament the fact that people suffer from injustices but assume we can do nothing about them. We will begin to brainstorm ways we can address both the symptoms and the systemic inequities behind these situations.

Listen Up! Joban Style

To cultivate the listening heart in Job is continually to reinforce a couple of key truths within ourselves.

1. The presence of suffering does not mean the absence of God

2. The answer to the question "Why do innocent people suffer?" is not answerable this side of the grave.

With these two truths in mind, we are to be on the lookout for signs of God's presence and care in the worst of situations in our own and others' lives. Job wants us to listen with our hearts for traces of a mysterious, transcendent God who does not withdraw when suffering draws near. Job calls us to shift our focus from seeking an answer to the question "Why do we suffer?" Instead he calls us to focus on the what of suffering: and that is the presence of God who has promised never to leave us or forsake us.

The person who would practice Job's version of the listening heart will seek examples of people who experience God's presence in the midst of suffering.

Sometimes, in the midst of severe suffering, a person is able to shift their attention from their own sense of injustice to an appreciation of God's presence in a moment that is both painful and beautiful. The experience of a friend of mine in his last few days of life is one such example. Before his death a few years ago, my friend, home under hospice care due to failing kidneys, told me of a glimmering moment he experienced late one afternoon.

Awakened by the tolling of his clock, he looked out his window, saw the pink of a gorgeous sunset beginning to thread the sky and heard the sound of children laughing as they played in the park across the street from his home. "And, even in the midst of my anger and hurt, I felt the presence of God and couldn't help but give thanks that everything God made is good and that those sights and sounds will continue when my time runs out."

The person who would practice Job's version of the listening heart will seek signs of God's presence amid her own painful moments. My father died in 2002 after a two-year struggle with liver cancer. I was to offer his funeral sermon at Grace United Methodist Church in Harrisburg, Pennsylvania. The faculty at Perkins School of Theology in Dallas, Texas where I teach, was holding its annual faculty retreat at the same time. When I got up to preach, a wave of calm washed over me, and I knew my colleagues had gathered, not, like Job's friends, to discuss why my dad had come down with liver cancer and died at age seventy-six. They had gathered to pray for me.

The person who would practice Job's version of the listening heart will cultivate sensitivity to the sufferings of others and seek to be an agent of God's presence in another's time of profound pain. That person will show up, not to explain the why, but to embody the what—the presence of our merciful God, whose ways are beyond our understanding, but who made a covenant to be our God in the Old Testament and "became flesh and dwelt among us . . . full of grace and truth" (John 1:14) in the New.

Listen Up! Jesus Style

What does "Listen up!" look like in the wisdom teachings of Jesus? Jesus, as he is depicted in the Synoptic Gospels, instructs us to turn our attention away from exclusive preoccupation with guaranteeing a secure future for ourselves. He encourages us to shift our focus from the accumulation of wealth, status, and power to the faces of those who are suffering. Jesus does not relate to such suffering with resigned regret. He names it as a sign of the dominion of the present era to the thrall of forces that oppose God. He calls us, not to resigned regret, but to a life of sacrificial compassion in action on behalf of this inbreaking reign of justice and joy.

To cultivate a listening heart as Jesus did, we will cultivate our attention to the motives, fears, and faith of others and of ourselves as well. As we engage in disciplines of prayer mentioned above, we will lose our ability to lie to ourselves about our true motives, and we will gain in our ability to be sensitive to the motives, needs, and situations of others.

Cultivating a listening heart involves listening to individuals and groups whom society does not consider worth listening to. I heard recently of a program matching college students with teenagers in the foster care system to encourage them to tell their stories and to gain confidence in applying to college. This effort is the result of the cultivation of a listening heart.

Let's listen to those who have fallen through the cracks of our national gospel of success that preaches, "If you can conceive it and believe it, you can achieve it." Let's cultivate the stories of those not listened to in our community, our nation. What are their stories? Let's be aware that their stories may make us aware that our perspectives and life experiences are more limited than we may have thought. Let's be attentive to how their stories can inspire us to exchange preoccupation with security and success defined by conventional wisdom for radical, sacrificial compassion. We don't have to look very far to exercise a listening heart.

I was once a guest preacher at a church and following the second service there was a coffee hour. As I walked around greeting people, I approached an elderly gentleman and asked "How are you?" "How am I?" he repeated. "It's kind of you to ask, but do you really have time to hear my answer? I come here every week. I have a lot of experience and insights to offer, but nobody has time to hear about them. So my short answer is, 'I'm fine.'"

Why don't we have the time to hear the answer to the question we glibly ask others several times a day? Why don't we have time to listen with our hearts to the concerns and wisdom of others? When King Solomon in 1 Kings 3 asks God for a listening heart he is asking for the energy to be radically attentive to people in the encounters with them in which his wise judgments will be crucial. He is asking to be attentive to the will of God as expressed through the interactions he has with his people. It sounds like hard work, because it is. Not to be too tough on Solomon, but the biblical witness indicates that he peaked young in the wisdom department. First Kings 3 seems to have been his finest hour. Jesus sustained the strenuous work of acute listening by his habit of prayer. The Gospels report that, periodically, Jesus withdrew to solitary places to pray, to listen attentively to God (Mark 1:35, 6:30, 14:32; Luke 4:42, 5:16). He prays at the crucial events in his life. Luke is particularly concerned to emphasize the role of prayer in Jesus' ministry. In Luke's gospel, Jesus is depicted as having prayed at his baptism (Luke 3:21). In Luke 6:12 he is said to have prayed all night before he chose his twelve disciples. Jesus was praying in Luke 9:18 when he asked his disciples "Who do the crowds say I am?" and "Who do you say I am?" In 9:28 he was at prayer on a mountain at the time of his transfiguration. Luke notes in 22:39 that when Jesus went to the Mount of Olives to pray it was "his custom" and indicates a particular place he habitually prayed when he was in Jerusalem (22:40).

Luke's account of Jesus in the garden of Gethsemane (22:39–46) suggests the themes of withdrawal for prayer and intensity in prayer. Jesus prayed to regenerate after periods of intense attentiveness to others and as preparation for such times to come. We do well to follow his example. If we found time to listen to God in prayer, chances are better that we would find time to listen to one another.

The Listening Heart: An Invitation to Make an Exchange

I began the Introduction with the scenario of approaching a customer service desk to make an exchange. We saw in chapter two how, with regard to the first wisdom virtue, the fear of the Lord, we are invited to exchange fear for faith. The second virtue, the listening heart, invites us to exchange self-centeredness for attentiveness to the needs of others and the work of God in the world, what the rabbis call *Tikkun Olam*, God at work repairing the world. Proverbs challenges the young to exchange immediate gratification for behaviors that benefit the whole community. Qohelet urges us to exchange melancholia over the worst in the world around us to thanksgiving for the best. Job invites us to exchange a focus on the suffering self for a focus on God's complex universe in which we are not the center, but in which we are strongly assured of God's faithful presence. Jesus' teachings prod us to exchange superficial religious ritual for sacrificial compassion out of love for the neighbor.

The Listening Heart as a "Great Exchange:

We Exchange Wants for Needs

Paying attention, listening with our hearts, is the way we learn wisdom. First of all, we exchange preoccupation with self-preservation and advancement for a focus on God's gift of wisdom within and around us. This is the fear of the Lord, and when we live listening to it we understand that wisdom is not a luxury but it is a necessity vital to our existence. We begin to crave wisdom, to require wisdom. And whenever our eyes encounter one of the other necessities of life, it reminds us of the one thing necessary: Wisdom herself.

Israel's sages compare wisdom to the necessities of life, food, water, and light. "The path of the righteous is like the light of dawn, which shines brighter and brighter until full day" (Prov 4:18). By contrast those who "forsake the paths of uprightness . . . walk in the ways of darkness" (2:13). Wisdom's teachings are a lamp (6:23). Wise words are "pleasant," like "honeycomb, sweetness to the soul and health to the body" (16:24). Wisdom is more honorable than a crown (14:18, 24; 16:31). Wisdom causes one to utter wise words that nourish like food (13:1; 15:15b; 17:22). One's mouth becomes a "fountain of life" (10:11; 18:4b). "The fear of the Lord is a fountain of life so one may avoid the snares of death" (14:27; 16:22).

We Exchange Glitter for True Treasure.

Over and over the sages look at the things that we value, that attract us in life. And they remind us that wisdom is more beautiful, valuable, and lasting than these things. The sages often compare wisdom to jewels and precious metals. "For wisdom is better than jewels, and all that you may desire cannot compare to her" (8:11). "My fruit is better than gold, even fine gold, and my yield than choice silver" (8:19; 16:16). "The tongue of the righteous is choice silver . . ." (10:20a). Wisdom brings to the seeker wealth, and it fills his treasuries (8:21). (See also 2:4–5; 3:14–15; 20:15; 10:20.) "In the house of the righteous there is much treasure" (15:6). We can appreciate material things that have beauty and value but remember that Wisdom exceeds them all.

We Exchange Crooked for Straight

When we live with our hearts attuned to the fear of the Lord, radical trust in God to guide our steps, we are able to discern the difference between crooked and straight. "Trust in the Lord with all your heart, and do not rely on your own insight. In all your ways acknowledge him, and he will make straight your paths" (3:5, 6).

The life of wisdom is often referred to as a path or way. We are told that God "guards the paths of justice and preserves the way of his faithful ones" (2:8). Fools are "those whose paths are crooked, and who are devious in their ways" (2:15). Their speech is crooked and devious (4:24). They are "crooked of mind" and "perverse of tongue" (17:20). Those who would be wise are advised to "walk in the way of good, and keep to the paths of the just" (2:20). Of Woman Wisdom it is said that "Her ways are ways of pleasantness, and all her paths are peace" (3:17). We are to avoid the path of folly (4:14) "which is like deep darkness" (4:19) in favor of "the path of the righteous which is like the light of dawn which shines brighter and brighter until full day" (4:18). Fools are often lazy and therefore their way is "overgrown with thorns, but the path of the upright is a level highway" (15:19). "The way of the guilty is crooked, but the conduct of the pure is right" (21:8). "Better to be poor and walk in integrity than to be crooked in one's ways even though rich" (28:6). "One who walks in integrity will be safe, but whoever follows crooked ways will fall into the Pit" (28:18).

We Exchange Danger for Security

When we live with a listening heart, we are able to discern the difference between those actions that bring short-term gain, but, in the long term, endanger our relationship with God and others in our family and community.

When one follows the path of wisdom, the sages say, "you will walk on your way securely and your foot will not stumble" (3:23). One will have no need to fear or panic, for "the Lord will be your confidence and keep your foot from being caught" (3:23–26). Repeatedly, the sages use the metaphor of a snare for the dangers of folly. "The evil are ensnared by the transgression of their lips, but the righteous escape from trouble" (12:13). "The mouths of fools are their ruin, and their lips a snare to themselves" (18:7; 12:13). "The fear of others lays a snare, but the one who trusts in the Lord is secure" (29:25). "In the transgression of the evil there is a snare, but the righteous sing and rejoice" (29:6). In addition to snare, they use the metaphor of ambush. "The words of the wicked are a deadly ambush, but the speech of the upright delivers them" (12:6; 17:12).

By contrast, the way of wisdom offers profound, though not always obvious, security (12:18). "In the fear of the Lord one has strong confidence and one's children will have a refuge" (14:26). "Wisdom is a shield to those who walk blamelessly" (2:7). "No one finds security by wickedness, but the root of the righteous will never be moved" (12:3; 12:12b). "The righteous find a refuge in their integrity (14:32b). "The Lord tears down the house of the proud, but maintains the widow's boundaries" (15:25). Pride goes before destruction and a haughty spirit before a fall" (16:17).

We Exchange Death for Life

The life of wisdom begins with an exchange of human anxieties for the fear of the Lord (faith). When we live life through the fear of the Lord, listening for God's guidance in interpreting life, we are able to exchange those attitudes and behaviors that lead to death for those that lead to life. For the sages, the fear of the Lord, understood as humble obedience to God's moral guidance in all of life, was the source of life itself. In part they understood *life* as one's physical well-being, longevity, and prosperity. Wise choices tended to nurture life understood in this way. But more deeply, *life* meant one's core connection with God that the most heinous of misfortune cannot sever. That meant that poverty, loss of reputation, and suffering at the hands of the wicked could not separate the wise person from God and therefore could not destroy his or her *life*. Conversely, one could have wealth and power and not have life, but rather, be marked as on the way to death.

Choosing wisdom was a matter of life and death. "There is a way that seems right to a person but its end is the way to death" (14:12). "The fear of the Lord is a fountain of life, so that one may avoid the snares of death" (14:27). "Do not be wise in your own eyes; fear the Lord, and turn away from evil. It will be a healing for your flesh, and a refreshment for your body" (3:7, 8). "The highway of the upright avoids evil; those who guard their way preserve their lives" (16:17). "The name of the Lord is a strong tower; the righteous run into it and are safe" (18:10). "The house of the wicked is destroyed, but the tent of the upright flourishes" (14:11). "Those who guard their mouths preserve their lives; those who open wide their lips come to ruin" (13:3). "The mouth of the righteous is a fountain of life" (10:11).

The one who heeds instruction is "on the path to life" (10:17). "The wicked earn no real gain, but those who sow righteousness get a true re- ward" (11:18). "A gentle tongue is a tree of life, but perverseness in it breaks the spirit" (15:4). "The violence of the wicked will sweep them away, because they refuse to do what is just" (21:7). Wisdom is "a tree of life to those who lay hold of her; those who hold her fast are called happy" (3:18). "My child, . . . keep sound wisdom and prudence, and they will be life for your soul and adornment for your neck" (3:22). "My child, be attentive to my words . . . For they are life to those who find them, and healing to all their flesh" (4:20–22).

We Exchange a Childhood God for a God for Grown-Ups

Job exchanged one set of responses to his undeserved sufferings for another. He exchanged passive acceptance, blaming self, or blaming God for an ac- tive search for God. Ultimately, he sacrifices his current notion of God as a God who is in control of everything, who has placed human beings at the very center of the universe, and who distributes divine retribution accord- ing to precise stipulations. He exchanges this human-shaped understanding of God for an encounter with the God he was not raised to expect, a God who may not micromanage the world's affairs, a God who affirms that di- vine retribution is a human invention, a God who has a lot of other things to be concerned about besides human beings. There is one thing about this God that is beyond dispute and uncertainty: this God will be present with us in times of trial and pain. This God always shows up.

We Exchange Complaints for Gratitude.

We have seen how Qohelet initially listens to an inward voice that repeatedly expresses its disappointment with life for not living up to traditional wisdom's affirmation that good actions lead to good fortune. He eschews denial and whining, however, exchanging them for facing in to the harsh realities of the limitations of human knowledge, the mystery of God and the sure approach of death. Having done so, he is able to find peace and even joy in the present moment, as fleeting and fragile as it is. He is able to exchange discontentment and resentment for gratitude.

We Exchange Self-Absorption for the Listening Heart

When I was growing up, my three siblings and I knew that our mother had the hearing of a bird dog. She heard things we didn't even remember saying, but we knew we had thought them! Jesus' spiritual hearing was divinely acute. He was always listening with his heart and had an uncanny ability to read the hearts of others. As he reads our hearts, he calls us to exchange fear and self-centeredness for faith, love of God and neighbor. If we are listening with our hearts, we will be able to hear the wisdom he has to direct and redirect our lives.

Jesus' spirit is reflected in the life and writings of Amy Carmichael (1867–1951), a missionary to India focusing on rescuing children being trafficked for sex. Her intense activism was matched by her intense prayer life. *In Candles in the Dark*, the best-known of her thirty-five books, she wrote "Keep close, keep close. If you are close, you will be keen. Your heart will be set on the things that abide. You will not be attracted by the world, but you will love the people in that world. You will live to share your joy. Nothing else will count for much."[9]

André Dubus, the late novelist and short story writer, lost one leg and the use of the other in a 1986 accident. In an essay titled "Song of Pity" he tells of a cold winter afternoon years before his accident when he was a graduate student at the University of Iowa Writers' Workshop. He came upon a man in a wheelchair who was unable to continue up a steep incline, and Dubus pushed the man's chair the rest of the way. Years later, Dubus found himself in a wheelchair. He reflects back on that afternoon. "I lacked imagination. Or I lacked the compassion and courage to imagine someone else's suffering. I never thought of my friend making his bed, sitting on a

---

9. Beasley-Topliffe, ed., *The Dictionary of Christian Spiritual Formation*, 51.

toilet, sitting in a shower, dressing himself, preparing breakfast and washing the dishes, just to leave the house, to go out into the freezing air of Iowa."[10]

Some years ago a young man named Andrew Miller Jr. was a student in one of my Doctor of Ministry classes. He was in his early thirties, filled with enthusiasm, intelligence, and good humor, a fourth-generation Salvation Army officer, then serving in Arlington, Texas, and affectionately known as Captain Andy.

His grandfather, Andy Miller Sr., died in 2011 at age eighty-eight after a long bout with Alzheimer's. He was a former national commander for the US in the Salvation Army. He was often referred to as "Mr. Salvation Army." Though short of stature, this smiling, peppy Irishman worked for the Lord, coaxed people to his church, called on captains of industry to raise money for his cause, met with presidents and popes, and was an usher at Robert Kennedy's funeral. The joke was told that a man at St. Peter's Square in Rome asked "Who is the guy on the balcony in the white robe (obviously the Pope) the reply was "I don't who he is, but the guy next to him is Andy Miller."

At his memorial service in Atlanta February 11, 2011 one speaker described him as "the Salvation Army's Godfather" for his ability to convince powerful people to give to the cause. Another described him as a "walking exclamation point!" because of his passion for Christ's kingdom.

His skill as a storyteller was exceeded only by his ability to listen to other people's stories. Here is just one Andy Miller story. Years ago, Andy visited a retreat where the leaders recognized and publicly asked him to come forward to assist with serving communion. The Salvation Army does not celebrate communion for various reasons. So he was chagrined and embarrassed at being put in an awkward situation. As he told it, "The only polite thing to do was to participate. I was already embarrassed when I went forward, but was even more so when I saw that communion would be served in paper Dixie cups. As I turned to walk down the aisle with the tray I was tempted to just walk out the back door and not return. Instead I went about distributing them, trying to avoid eye contact and just get it done. In the process I accidentally locked eyes with a couple at the end of the third row and felt compelled to move toward them, hold out the tray and say, "I offer you the forgiveness of God." Whereupon the woman hissed at me "Who told you about us?" This led to a conversation with the couple after the service in which her husband was able to ask forgiveness for what he had done and she was able to give it." Said Andy, "I think William Booth, founder of the Salvation Army, would have said I did the right thing!"

10. McKenzie, *Novel Preaching*, 18.

It is because God has a listening heart that God sent Jesus the Son. It is because Jesus had a listening heart that he lived, died, and lives on for each of us. When you step up to the divine return desk and ask to exchange self-absorption for a listening heart, remember who stood here before you, one who, because he trusted God, exchanged his fear of experiencing pain for a listening heart, one that led him to a cross and a resurrection. There he proved before our eyes the power that comes from trusting and taking directions from God, and listening with our hearts to the beating hearts of those around us.

Meditation

The Listening Heart

Psalm 34:1–10; 1 Kings 3:3–12; Mark 10:46–52

Earlier I mentioned my clergy colleague who had anxiety about his first senior pastor position and the dream he had the night before his first day on the job. "I dreamed I was a little boy with daddy's briefcase walking into work." We may put on our game face during the daylight hours, but after midnight, in our dreams, our fears come out. That's what happened to people in the Bible.

Solomon's dream in 1 Kings chapter 3 was similar to my friend's. "You have made me king to fill Big Daddy's shoes, and I am only a child. There are so many of them and just one of me . . . help!"

I wonder if Bartimaeus had a recurring dream in which he was an old, old man, still with veiled, sightless eyes, still sitting on his cloak, with it all spread around him to catch the coins passersby tossed at him. Nothing changed. Just old and blind and alone.

God instructs Solomon "Ask what I should give you."

Jesus asks Bartimaeus, "What do you want me to do for you?"

When he turns to you, what's your answer?

I want things to stay just like they are.

I want everything to work out painlessly and perfectly for me and my family.

I want to reach my dreams without making any sacrifices.

Bartimaeus has the right answer: Too long I have lived in this dark and enclosed place. Too long I have focused on my own sufferings and the unfairness of it all. Let me see again so I can emerge from this prison.

Solomon has the right answer: "I am overwhelmed by my new responsibilities. Give me a listening mind, or a hearing heart." It doesn't really matter how you translate it, because for the Hebrew mind, the heart was the source, not just of emotions, but of thought and decision-making as well. Solomon was saying something like, "Help me to give my full attention to the encounters with people that lie ahead of me, where I will be called on to judge wisely. Help me to listen attentively to what they say and to what God is saying when we are face to face."

Don't you imagine that Jesus had plenty of his own fears to preoccupy him on his way to Jerusalem? "Oh, God, I'm afraid they're going to kill me. I don't want to die. Oh, God, I don't want to suffer." In light of that, the four most beautiful words in the passage to me are these: *But Jesus stood still.*

How typical of Jesus is this action! He always notices our fears: whether we are terrified in our storm-battered boat, kneeling at his feet, worn out with illness or sorrow, not thinking ourselves worthy to so much as touch the hem of his cloak, or cowering behind locked doors Easter evening because all our hopes are presumed dead. Our Risen Jesus always passes through the thickest wall of our fears and stands before us. *Jesus stood still.* With these words on his lips: "Take heart. I am with you. Be healed of your diseases. Do not be afraid."

How typical of Jesus is his command to anyone who would prevent another's coming to him. Act like a poor, blind person in this society should, says the crowd to Bartimaeus. "Sit down and shut up!" "Call him here," says Jesus.

Jesus' question to Bartimaeus doesn't assume Bartimaeus's answer. Rather, it respects Bartimaeus's ability to articulate and choose his healing, conveying that the choice belongs to him. "What do you want me to do for you?" he asks Bartimaeus.

Years ago when I was serving a church in Pennsylvania, a parishioner called me—it was around 10:30 PM. "I'm so sorry to bother you. My nephew needs to talk to somebody really badly. He is not a churchgoer but he said he wanted to talk to my pastor." A half hour later I sat in my living room across from a young man in his late twenties, pale as a ghost, with a red gash in his forehead. He launched into a story that you have heard all too often. Of how he'd had several drinks out with his friends, then how he and his friend had left to go home, with him driving and how he was now sitting here with one surface head wound while his buddy was fighting for his life in the ICU. While he talked he picked up the big Bible we had on the coffee table, the kind with the face of Jesus on the front. He started tracing the face of Jesus while he told his tale. Around the face, tracing his hair, circling his eyes, down the line of his nose, the outline of his lips, his ears, back around the route—his face, his hair, his eyes, his nose, his lips, his ears, his face, his hair, his eyes, his nose, his lips, his ears, tracing the face. Suddenly, he looked up at me his eyes wet and blurted out, "Jesus Christ, what am I going to do?"

There are a lot of people out there in hospital waiting rooms, on reservations, in upscale neighborhoods, in section eight housing, saying the name of Jesus, halfway between a curse and a prayer, people who think praying is out so cursing is all that's left: because it's too late for them to start again, because the path of their life has gotten so far off the map, because people like them have no futures, because peace of mind is a thing of the past.

Are we paying enough attention to notice and offer the gospel they need: the news that it's not too late to fear the Lord. That whenever we turn to God trembling, receptive, repentant, God comes to meet us bearing gifts: a peace that seems impossible under the circumstances, a joy we could never earn, and some directions for our lives that are a whole lot more reliable than the wandering around we've been doing. Can we tell them from our own experience: the Lord is listening with his heart; the Lord is asking from his heart.

He had read all the statistics on Alzheimer's, knew the clinical symptoms, had been to a couple of workshops on nursing care for these people because the center he administered had just finished a new Alzheimer's wing. It was brand spanking new with all the modern conveniences. Then he saw them, a couple, the woman walking with the assistance of her husband, her eyes filled with confusion and fear, looking around at the unfamiliar surroundings, her new home. He greeted them warmly, with the hearty assurance, "Things seem a little strange now, but you'll feel at home in no time." Two weeks later he noticed Mary still had the fear look in her eyes. Her children and husband brought in memorabilia from home to brighten up her room. An afghan, family pictures, a favorite lamp. He noticed that Mary came to meals but didn't stay in the common rooms any longer than she had to. Neither did the other guests. He decided to talk with colleagues at other centers. He made several visits and noted that some of them had "Memory Lane Rooms." Rooms that were decorated in the time in which many of these people mentally live—the fifties. So he came home and decorated the whole wing that way. He put a Judy Garland movie in the DVD player. He got a small CD player and kept a stack of big band CDs next to it. The Campbell's Soup girl emblem graced the wall.

The last time he walked down the hall, many of the guests rooms were empty, including Mary's. She was sitting with her friends in the Memory Lane Room, listening to Tommy Dorsey, and he noticed there was not nearly so much fear in her eyes.

There is someone in your life and mine waiting for us to notice them and in that noticing to unleash a divine repair. I wonder who . . .

The listening heart describes our discipleship in a nutshell: exchanging a life of self-absorption for a life of radical attentiveness to others' perspectives and pains. The life of the listening heart is not an easy path. We hear things we would rather not hear and learn things it is easier not to know and feel things it is more comfortable not to feel. So that's how it feels to be fourteen and without a future. That's how it feels to wake up to racist graffiti spray painted on your storefront. That's how it feels to hope for a last-minute pardon from the governor. That's how it feels to dread your daddy's visits to your room at night. We go places we never thought we'd go. We cry tears we would rather not cry. Sometimes we lie awake when we would rather be sleeping just because someone else is in too much pain to sleep. Mystic Henry Nouwen defines Christian maturity as "the ability and willingness to be led where you would rather not go." The way of the Christian leader is not the way of upward mobility in which our world has invested so much energy, but the way of downward mobility with outstretched arms that ends on the cross."[11]

Not everyone wants to live that way. Just before the story of Bartimaeus is the story of two disciples, James and John the sons of Zebedee. They came forward to Jesus and said to him, "Teacher, we want you to do for us whatever we ask of you." He said to them, "What is it you want me to do for you?' They said to him, "Grant us to sit , one at your right hand and one at your left, in your glory." Well, that's one vision for discipleship.

But here's another. "What do you want me to do for you?" Jesus asks Bartimaeus. "Lord, let me see again," says the blind man. "And immediately he regained his sight and followed Jesus on the road to Jerusalem."

In Chapter 4 we'll take a look at the third wisdom virtue, the cool spirit.

Questions for Reflection on the Listening Heart

1. Who is the best listener you know?

2. How good a listener are you?

3. Can you think of a time when someone really listened to you and made a difference in your life?

4. Can you think of a time when you listened with care and compassion to someone else and made a difference in their life?

11. Nouwen, *In the Name of Jesus*, 62.

5. Who in our society is not listened to?

6. Who is listened to?

7. How would our families and communities be different if we practiced the virtue of the listening heart?

Chapter 4

Part One—The Third Wisdom Virtue
The Cool Spirit

"One who spares words is knowledgeable; one who is cool in spirit has understanding" (Prov 17:27).

A Virtue We'd Rather Forget?

Author J. D. Vance tells of a time he was driving in Cincinnati with his wife Usha when someone cut him off in traffic. He honked, the guy gave him the middle finger salute, and, when both cars stopped at a red light, J. D. unbuckled his seat belt and opened the car door. He planned to demand an apology and fight the man if necessary.

Then common sense prevailed. He shut the door and stayed in his car. In that moment between getting out of the car and deciding to shut the door J. D. exercised what the sages of Israel would call the "cool spirit:" self-control.[1]

Self-control is the third wisdom virtue. It is the hallmark of the wise person, according to Proverbs. This ability to rein oneself in is not solely a matter of personal willpower. It is a discipline that flows from living connected to God through the fear of the Lord. Fearing the Lord in turn means listening for divine guidance in the sometimes conflictual encounters of daily life, the "listening heart," the second wisdom pillar. The third pillar of wisdom, what the sages called the "cool spirit," describes the ability to

1. Vance, *Hillbilly Elegy.*

forego the short-term gratification of venting our temper or indulging our appetites to gain the longer-term benefits that restraint brings to individuals and communities. It is an exchange of hot for "cool."

Proverbs was written to instill self-control in both young and old, the "simple" (1:4) and those who had been around the block a few times (1:5), the "wise." Instilling wisdom in the young and gullible was crucial. For in the tumultuous postexilic time, there was no longer a king or a temple, and the nation's identity depended on being able to hold onto the young. The sages' mission was to train them in the way they should go, and to warn them of the way they should not go.

Offering a refresher course to those who should be no strangers to wisdom was another goal of the sages of Proverbs. I have kept a journal for many years and purposely do not go back and reread long ago portions. I am sure it would help me see patterns that would help me discern my spiritual growth needs moving forward. But I am pretty sure it would also show that I am a living example of the Pennsylvania Dutch saying: "Too soon olt, too late schmart!" I hope it would show that, while I may still be working on some of the same issues, I have grown in unselfishness, maturity, and wisdom. The sages knew that the young can be short on years and long on wisdom, and the old can be long on years but short on wisdom.

Waiting in line at a rental car counter at 11:30 PM one evening in Buffalo, New York, my then college-aged daughter and I witnessed a man in his fifties losing his temper at the clerk because he had to wait in line behind others. His face got red. He raised his voice. He leaned well into the physical space of the young clerk. "Why is he acting like that, Mom?" my daughter asked. Good question.

This past weekend I performed the wedding ceremony of a high school friend of my son's and his bride. Our cultural stereotype is of bridezillas, young women who are so focused on perfection in their weddings that any glitch sends them into a rage. This young bride destroyed that stereotype. Everything went perfectly in the wedding ceremony until the exchange of rings. The best man handed me the rings. The bride put the larger ring on her groom's left ring finger. I then, with uncharacteristic clumsiness, dropped her ring. A ridiculous scene ensued in which the best man, the bride, and I searched the carpet under her train for the ring. In the process she stepped on it and bent it out of shape so that it would not fit on her finger. We got through the rest of the service, but I could sense her dismay. At the reception, I went up to her and thanked her for the honor of performing her wedding and told her to send me the bill for having the ring restored and reshaped by a jeweler. She hugged me, thanked me for doing the wedding, said she was the one who stepped on it, and that it would make for a great wedding story to tell in the future.

Her kind words banished my mental image of appearing in *People's Court*! I thought to myself, what maturity! You can be twenty-seven and really mature and gracious, and you can be fifty-five and kind of a jerk.

What makes the difference? It depends in part on the degree to which one can exercise this third wisdom virtue, the "cool spirit," or impulse control. The key quality of a fool is lack of self-control. "Fools despise wisdom and instruction"(Prov 1:7b). Self-control comes from the fear of the Lord. If you tremble, trust, and take directions from God, self-control will be one important result. Self-control also flows from the listening heart. If you care about the welfare of others and not just yourself, if you are on the lookout for divine guidance in daily situations, you're more likely to exercise self-control than not.

Whenever I try to remember all four of these wisdom virtues covered in this book, I inevitably leave one out. And guess which one? If you guessed self-control, you are correct! In this omission, I am a mirror of our culture and a condition cultural critics have baptized "affluenza."

In 2001 John De Graaf, David Wann, and Thomas Naylor wrote a book entitled *Affluenza: The All-Consuming Epidemic*. They defined affluenza as "a painful, contagious, socially transmitted condition of overload, debt, anxiety and waste resulting from the dogged pursuit of more."[2] It is the bloated sense of unfulfillment that results from efforts to keep up with the Joneses. It is the stress, waste, and indebtedness caused when we pursue a materialistic version of the American Dream.

I used to have an exercise video that featured a women twenty years older than I was at the time, but who looked twenty years younger. She kept up a peppy repartee throughout the painful workout, repeatedly reminding us: "Remember, don't skip the exercises that are most painful to you. They are the ones you need to work on most!" Self-control may be a wisdom virtue we badly need but would rather forget.

The Backstory to the Virtue of Self-Control

We twenty-first–century types tend to define virtue in purely personal terms as sexual purity and abstinence from alcoholic beverages. The ancient Greeks had a deeper view. For them, the virtues were persistent habits of the heart and mind that made for personal and social harmony. They believed that attributes such as musical or athletic ability, while they can be honed

2. De Graaf, Wann, and Naylor, *Affluenza*, 2.

with practice, are largely inborn. By contrast, virtues are largely acquired through education. They need to be deepened through daily practice until they become habits. The Greeks believed we develop character by exercising its virtues. They did not believe that the virtues necessarily led to material success. Rather, their reward is intrinsic.[3]

The classical Greek notion of character articulated by Plato and Aristotle, Greek philosophers of the third century BCE, identified four virtues: prudence, justice, fortitude, and temperance. These constitute a cluster of human qualities necessary for personal and social harmony in all the activities of daily life. These are often called "cardinal virtues," a term that indicates that they are the most basic and highly valued virtues.

The master virtue that makes all others possible for Aristotle is prudence (in Greek, *phronesis*). He defined it as the practical wisdom that recognizes and makes the right choices in specific situations. It helps us get clear about why we're doing what we're doing in a given situation and what we ought to be doing instead. It is the moderator in the panel discussion among the virtues. It helps us rank them in order of importance as they lead us to action in particular instances. Its role is akin to a combination of the biblical wisdom virtues of the fear of the Lord and the listening heart (or discerning mind).

Justice in Greek thought includes fairness, honesty, and keeping promises.

Fortitude means courage, both in battle and in the pursuit of justice against all odds. This virtue could be seen as a secular version of the subversive voice I'll talk about in chapter 5.

The final virtue in Greek understanding is temperance, which has much in common with our wisdom virtue of self-control or the "cool spirit." Temperance is the self-discipline necessary to minimize life's chaos and to accomplish any worthwhile end.[4]

Theologian and philosopher Thomas Aquinas, writing in the thirteenth century, sought a theological context for the formation of character. Not prudence, but charity (*caritas:* love) took the lead with faith and hope close behind. "Charity is the mother and root of all virtues."[5]

He outlined the three theological virtues with some help from the Apostle Paul (1 Corinthians 13:13). They are faith, hope, and love. They differ from the Greek virtues in that they are regarded as gifts from God. The virtuous person for Aquinas is one who is filled with divine love or

3. Brown, *Character in Crisis*, 12.

4. Aristotle, *Nichomachean Ethics*, quoted in Brown, *Character in Crisis*, 12.

5. Brown, *Character in Crisis*, 12.

charity. This person is, first and foremost, a recipient of that *caritas*. While Christians are expected to respond to God's grace, there is a sense in which our virtues are fundamentally not our own.[6]

For Aquinas, virtue is an infusion of God's grace that saves and enables us. Faith generates hope and hope generates charity (*caritas*) defined as love of God and love of neighbor. The theological virtues initiated by the action of God bring us into relationship with God. In the process our characters are not just formed. They are transformed (2 Corinthians 3:17–18).[7]

Character Counts!

In the mid 1990s a group of political and civic leaders formed a program called "Character Counts!" to instill qualities of character in school children and youth groups. Their pillars rely heavily on a classical Greek understanding of virtue. They identified six "pillars of character" and produced curriculum to support their goals. The six pillars are trustworthiness (including honesty and loyalty), respect, responsibility (including self-discipline and hard work), fairness (caring), and citizenship (including obeying laws, staying informed, and voting).They are outlined in Michael Josephson's book *Making Ethical Decisions: The Basic Primer on Using the Six Pillars of Character to Make Better Decisions and a Better Life*.[8]

The four cardinal wisdom virtues I have discerned in biblical wisdom literature have some common ground with Greek virtues in that their value is intrinsic and they are to be exercised not just for personal but also for public benefit. Yet their source and destination are different from the Greek virtues. They come from God and they lead the community to God by fostering *shalom*, peace with justice in the Old Testament and participation in the kingdom of God through the church, the body of Christ, in the New Testament.

What impact does this have on our understanding of biblical wisdom's virtue of self-control? It means that God helps us in exercising it. It's not all on us! God helps us overcome our tendency toward what the Apostle Paul called the "works of the flesh," and offers us the opportunity to instead display the "fruits of the Spirit."

> Now the works of the flesh are . . . fornication, impurity, licentiousness, idolatry, sorcery, enmities, strike, jealousy, anger,

6. McKenzie, *Preaching Biblical Wisdom in a Self-Help Society*, 56.

7. Ibid., 54–57.

8. Josephson, *Making Ethical Decisions*.

quarrels, dissensions, factions, envy, drunkenness, carousing
and things like these . . . those who do such things cannot inherit the kingdom of God.

By contrast, the fruit of the Spirit is love, joy, peace, forbearance,
kindness, goodness, faithfulness, gentleness and self-control . . .
those who belong to Christ Jesus have crucified the flesh with its
passions and desires (Gal 5:19–24).

The Greek translated as "self-control" is *egkráteia*, literally "dominion or
mastery within." In the context of the books of Proverbs, it is an impulse
control that proceeds from within oneself, but which one does not exercise
by oneself. For it is portrayed as a result of appropriating the gift of divine
Wisdom in Proverbs and as the work of God's Spirit in the inner life in the
writings of Paul in the New Testament.

The Foolish Person as a Hothead

If self-control is one of the hallmarks of the wise person, it is no surprise
that lack of self-control is one of the quintessential traits of the fool. Self-
control, or the lack thereof, affects a whole spectrum of choices: to exercise
prudent speech and silence, or to speak impulsively and fly off the handle;
to work hard or to be a slacker; to be moderate in one's eating and drinking or to overindulge; to be faithful to one's sexual partner or to veer into
promiscuity. In their proverbial advice the sages did not debate the relative
role of nature and nurture with regard to destructive patterns of behavior.
They did not describe the dynamics of addiction and disease. They did not
take into account how family anger and violence often have their roots in
childhood abuse that creates adult abusers. The book of Proverbs simply
describes negative behaviors and their results and warns the young, in the
strongest possible terms, to avoid them. As twenty-first–century people, we
need to understand the psychological and social dynamics that keep people
trapped in cycles of addiction, violence, and other destructive behaviors.
At the same time, the clarity of Israel's sages is useful. In a matter-of-fact
manner, they point to the path of wisdom that leads to life and to the path
of folly that leads to spiritual death and say, "Pick one!"

Proverbs scholar Dave Bland contrasts the values clarification approach of much contemporary values education, which leaves the choices

of values to each individual, with the sage's practice of teaching specific core values to impressionable minds.[9]

The book of Proverbs is filled with in-your-face wisdom sayings intended to nip uncontrolled behaviors by the young in the bud. When I was a young mother, a neighbor told me that the cure for a toddler's tantrum was to toss a glass of cold water in their face. I found out the hard way that this was not a successful strategy. I suspect when Jesus spoke of offering "a cup of cold water in my name," this isn't exactly what he meant! (Mark 9:41; Matt 10:42).

We often use the term *hothead* to describe someone who is unable to control his or her speech and temper. There is a physiological basis for the term. We've all felt our faces flush with anger or embarrassment. The blood pressure rise that accompanies anger can cause a flushed face. The feeling of heat in such situations goes back to our early survival instinct. When we are in survival mode, our body increases blood flow to our extremities so we have a better response time in either fighting or fleeing. An eruption of anger from someone who lacks impulse control can function like a lighted match thrown onto a pool of gasoline. By contrast, the person with self-control knows how to "rein in the rage," and to act as a coolant in a dicey situation.

"Those who are hot tempered stir up strife, but those who are slow to anger calm contention" (Prov 15:18).

"Make no friends with those given to anger, and do not associate with hotheads, or you may learn their ways and entangle yourselves in a snare" (Prov 22:24–25).

When self-control is lacking, the result is behaviors that produce strife: drunkenness, quarreling, anger, hatred, and greed. "The angry man stirs up strife, but one who is slow to anger heals discords" (Prov 15:18). "Hatred stirs up strife, but love covers all offences" (Prov 10:12). Greed is the breeding ground for a whole battery of crimes against individuals and society. It stems, like anger and hatred, from a breakdown of self-control. The wise teachers of Israel characterized these actions, and the attitudes from which they stem, as typical of the vicious fool (*nabal*).[10]

An anonymous sage once said, "Discipline puts back in its place that something in us which should serve but wants to rule."[11] That is a good description of what self-control does. Clearly, it is a particularly important virtue in leaders. Without it the king might allow the desire for wealth and

9. Bland, *Proverbs and the Formation of Character*, 9.

10. Toombs, "The Theology and Ethics of the Book of Proverbs," 19.

11. Manser, *The Westminster Collection of Christian Quotations*, 76.

power to get the better of him. He might then forget to fulfill his communal responsibilities to speak for the silent, the poor, and the needy, and to champion the rights of those left desolate (21:8, 9). Self-indulgence in a ruler harms the whole community.[12]

I recently listened to a news magazine that featured a panel of five people who have worked in various capacities as presidential advisors over the past several decades. The moderator asked them what qualities they felt were most important in a leader. One respondent likened the president's role to that of an air traffic controller with 500 planes in air, all about out of fuel and awaiting directions. The panel listed qualities like the intelligence to be well-informed and to reflect deeply on a broad range of issues, the ability to make crisp decisions amid a cacophony of information and opinions, and the willingness to listen to views different from their own. Several of the panelists listed one more crucial quality: self-control.[13]

Lack of self-control leads to behaviors that disrupt the harmony of interpersonal relationships as well as the orderly functioning of society. In the folklore of many cultures, there are reports of the activity of "poltergeists" (German for "noisy ghosts"). Their goal seems to be to disrupt the peace of a family by their unpredictable behavior. Reports are that they cause loud noises; they levitate objects; and they have been known to pinch and bite. The person who lacks self-control has this same disruptive effect on a group. If these behaviors are allowed to persist, they tear a society apart. To lack self-control is to be antisocial and to live in a way that is incompatible with both the fear of the Lord and the listening heart.[14]

The "Cool Man" in Proverbs

Throughout Proverbs those who live by wisdom are described as following a path (4:18; 5:06; 10:17; 12:28; 15:19, 24). Self-control is a crucial communal value that helps ensure that the community is traveling along together on the path of wisdom that leads to *shalom*, peace with justice.[15]

The ideal of the sages of Proverbs is the one who is "cool in spirit" (17:27). Primarily used to refer to self-control in matters of speech, it also applies to behavior across a broad spectrum of situations. Injunctions to self-restraint appear in the ethical instructions, not only of Israel, but also of other Ancient Near Eastern cultures, especially those of Egyptian origin.

12. Melchert, *Wise Teaching*, 45.

13. *Face the Nation*, August 14, 2016.

14. Toombs, "The Theology and Ethics of the Book of Proverbs," 20.

15. Brown, *Character in Crisis*, 34–35.

The sayings of Proverbs 22:20—24:22 show the influence of *The Sayings of Amenemope*, an Egyptian work of instruction for young courtiers that pre-dates Proverbs, probably dating to 1200 BCE.[16]

Frequent in the instructions of *Amenemope* and other Egyptian writings is the contrast between the one who is "slow to anger" and the "heated man." This theme is found in Proverbs 15:18, 22:24, and 29:22.[17]

In Proverbs 17:27, the expressive phrase "cool of spirit" is used to indicate self-control in speaking. "One who spares words is knowledgeable; one who is cool in spirit has understanding."

The cool spirit has at its core the ability to control oneself (see 10:1–22; 16 and 25:1—29:27). The "cool man" recognizes self-control as the leash which restrains destructive emotions and the actions to which they give rise.

> Like a city breached, without walls is one who lacks self-control
> (25:28).

The value of self-control in matters of the temper spans religious boundaries. There is a story about Buddha that makes this clear. It seems a man had heard of the reputation Buddha had for being peaceful and nonviolent regardless of what he encountered in life. This man decided to test the divine one, and he traveled a long distance to be in his presence. For three days he was rude and obnoxious to the Buddha. He criticized and found fault with everything the Buddha said or did. He verbally abused the Buddha, attempting to get him to react angrily. Yet the Buddha never faltered. Each time he responded with love and kindness. Finally the man could take it no longer. "How can you be so peaceful and kind when all I've ever said to you was antagonistic?" The Buddha's response was in the form of a question to the man. "If someone offers you a gift, and you do not accept that gift, to whom does the gift belong?" The man had his answer.[18]

For the Hebrew sages, the "cool" man avoids public intoxication (23:33) and foolish companions (13:20).[19] The "cool" man (17:27) will not give way to fits of temper and will ignore insults (12:16). He resists sexual temptation and honors the marital relationship. The one who lacks self-control in such matters is compared with a person carrying "fire in one's clothes" or "walking on hot coals" (6:27–29).

"Can fire be carried in the bosom without burning one's clothes?" (6:27).

16. Murphy, *The Tree of Life*, 166.
17. Ibid., 25.
18. Dyer, *Wisdom of the Ages*, 251.
19. Blekinsopp, *Sage, Priest, Prophet*, 34–35.

Hard work

So much for what the cool person avoids. What positive actions character-ize his/her life? The "cool man" or disciplined person embraces hard work, realizing that hard work is one of the fruits of self-control. The sages ad-monished their students to be diligent and not to despise discipline and cor-rection (1:7b). They warned them not to sleep too much. The sages learned these lessons, in part, from observing the animal kingdom (6:6; 30:24–31) as well as the human realm (24:30–34).[20] They contrasted the industry of the ant community with the laziness of a foolish vineyard owner. From their observations they deduced that actions have consequences and that the consequences of diligence are preferable to those of sloth.

John Wesley, the founder, along with his brother Charles, of the Meth-odist movement in England in the 1700s, was an enthusiastic advocate of hard work. Methodist folk wisdom attributes to John Wesley the saying "The more labor, the more blessing."[21]

The sages of Proverbs affirmed that hard work is the road to wealth (12:27; 13:4; 14:23; 20:13). While it doesn't necessarily bring happiness (11:3; 16:16; 22:1–2), it is essential to security (10:15; 18:11). According to the sages of Proverbs, its possession contributes to the wholesome living that results in the divine blessing of the wealthy person (10:22; 13:21,25; 15:6; 22:4).[22]

Cool Speech

The sages realized that speech was an area of human life that demanded rigorous self-control. They recognized the destructive power of the tongue centuries before the writing of the New Testament book of James, which warned of its power in chapter 3:5–12. Say the sages, "Death and life are in the tongue" (Prov 18:21). The fool, the "hot" man, is one who does not know when to keep quiet, and who has no control over his tongue (10:8,14; 12:23; 18:2). "Truthful lips last forever, but a lying tongue lasts only a moment" (Prov 12:19). "A poor man is better than a liar" (19:22).

The "cool man" controls his speech. He uses it sparingly and carefully considers each word. "He who guards his mouth preserves his life, but he who talks too much courts disaster" (13:3). "The mind of the righteous man

---

20. Melchert, *Wise Teaching,* 43.

21. Wesley, *Works XIII,* 29.

22. Blekinsopp, *Sage, Priest, Prophet,* 35–36.

ponders how to answer, but the mouth of the wicked pours out evil things" (15:28).

Chapter 10 is a cluster of proverbs that deal with wise and foolish speech. The theme is prominent in chapters 10–15 and chapters 17 and 18, as well as chapter 25:11–20. The choice of strategy with regard to speech is to be thoughtful rather than rash and to contribute to making a situation life-giving rather than death-dealing. At times harsh speech and rebuke are called for (10:10; 25:12; 28:23). But often silence or gentleness in speech is a wiser course of action (15:1).[23]

Bobby LaKind and Michael McDonald of the Doobie Brothers wrote lyrics for the song "One by One," in 1980. One line has always stuck with me: "You'll always have the chance to give up. Why do it now?"

I apply this philosophy to wise and foolish speech. Because I have never come home from a social interaction and thought, "I had a chance to say something really insulting to that person, and now the unique opportunity may never come again." We always have the chance to say something obnoxious and incendiary, so why do it now?

"A gentle tongue is a tree of life" (15:4).
"A soft answer turns away wrath but harsh words stir up strife" (15:1).

Knowing when to be silent and listen is an important aspect of self-control (18:15b; 12:15; 18:13; 25:12). The sages realized that it is especially difficult to maintain silence when one is being criticized. The wise person does not resent criticism but listens to it and evaluates it.

"Whoever loves discipline loves knowledge, but those who hate to be rebuked are stupid" (12:1).

The wise person refrains from boasting.
"If you have been foolish, exalting yourself, or if you have been devising evil,
    put your hand on your mouth" (30:32).
With regard to his speech, the "cool man" knows the value of speaking from a well-informed mind (20:15). He knows the danger of slander, gossip, and quarreling (10:18; 11:12–13; 26:21). He avoids unnecessary involvement in the quarrels of others.

"Like somebody who takes a passing dog by the ears
Is one who meddles in the quarrel of another" (Prov 26:17).

---

23. McKenzie, *Preaching Proverbs*, 33.

Silence can also be an effective strategy. Simply staying silent can work wonders, even for one of limited talent. I remember hearing an interview a few years ago with the actor Luke Wilson. He said he learned to act in math class, where, though he had no clue what was going on, he would frequently nod in agreement with the teacher and keep a thoughtful expression on his face throughout class. Apparently, this had a positive effect on his final grade!

"Even fools who keep silent are considered wise,
When they close their lips they are deemed intelligent" (17:28).[24]

If you have ever had laryngitis, you know the feeling of wanting to speak and not being able to. The sages urge us to exercise a sort of self-selective laryngitis, and, taking the time to think before we speak, to maintain silence when silence is preferable to what we would like to say.

Throughout religious history, silence has been an integral part of the spiritual journey, as we quiet the impulse to do all the talking in times of prayer and come to recognize that silence before God is a prelude to insight.

The Cool Spirit of Ecclesiastes

While Job is all about a passion for vindication, Qohelet is all about being cool. Qohelet, the name given to the "gatherer" of the wisdom reflections and sayings in Ecclesiastes, was a cool character. Lacking the passionate anger of Job, Ecclesiastes is characterized by melancholy and a depiction of God as distant. His is a lean, taut book, knit together with tremendous literary discipline. The author's agenda is to undercut the peppy optimism of the book of Proverbs by coining sayings of his own that highlight the inequities of life Proverbs would prefer to ignore. Chapter seven is a series of such sayings.

"A good name is better than precious ointment, and the day of death, than the day of birth" (Eccl 7:1).

We have seen how he uses the word *hebel* (vapor, often translated "vanity") to describe things that disappointed him in life around him. He was disappointed that the fear of the Lord doesn't always lead to knowledge that is useful for figuring out life, but instead leads us to the insight that our human understanding is limited (1:17–18). He was disappointed that hard work and wise living don't guarantee us a free pass to a life free of misfortune and death (2:14b-17; 8:14–23; 9:11–12). He was disappointed that the powerless and the poor suffer at the hands of the rich and the powerful (4:1–3).

24. Blekinsopp, *Sage, Priest, Prophet*, 34–35.

Though he does admit to feeling anger and despair (2:17; 2:20) his book is not a twelve-chapter long ventfest. Rather, he shows us how to channel those emotions into a realistic view of life that focuses on gratitude for the good gifts of wisdom, food, drink, work, and human companionship in each passing moment (2:13–14a; 2:24–25; 9:7–8).

Qohelet counsels self-discipline with regard to speech and the accumulation of wealth in terms reminiscent of Proverbs' more conventional wisdom collection.

"Words spoken by the wise bring them favor, but the lips of fools consume them. The words of their mouths begin in foolishness, and their talk ends in wicked madness; yet fools talk on and on" (10:13,14).

"Better is a handful with quiet than two handfuls with toil, and a chasing after wind" (4:6).

"Do not let your mouth lead you into sin . . ." (5:6).

"If the anger of the ruler rises against you, do not leave your post, for calmness will undo great offenses" (10:4).

This saying of Qohelet's reminds me of the "Keep Calm and . . ." posters that abound these days. They originate from a motivational poster that read "Keep Calm and Carry On," produced by the British government in 1939 to raise the morale of the British public, threatened by mass air attacks on major cities. The poster was hardly ever publicly displayed and was little known until a copy was rediscovered in 2000 at Barter Books, a bookshop in the town of Alnwick.[25]

It has since been reissued by a number of private companies, and has been used as the advertising theme for a range of products. Knockoffs include "Keep Calm and Keep Selling"; "Keep Calm and Eat a Cookie" (featuring a picture of *Sesame Street*'s "Cookie Monster" character); "Keep Calm and Stay Cool," and many more. A website sells pillows, tote bags, aprons, hoodies, coffee mugs, T-shirts, and key chains with the "Keep Calm and Carry On" slogan.[26]

Qohelet warns us not to lose our cool over money! He cautions against being rash and greedy for gain. Why? Because such attitudes and actions are futile. They cannot increase our good. They are just so much wasted energy. They distract us from our enjoying our portion in the present moment, the only good that life holds in Qohelet's view.

"The lover of money will not be satisfied with money; nor the lover of wealth, with gain. This also is vanity. When goods increase, those who

25. McMeel, *Keep Calm and Carry On.*

26. "Keep Calm Memes, Variations and Customised Keep Calm and Carry on Posters, Mugs, iPhone Cases, T-Shirts and Downloads," http://www.keepcalmandcarryon. com/buy-keep-calm-variations-and-memes/?shortcode=NQOxtJXW.

eat them increase; and what gain has their owner but to see them with his eyes?" (5:10–11).

Throughout the book he sets positive statements about wisdom next to observations about the aspects of life that seem to undercut the point of pursuing wisdom. "Then I saw that wisdom excels folly as light excels darkness. The wise have eyes in their head, but fools walk in darkness. Yet I perceived that the same fate befalls all of them" (2:13–14a). This is not just a ploy to confuse the reader. Nor is it, in my view, evidence of a later editor who inserted positive statements about wisdom as a sprinkling of sugar over Qohelet's dose of reality to make it go down easier. Qohelet juxtaposes conventional and subversive wisdom because he wants us to live with two truths in sight. One is that the "cool man" can avoid many of the pitfalls of life by disciplining his appetites. Conventional wisdom is an aid in helping a person control unruly, destructive impulses. The second is that there are some events and conditions the coolest of cool people cannot avoid. We must face the fact that our human knowledge is limited and God is mysterious (5:1–7). We must live with the reality that life is unpredictable (9:11, 12), and that social systems are unequal (4:1–3). All the more reason, Qohelet thinks, to be cool. Because it does no good not to be.

We've all heard the common saying "It is what it is." Qohelet could have coined that saying. Because his goal was to discipline himself to focus on the present with a grateful heart rather than to be buffeted by heated waves of anxiety and anger over the inequities and unpredictabilities of life.

As we move to explore the cool spirit of Jesus the Sage, a more apt saying would be "It is what it is, but it could be better, with God's help."

The Cool Spirit of Jesus the Sage

There is some continuity between the sages of Proverbs and Jesus the sage with regard to this wisdom virtue of self-control. Both warn against greed that makes accumulating money one's highest priority (Prov 4:23; Matt 6:19). Both discern that the heart is the wellspring of conduct (Prov 4:23; Matt 15:19; Mark 8:21). Both deal with how one is to relate to the poor. Proverbs encourages respectful charity to the poor (Prov 14:21,31). Jesus goes a step further, pronouncing God's blessing on the poor and joining them in table fellowship (Luke 6:20).

Beneath the similarities there are significant differences between conventional wisdom and Jesus' wisdom when it comes to self-control. For one thing there is a different purpose for exercising self-control. The sages of Proverbs urged the young to rein in their physical cravings so they could stabilize the tumultuous postexilic community. Jesus, by contrast, urged followers to rein in their cravings for security so they could destabilize the religious, political status quo of his day. The nature of the cravings followers were advised to control was different. The sages urged self-control over appetites. Jesus urged self-control over cravings for security and status.

Jesus is in agreement with the sages on the need to restrain oneself from anger (Matt 5:21), adultery (5:27), and gullibility with regard to false teachers (Matt 7:15–16). Beyond that the differences begin to appear.

You can tell a lot about a person's priorities by what he or she talks most about. And you can tell what is not as important to him by what he doesn't talk much about. Several of the appetites and actions the sages warn against get little play in Jesus' teachings. He does not talk about avoiding foolish companions. In fact, he habitually dined with those society had labeled "expendables."[27] He offers no conventional wisdom about moderation in food and drink, foresight in planning one's earthly affairs for the future, or the value of hard work. He includes not a single saying warning of the evil influence of women as nags or temptresses, a theme that, unfortunately, is rather prominent in Proverbs (Prov 27:15; Prov 7).

Not only does Jesus not emphasize certain prudent advice of Proverbs. At times he seems to undercut its conventional advice. Proverbs highlights the importance of prudent, close-mouthed public behavior as a means to a good reputation (21:23; 22:1; 30:32). Jesus modeled and taught bold speech and the blessedness of gaining a bad reputation and even being even ill-treated in the service of God's kingdom (Matt 5:11–12).

Proverbial wisdom underscores the importance of planning ahead and hard work as means to a degree of prosperity and security. Jesus encouraged his followers to restrain their urge to worry about the necessities of life (Matt 6:25ff) and resist a preoccupation with personal security (Matt 16:24–26). They were to rein in their appetites for flaunting their piety in public (Matt 6:1), piling up material goods (Matt 6:19), judging others (Matt 7:1), and retaliating for wrongs done to them (Matt 5:38).

Proverbs warns the young not to be in the company of with those who would hinder them in their pursuit of wisdom. Jesus warns his disciples not to be people who hinder others they judge unworthy of divine attention from approaching Jesus. His rebuke of the disciples who seek to send the children away from his presence is a prime example of this dynamic (Luke 18:15–17).

While Proverbs acknowledges that there were times when harsh speech and rebuke are called for (10:10; 25:12; 28:23), the sages mostly favor

---

27. Patterson, *The God of Jesus*, 55–88.

conciliatory speech and silence as modes of ensuring community harmony. They favor conciliatory speech toward rulers and social superiors as a means of survival (20:2; 22:11). Jesus models the opposite speech pattern. He doles out challenging speech to religious and political authorities and comforting, conciliatory speech to those on the social margins, the desperate, and the ill.

Examples of Jesus' challenge to the religious elite, and, at times, to his own disciples, include the following: Matthew 11:7; 12:1–8; 15:1–12; Mark 8:11–12; 9:19; 10:35–45; 11:15–19; Luke 5:17–24; 5:33–6:5; Luke 22:24–30; John 3:10.

Examples of his comforting of the desperate, the marginal and the poor include: Matthew 9:2; 9:27; Mark 5:34; Luke 7:36–50; John 19:26–27.

Jesus could also be kind to the prestigious who evidenced faith (Matt 8:5ff) and curt with the desperate: John 4: 17–18; 5:6; Matthew 15:24.

He did not hesitate to be blunt and challenging with his own disciples and even his own family: Matthew 20:22; Mark 3:35; 8:33; 10:38; 20:22; 3:35.

Luke 7:36–50 is an excellent example of Jesus' pattern of challenge to the powerful and comfort to the powerless. We hear the contrast between his challenging words to Simon and his comforting words to the woman who bathes his feet with ointment and her tears.

Both Proverbs and Jesus remind us that outer actions come from the inner life of a person. Proverbs 4:23 reminds us "Keep your heart with all vigilance, for from it flow the springs of life," and "The thoughts of the righteous are just" (12:5), and "Whoever is slow to anger has great understanding" (Prov 14:29). The cool spirit is very much a function of the inward person, the heart, the seedbed of volition, emotion, and thought. Jesus would not disagree that one should restrain destructive, lustful thoughts from which violent and adulterous actions spring (Mark 7:17–23; Matt 6:21).

Yet he commands us to rein in certain cautious, conventional impulses like the desire for retaliation, the craving for a secure future, and the desire to determine who is worthy of our time and who detracts from our goals. He urges us to give freer rein to certain bold and personally risky impulses, that may be at odds with conventional wisdom. Loving one's enemies, we don't retaliate. We forgive. Striving for God's kingdom and righteousness, we don't live with a paralyzing preoccupation with personal security. Rather, we experience a carefree life that trusts God for provisions for each day. Being pure in heart doesn't mean determining who is included and who is excluded at God's table. It means offering welcoming, forgiving speech to others. These unconventional impulses, activated over time, result in scenarios in which the kingdom of God breaks through into our mundane days.

Jesus had a cool head, but he used it not to promote his reputation, but to strategically convey his subversive teachings. Jesus offers proverbial sayings to live by, but they are paradoxical and life-shaking. Proverbs tells us self-control can bring us security and life. Jesus tells us that if we would save our life we must lose it. Proverbs tells us that if we exercise self-control we will have a good reputation. Jesus says that we are blessed when we are persecuted for the sake of the gospel. Proverbs warns against harsh words that stir up wrath. When the occasion called for plain speaking, Jesus did not care whose hackles he raised.

Versions of an emphasis on self-control anchor the world's great religions. Confucius counseled "nothing in excess," a way of life that charts a middle course between unworkable extremes and brings harmony and balance to family and social relationships.[28] Sufism, a manifestation of Islam especially focused on one's present, inward life, counsels the control of one's anger and addictions as a way of subduing the ego (*nafs*) that impedes one's surrender to Allah. Hinduism offers the discipline of yoga, with its emphasis on diet, posture, breathing, and concentration as a means of connecting with *Atman*. *Atman* is that dimension of the human self that reflects *Brahman*, the hidden ground of all existence that pervades, sustains, and inspires human life.[29] Buddhism recommends self-control in matters of speech and behavior. Speech should be both true and charitable. Those who follow "The Way" seek the gradual liberation from delusions and cravings and the attainment of *nirvana*, eternal and imponderable peace. Such followers should practice gentle, caring actions and eschew anger, unchastity, and the consumption of intoxicants.[30]

John Wesley repeatedly preached and taught that the Christian life is a gift of grace. He warned his followers not to forget that "we are saved by faith, producing all inward holiness, not by works, by any externals whatever."[31] At the same time he insisted that the Christian life also involved a concerted, consistent human response. One made use of what he called the "means of grace": searching the Scriptures, public and private prayer, worship and the sacraments, attendance at societies (small groups for spiritual accountability), and acts of charity. Responding intentionally to God's grace meant self-discipline. In one of his letters he wrote, "Better forty members

---

28. Smith, *The Illustrated World's Religions*, 110.

29. Armstrong, *The History of God*, 30.

30. Smith, *The Illustrated World Religions*, 74.

31. Jarboe, *Wesley Quotations*, 86.

should be lost than our discipline lost: They are no Methodists that will bear no restraints."[32]

For Christians, ironically, a key craving we need to get control over is our compulsion to be in control. This, I think, is part of what Jesus meant when he coined the aphorism "If anyone would find his life, he will lose it." We need to give control over to God.

A few years ago I was having a conversation with a United Methodist pastor serving a church in central Texas. He made an intriguing connection between faith and relinquishment of control. He said:

> To be a person of faith who lives by grace, you can't be in con-
> trol. You have to relinquish that. Of course, we give our best to
> the task at hand, but we are not completely in control of life. We
> must have the ability to laugh at ourselves. People make faith a
> set of religious principles, a program and they miss the point.
> It's about living life in a fulsome way. It is like people planning
> or going to a wedding. They get all fussy with the pictures and
> the clothing, and they completely miss the experience. It's like
> parents so hell bent on making something out of their children
> and their children making something out of themselves that
> they miss the relationship.[33]

In the news this week was a story of a public figure whose inability to control his urge to tweet suggestive pictures of himself has destroyed his marriage and his career. There was still another story of a social activist whose inability to control his temper in his personal life has led to a prison sentence and to his inability to be available to lead his movement. Lack of self-control destroys one's reputation and the credibility needed to bring about positive change in the world. On the flip side, exercising impulse-control in temper, speech, physical appetites, and relationships, one gains the respect of the community. One earns a reputation for morality, moderation, and discipline. This is a foundation that takes time to construct. It is a groundwork that must be laid if we seek to raise our subversive voices: that is, to articulate strategic, credible, and premeditated challenges to the status quo.

In the next part of this chapter we will explore how to cultivate the virtue of the cool spirit.

---

32 Ibid.

33. McKenzie, *Hear and Be Wise*, 118.

Chapter 4

Part Two—Cool Off!
Cultivating the Virtue of the Cool Spirit

Why is Self-Control So Important?

PERHAPS YOU HAVE HEARD someone say (or said yourself), "It's my life. My choices are nobody's business but my own." The belief that anyone is an island with no impact on others is an illusion. Rabbi Simeon ben Yohai, a first-century rabbinic teacher, told this parable to illustrate Leviticus 4:6 and to make the point that many may suffer because of the actions of one.

It is like men who were sitting in a ship. One took a drill and began boring beneath his own place. His fellow travelers said to him: "What are you doing?" He said to them: "What does that matter to you? Am I not drilling under my own place?" They said, "Because the water will come up and flood the ship for us all."[1]

The cool spirit may not be the most exciting of the four wisdom virtues, but when it is missing, our erratic actions have an impact far beyond ourselves. Nobody wants to be that person who has faith (fear of the Lord), compassion (listening heart), and moral courage (subversive voice) but lacks self-discipline. The educational slogan "The mind is a terrible thing to waste" in this context could become "Self-control is a terrible thing to lack."

Do we need convincing that self-control is an important virtue? Then let's first look within and around ourselves for signs of its presence. Here

1. Johnston and McArthur, *They Also Taught in Parables*, 82.

is someone who has impulse control and discernment. She knows what it is appropriate to share about herself and what is not. Here is someone who is able to hold her tongue and not join in maligning an absent friend. Here is someone who has the ability to hold his temper when disrespected and avoid a violent confrontation that would involve bystanders. Here is someone who recognizes that she is out of control and seeks help in the face of an addiction that hurts not only her, but those who love her. Here is someone who is able to resist an extramarital affair event though the desire and opportunity are close at hand. Here is someone who can ask "Do I need this or do I just want it?" and conserve his resources for future use. Here is someone who is able to rein in her rationalizations and recognize her true motivations in a situation. Here is someone who can allow the desire to be right to give way to the desire to continue in relationship. Here is someone who has appropriate physical boundaries and resists the temptation to misuse her power.

Do we still need convincing that self-control is an important virtue? Just because we notice it most when it is missing? You know the old saying "You don't know what you've got 'til it's gone." If that is true of our self-control, it may be too late to recover our reputations and our relationships.

But let's not strike too somber a tone. There is hope for those who struggle with self-control, which is just about all of us, except for those self-righteous and rather boring people who lack the imagination required to experience temptation.

A few years ago I read about a new food sprinkle that convinces the brain that you are full and helps you avoid overeating. It was called SENSA. The claim was that if you used the SENSA crystals you could lose up to thirty pounds in six months without diet or exercise. Imagine my surprise to learn that the product lacked scientific evidence as to its effectiveness and became the subject of controversy and lawsuits! Following a $26 million fine by the US Federal Trade Commission in 2014, the company ceased operations.[2]

The sages of Israel didn't fool themselves that self-control was something you could sprinkle over your life and you wouldn't be tempted to overeat, engage in sexual misconduct, lose your temper, confuse your priorities, overspend, or overindulge.

While Scripture presents the four wisdom virtues as gifts from God, it also repeatedly emphasizes that we need to respond to that gift. We need

2. Bishop, "Misleading 'Sprinkle, eat, and lose Weight' Claims Result in $26M Refund."

to cultivate the four virtues, in this case, the cool spirit, self-control or self-discipline. How does one gain self-discipline?

We've probably all heard the old joke "How do you get to Carnegie Hall?" The origin of the joke will probably always remain a mystery, but the best explanation comes from the wife of violinist Mischa Elman. One day, after a rehearsal that hadn't pleased Elman, the couple was leaving Carnegie Hall by the backstage entrance when they were approached by two tourists looking for the hall's entrance. Seeing his violin case, they asked, "How do you get to Carnegie Hall?" Continuing on his way and without looking up, Elman simply replied, "Practice."[3]

A contemporary way to express the ideal of the person who has practiced self-control would be to call him or her "clutch." *New York Times* columnist Paul Sullivan's book 2010 *Clutch: Why Some People Excel Under Pressure and Others Don't* describes the difference between someone who is "clutch" and someone who chokes under pressure. Somebody who is clutch reacts in a pressure-filled situation the same way they would in a relaxed, normal situation. They come through in a crisis. A golfer swings just as fluidly in moments of intense pressure as he does as if he were playing with friends is clutch. Clutch performers have in common that they have focus and that they practice.

Chokers, by contrast, tend to be overconfident, holding very high opinions of themselves. They may allow reputation to compensate for preparation. They tend to not take responsibility for their own mistakes.

If we asked the sages the question "How do you get self-control?" their answer would be practice, practice, practice. Self-control is described in Proverbs as both a gift (from God and Woman Wisdom) and as an accomplishment that comes from earnest, consistent effort by the learner (Prov 2—7).[4]

My yoga teacher Anya is fond of saying "While there is some discomfort now, with time and consistent practice, this may become one of your favorite poses." Maybe there is an analogy here. A limber body is not something that can be accomplished by taking a supplement, sprinkling magic limber crystals over my food, or by wishful thinking. Practice. Practice. Practice. This is required if one wishes not to lose the ground she has gained, much less if she wishes to advance in her skills. Hillel the Elder (110 BCE–10 CE) said, "Put no trust in thyself until the day of thy death."[5]

3. "History of the Hall."
4. Melchert, *Wise Teaching,* 45.
5. Goldin, *The Living Talmud,* 86.

The rabbis who, in the Talmud, commented on Torah, believed that every day is a struggle between one's evil inclination (the *yetzer harah* mentioned in Genesis 6:5) and the *yetzer hatov*. Study of Torah is the means by which one's destructive tendencies can be reigned in. Every day we will face new challenges or lower our guard to old ones. As this applies to self-control, it means that its cultivation is the work of a lifetime and that we should never let down our guard.

Self-control is not just a private virtue. It is learned in community. The learner's self-discipline is fostered and modeled by family, mentors, and teachers. It is learned from the support and discipline of one's family, as in the case of King Lemuel's mother (Prov 31:1, 4) and the "father and mother" referred to so often in Proverbs 1—7. The learner's self-discipline has beneficial effects on the whole community. Conversely, the fool's lack of impulse control can do harm to many.

"The wise lay up knowledge,
But the babbling of a fool brings ruin near" (Prov 10:14).

"Wisdom is better than weapons of war, but one bungler destroys much good" (Eccl 9:18).

The students of Israel's sages learned self-control not only by practicing it, but also by observing the lives of their teachers. So we can learn about self-control not only from Jesus' teachings, but also from his life. Here is a subversive sage with a cool character—one who, while he experienced the gamut of human emotions, did not act or speak impulsively. He responded spontaneously but also strategically. Instances of Jesus' own self-control abound in the Gospels. He resisted the temptation of Satan to allow greed and ego to get out of hand and become his motivations (Matt 4:1–11; Mark 1:12–13; Luke 4:4:1–13). Energized by compassion, he suppressed his own fatigue and hunger, rising to the occasion when human need surrounded him (Mark 6:30–44). Far more than once, he exercised the "cool man's" ability to ignore an insult. His followers were not always so strong. When one of his followers sliced off the ear of one of the high priest's slaves in the garden of Gethsemane, Jesus, pointed out the folly of anger as a way of life (Luke 22:51; Matt 26:51–52) . His symbolic action of turning over the tables in the Temple was motivated by a sense that God was being done an injustice, not that he was himself was being issued a personal affront. The action, though dramatic, did not take the form of violence against other people.

Self-control was so prized by Israel's sages because it stabilizes the community in keeping with God's will for an orderly world. By contrast, when we throw restraint to the winds, we undermine this harmony and act as enemies of our Creator. When self-control is lacking, the result is behaviors that produce strife both in personal and social life. To lack self-control is to be antisocial and to live in a way that is incompatible with the fear of the Lord.[6] Everyone goes off on his own path, and most are crooked and choked with thorns.

The wise teachers of Israel did not allow for a middle ground between wisdom and folly. But they did make nuanced distinctions among fools. They varied the language they used to describe fools. James Crenshaw, in his classic text *Old Testament Wisdom,* identified eight different terms for "fool" in the book of Proverbs.[7] The five that occur most frequently are:

Peti
Kesil
Ewil
Nabal
Les

While there is overlap, there are distinctive emphases for each fool. The *peti* is gullible. The *kesil* is ignorant of wisdom and lacks restraint in speech and temper. The *ewil* intentionally disregards wise counsel to pursue selfish ends. The *nabal* can be malicious in relating to others and is best avoided altogether. By no coincidence, Nabal is the name of the brutish husband of the lovely Abigail whose story is told in 2 Samuel 25. The *les* is a "know it all" with a disrespect for wisdom.

Peti (simple; gullible fool)

1:4—The purpose of the book of Proverbs is "to teach shrewdness to the simple."

1:22—"How long, O simple ones, will you love being simple?"

1:32—"Waywardness kills the simple and the complacency of fools destroys them."

7:7—"I saw among the simple ones, I observed among the youths, a young man without sense."

8:5—"O simple ones, learn prudence; acquire intelligence you who lack it."

9:4, 6, 16—"You that are simple, turn in here! . . . Lay aside immaturity and live . . . . You who are simple, turn in here!"

14:15—"The simple believe everything. The clever consider their steps."

6. Toombs, "The Theology and Ethics of the Book of Proverbs," 20.

7. Crenshaw, *Old Testament Wisdom,* 80–81

Kesil (ignorant fool)

3:35—"The wise inherit honor, stubborn fools, disgrace."

10:18—"Lying lips conceal hatred and whoever utters slander is a fool."

14:16—"The wise are cautious and turn away from evil, but the fool throws off restraint and is careless."

17:12—"Better to meet a she-bear robbed of its cubs than to confront a fool immersed in folly."

18:2—"A fool takes no pleasure in understanding but only in expressing personal opinion."

18:6—"A fool's lips bring strife and a fool's mouth invites a flogging."

18:7—"The mouths of fools are their ruin; their lips are a snare to themselves."

26:4—"Do not answer fools according to their folly or you will be a fool yourself."

26:5— "Answer fools according to their folly or they will be wise in their own eyes."

26:11—"Like a dog that returns to its vomit is a fool who reverts to his folly."

26:12—"Do you see persons wise in their own eyes? There is more hope for fools than for them."

29:11—"A fool gives full vent to anger, but the wise quietly holds it back."

Ewil (obstinate fool)

1:7—"The fear of the Lord is the beginning of wisdom, fools despise wisdom and instruction."

10:21—"The lips of the wise feed many, but fools die for lack of sense."

14:9—"Fools mock at the guilt offering, but the upright enjoy God's favor."

15:5—"A fool despises a parent's instruction, but the one who heeds admonition is prudent."

16:22—"Wisdom is a fountain of life to one who has it, but folly is the punishment of fools."

17:28—"Even fools who keep silent are considered wise; when they close their lips, they are deemed intelligent."

20:3—"It is honorable to refrain from strife, but every fool is quick to quarrel."

24:7—"Wisdom is too high for fools. In the gate they do not open their mouths."

Nabal (malicious fool)

17:7—"Fine speech is not becoming to a fool, much less is false speech to a ruler."

30:22—"Under three things the earth trembles; under four it cannot bear up . . .

A slave when he becomes king and a fool when glutted with food."

30:32—"If you have been foolish, exalting yourself, or if you have been devising evil, put your hand on your mouth."

Les (scornful fool)

3:34—"Toward the scorners he is scornful, but to the humble he shows favor."

9:7—"Whoever corrects a scoffer wins abuse; whoever rebukes the wicked gets hurt."

9:8—"A scoffer who is rebuked will only hate you; the wise, when rebuked, will love you.

13:1—"A wise child loves discipline, but a scoffer does not listen to rebuke."

13:20—"Whoever walks with the wise becomes wise, but the companion of fools suffers harm."

14:6—"A scoffer seeks wisdom in vain, but knowledge is easy for one who understands."

14:7—"Leave the presence of a fool, for there you do not find words of wisdom."

15:12—"Scoffers do not like to be rebuked. They will not go to the wise."

19:25—"Strike a scoffer and the simple will learn prudence."

21:24—"The proud, haughty person named 'Scoffer' acts with arrogant pride."

22:10—"Drive out a scoffer and strife goes out. Quarreling and abuse will cease."

24:9—"The devising of folly is sin and the scoffer is an abomination to all."

29:8—"Scoffers set a city aflame but the wise turn away wrath."

Avoiding the Path of Folly

We have seen how wisdom is a path paved by the fear of the Lord that leads to compassion, self-control, and moral courage. Old Testament scholar Dianne Bergant points out that the designation of wisdom in the book of Proverbs as "the Way" calls to mind a path worn by constant use. The implication is that wisdom involves patterns of behavior, not isolated acts. The purpose of this "way" is the formation of an interior disposition. Biblical wisdom affirms that this "way" can also be regarded as a divine gift.[8]

The sages of Proverbs contrast the way of wisdom that leads to life and the way of folly that leads to death.
"The path of the righteous is like the light of dawn, which shines brighter and brighter until full day."
"The way of the wicked is like deep darkness; they do not know what they stumble over" (Prov 4:18–19).

Folly is a path as surely as wisdom is. Both are paved by repeated choices in small matters. All the nuanced types of fools we have mentioned begun their careers with an isolate act or two when they threw restraint to the winds for short-term gratification. In time, those actions harden into patterns of consistent folly—the opposite of the wisdom virtues of the fear of the Lord, the listening heart, self-control, and the subversive voice.

We hear weekly of celebrities who lack self-control. Their antics make us shake our heads and feel good about how much more stable we are than they are, even though they have more money and perhaps are slightly better looking than we are. They throw a phone at a bellman, smash a photographer's camera, or get drunk, call their daughter, and get verbally abusive over the phone. They send suggestive pictures of themselves to the world on Twitter. While on probation for drunk driving charges, they shoplift necklaces at airport jewelry boutiques in full view of the security camera.

It's not just celebrities who lack self-control and act in self-destructive ways. While we might view destructive life patterns through the lens of

8. Bergant, *Israel's Wisdom Literature*, 81–82.

what we know about compulsive behavior and addiction, the sages of Israel would simply offer a one-word commentary on the following scenarios: self-control!

She overspends and gets $17,000 into credit card debt. He speeds through a stop sign because he's angry at the driver in front of him and hits a man in a wheelchair crossing the intersection. He loses his temper and drags his fiancée out of an elevator by her hair. She gets drunk and falls asleep on the sofa while her three-year-old daughter plays unsupervised in their front yard on a busy street. And so on and so forth. Sometimes these lapses in judgment are aberrations, anomalies in otherwise prudent, self-disciplined lives. But just as often, they are part of a pattern that has been forming over days, months, and years, mile markers on the road to folly.

There is a path of wisdom and there is a path of folly according to Israel's wise teachers. Wisdom scholar Glenn Pemberton describes it as a gradual "deformation of character." Being a fool is not something anyone decides when they're young they want to be when they grow up. It happens gradually, because folly is seductive. Pemberton marks four stages in the career of the fool. The first stage is the isolated foolish action. Most foolish actions, according to Proverbs, result from a lack of self-control. Where self-control is lacking, behaviors that produce strife in individual and communal life occur: drunkenness, quarreling, anger, hatred, and greed. "Hatred stirs up strife, but love covers all offenses" (10:12). Greed is the breeding ground for a whole battery of crimes against individuals and society. "Do not wear yourself out to get rich; be wise enough to desist" (23:24). Greed stems from a breakdown of self-control. And so does anger. The ideal of the sages of Proverbs is one who is "cool in spirit" (17:27). "One who spares words is knowledgeable; one who is cool in spirit has understanding." "Those who are hot-tempered stir up strife, but those who are slow to anger calm contention" (15:18).

An isolated foolish act doesn't make someone a fool any more than an isolated wise act makes someone a sage. But continued foolish acts lead to the second stage of folly when folly becomes a sport. The sages put it graphically, "Like a dog that returns to its vomit is a fool who reverts to his folly" (26:1). The fool comes to enjoy his folly even if it makes him sick. Its destructiveness has become part of its allure. It is wisdom that the fool can't stand. "A desire realized is sweet to the soul, but to turn away from evil is an abomination to fools" (13:19).[9]

The third stage in the career of the fool is when the fool is beyond correction. "Fools despise wisdom and instruction" (1:7). They follow the

---

9. Pemberton, "It's a Fool's Life," 220–21.

path of least resistance to quick rewards, fast money (1:13), excitement (1:11–12), sexual pleasure (5:3–6), and acceptance (1:14).[10] The sages urge the young to avoid the company of third-stage fools—they are corrupt beyond correction and nothing good can come of associating with them. To quote a non-biblical but time-honored proverb, "You lie down with dogs, you rise up with fleas."

The final stage in the career of the fool is what Pemberton calls "collapse and rage." We all know people whose lives are littered with destructive behaviors that impact others as well as themselves. They often blame everyone and everything but themselves for their ongoing predicament. They even blame God. This is the stage four fool. "Fools self-destruct and then hold God responsible for all their problems. Nothing is their fault. Family, friends, society, and God are to blame for the disarray of their lives."[11]

Such is the career of the fool, if he or she is not intercepted early on by the teachings of the sages. It goes from initial foolish act born out of lack of self-control common to the young. It proceeds to the enjoyment of repeated foolish acts. It moves on to the state of being beyond correction. It ends in collapse and rage. Throughout the process the fool is dangerous, not only to himself but to those whose lives he touches. We might view the career path of the fool as paved by repeated rejections of the gift of divine Wisdom in specific situations.

Since the path of folly, the flip side of wisdom, can be gradual, I thought it might be a good idea to invent a game called "You May be a Fool If . . ." to hold a mirror up to our lives and that of our culture to see what path we are on. The game can easily be switched to "You May be Wise If . . ." by proposing the opposite attitude or action.

"You May Be a Fool If . . ." in the Book of Proverbs

Speech

> You blurt out angry words that make bad situations worse or ruin good ones (15:1,4,18; 16:32; 17:27; 22:24; 29:22).
>
> You don't know the value of judicious, pleasant speech (16:21; 23; 24).
>
> You slander others (10:18).
>
> You gossip, ruining others' reputations (11:12–13).

---

10. Ibid, 221.
11. Ibid, 223.

You pick fights (26:21).

You say dishonest things (12:19; 19:22).

You blather on, saying little of importance (10:8; 12:23; 13:3; 18:2).

You brag and boast about your accomplishments (30:2).

You can't ignore an insult (12:16).

You have not learned the importance of listening (18:2; 17:28).

You are a know-it-all (12:15; 18:13).

Possessions

You think having lots of material possessions will make you happy and contented (15:16; 17:1; 16:16–19).

You place gaining money above your integrity and relationships (17:23).

Appetites

You cannot control yourself in certain areas of your life. This is having a negative effect, and you are not doing anything about it (6:6; 30:24–31; 24:30–34; 23:30; 25:28).

You lack self-control (25:27–28).

You are lazy (1:7b; 6:6; 18:9; 24:30–34; 30:24–31).

Relationships

You are unfaithful to primary relationship and betray the one closest to you (6:27–29; 15:6; 22:4).

You keep company with people who bring out the worst in you (13:20).

You enjoy spoiling the good fortune and happiness of others through deceitful speech and actions (16:27–30; 17:19; 17:23; 18:6–8).

You meddle in other people's concerns that are none of your business (26:17).

You cannot stand to be corrected (1:7b; 25:11–12).

You disdain those who are poor (17:5).

You hold grudges (17:9).

"You May Be a Fool If . . . " in the Book of Ecclesiastes

You're always looking for a future lucky break rather than dealing with the unchanging realities of the present (1:4–11).

You think your hard work can bring security (2:18–22; 9:11–12).

You think wealth will bring you contentment (5:10–12).

You think your accomplishments can bring you a lasting memory (2:18–22).

You think your wise living can help you escape from death (3:16–22).

You think you can know all there is to know about life and God (5:1–7; 8:10–17).

You are impatient and try to force events to premature conclusions (3:1–8).

You live as if you will never get old (12:1–8).

You think you can live life without coming in contact with tragedy and injustice (4:1–7).

"You May Be a Fool If . . ." in the Teachings of Jesus

You think you can harbor evil, foolish thoughts and they will stay your little secret (Matt 5:21; 5:27).

You think wealth can bring you lasting benefit (Matt 6:29).

You are gullible to false teachers and resistant to Jesus' message (Matt 7:15–16).

You think obsessive worry does any good (Matt 6:25ff).

You are preoccupied with personal security (Matt 16:24–26).

Your desire to be well thought of leads you to engage in displays of public religiosity (Matt 6:2).

You believe you are in a position to judge others (Matt 7:1).

You believe you are entitled to retaliate for wrongs done to you (Matt 5:38).

You hinder the approach of others to God (Mark 9:33–37; Matt 18:10–14).

You cannot ignore an insult (Luke 22:51; Matt 26:51–52).

You have no trouble sleeping while others suffer (Gethsemane).

Two Meditations on Self-Control

Meditation One: Self–Control: A Building Block of the Wise Life

(Proverbs 25:28; Philippians 4:6–7)

My topic is something we only notice when it is missing: the virtue of self-control. You can be humble, magnanimous, resilient, committed, and passionate, but if you live at the mercy of your impulses, if you lack self-control you sabotage yourself. It's like a house of cards. Take out the self-control card and the whole thing clatters to the ground.

Do you know anybody who lacks self-control and is therefore a prisoner of their own impulses?

Every week brings a new slate of very public, very stupid, often very sad examples of the consequences of the lack of self-control. They may entail loss of reputation, loss of health, even loss of life, one's own or another's. The practice of self-control is no trivial matter. It can be a matter of life or death.

Here is how the wise teachers of Israel in the chaotic period when they were in exile expressed the importance of self-control: "Like a city breached, without walls, is the one who lacks self-control" (Prov 25:28).

They were picturing a city with walls to keep out destroying forces with a guard at every gate and a night watch to patrol the perimeter. But now the walls have fallen and there is no one to guard your gates. You are at the mercy of anything or anyone that wants to come in and take your city. You have no defense against your own impulses.

The sages of Israel were desperate to keep their community together. And they knew that lack of impulse control destroys communities. They knew we are often are at the mercy of appetites for sex, money, food and drink, and personal power. They knew we can be at the mercy of our unrestrained tempers and our inflammatory speech. The hallmark of the fool is that he/she lacks self-control. He is a "hothead." By contrast, they called the wise person "a cool man." He is not a prisoner of, at the mercy of his impulses. He has trained himself to listen to God's wisdom in his ear, to remember that his actions affect those beyond himself, to think before he speaks or acts, to rein himself in before it's too late.

Some people are at the mercy of their own tempers.

If that is you, the sages would advise you: "Make no friends with those given to anger and do not associate with hotheads" (Prov 22:24).

I am a patient woman. I like to think. But my university-issued laptop crashed twice in the last two weeks. The first time it happened I took it to the IT office and they supposedly fixed the problem. Then, a week later it happened again. I had just opened up a sermon I was writing on the virtue of self-control. Up popped the dreaded box "Error detected in start-up. There may be a problem with your hard drive. Contact the help desk."

"I'll contact the help desk!" I said to myself. And I'll say to whomever had the bad luck to answer the phone, "HELP DESK? You call this a HELP DESK? How is this helping me for my computer to melt down twice in two weeks while I'm trying to do crucial work?"

But I didn't say that. Why? Because I can always say it tomorrow, but I can't retract it if I say it today. I didn't fly off the handle because I've never come home from an event and thought "I missed a chance to say something offensive and insulting to her, to him, and it may never come again!"

Some people are at the mercy of an addiction.

If that's you , the sages would advise you: "Wine is a mocker, strong drink is a brawler, and whoever is led astray by it is not wise" (Prov 20:1).

I know of a young dad, Scott, who had a problem with alcohol. He has been sober now for five years with the help of Alcoholics Anonymous. He moved with his wife and two young boys to a new neighborhood. A neighbor invited them to a backyard picnic. Scott came into the kitchen to get a soda. His host handed him a bottle of wine and said, "Hey, Scott, will you open this—you'll have to take it out in the garage; there is a corkscrew in the top drawer of the tool cabinet. He is alone with a bottle—he opens it, smells it, puts it to his lips, then hears the sound of children playing in the backyard, pictures his boys, carries the bottle into the kitchen, hands it to his host, grabs a Coke out of the cooler, and heads outside to play with his sons.

Some people are at the mercy of their desire to accumulate money.
Some people with their need to spend money.

The sages would us say this: "Do not wear yourself out to get rich. Be wise enough to desist" (23:4).

Some people are at the mercy of their sexual impulses.

The sages were also concerned with sexual relationships that destroyed families and communities. They would ask us this: "Can one carry fire in one's clothes without getting burned?" (Prov 6:27).

Years ago I was sitting in my office at the first church I was appointed to one evening around seven. I was still in the process of moving into my new office, putting books and knickknacks on the shelves. I had been studying the church directory to try to familiarize myself with the various couples and family groupings.

A woman's face appeared at my window and she knocked lightly on the door.

I motioned her to come in. "I'm sorry to barge in like this, but I was passing by and saw your light on. You don't know this because you just got here, but I recently lost fifty pounds. I'm feeling so much better about myself! There is a man at work I've been attracted to since I started working there. Lately he has been paying me more attention. I'm thinking about taking it to the next level with him. And I wondered what you would think about that."

I answered, "The more important question, is what does your husband think about that?"

She looked startled, then said, "Well, he's sitting out in the car waiting right now to hear what you're going to tell me."

Some people are at the mercy of poor lifestyle choices that jeopardize their health.

My brother-in-law is a physician in Hershey, Pennsylvania. He is a wonderful, caring man, but very no-nonsense. One of his side gigs is to be the on-site physician when insurance companies sponsor health screenings at local companies. He then makes follow-up phone calls with people who need to make changes in their habits. My sister calls them "Dr. Rob's Grim Reaper calls." I was visiting them last month and one evening sat at their kitchen table and couldn't help but overhear a couple of his calls. "This is Dr. Rob Weil. I was the on-site physician at your company health screening yesterday. Are you aware that a blood pressure level of 180 over 90 carries with a significant risk of stroke and or death? Have you thought about changes in diet and exercise that could help address this problem? Do you have a primary care physician? Good, well contact them tomorrow and make an appointment to take control of this situation. Your family will thank you. You're welcome."

My brother-in-law is a wisdom teacher the sages of Proverbs would approve of. He is saying "Get a grip. Take control of your health before your poor choices get the better of you. Do it for the sake of those who care about you!"

Self-control can do a lot of good. The sages of Israel remind us that there are many situations in which impulse control can improve our lives and lead to better outcomes than a foolish lack of restraint. But the sages responsible for the books of Ecclesiastes and Job remind us that we can't control everything that happens to us in life by the sheer exercise of our wills. Unfair, painful things happen to the wisest among us.

It's not just things that happen in the outer world that elude our efforts at total control. We also know from experience that we can't control everything that goes on within us by a sheer exercise of our wills. Genesis 6:5 warns us of the evil inclination that challenges our desire to do good and work for the *shalom* of the community. In chapter 7 of Romans Paul confesses his inward struggles between his knowledge of what is right and his self-destructive tendency to do exactly the opposite (Rom 7:24).

We can't always control our anxiety about the future by sheer human will. I have often wondered how Paul overcame his, as he sat in prison in Rome writing Philippians with a Roman centurion guarding his door and execution a daily possibility.

We can't always control our guilt over the past by sheer human will—the way our past choices have hurt others. I have often wondered how Paul overcame his guilt for what he had done in the past.

We can't always control our sorrow at the losses of life by sheer human will.

We can't always control an addiction or persistent condition we can't seem to shake by sheer human will. I have often wondered how Paul came to terms with his thorn in the flesh mentioned in 2 Corinthians 12.

I can only surmise that, at some point, probably his lowest point, he decided to exchange fear for faith. Having come to the end of his self-control, he had no choice but to give control over to God. Hence his advice, "Do not worry about anything, but in everything by prayer and supplication with thanksgiving let your requests be made known to God" (Phil 4:6).

When you come to the end of your self-control, give control to God. Self-control, says Paul in Galatians 5:23 and 2 Timothy 2:7, is a gift of God's

Spirit. The word in Greek is not self-control, but "strength within." We have more than sheer human willpower to power us. We have strength within, inner strength and wisdom as a gift of God's Spirit.

I believe as Paul, imprisoned when he wrote to the Philippians, gazed at his human guard and in his face he began to see the face of Christ at his door. He began to see that we are not cities with breached walls, at the mercy of our own impulses, anxieties, and guilt. No, rather, "The peace of God which surpasses all understanding guards our hearts and our minds in Christ Jesus" (Phil 4:7). Jesus is the night watch. Jesus is the guard at the gate. Jesus is more than a match for impulses, anxieties, and guilt, no matter what adversities may come in this uncertain life.

Several years ago I had a student whose name was John. He and his wife Sandy had a five-year-old daughter named Christie. Sandy became ill and John cared for her with great tenderness through a yearlong illness. She passed away and, once the family had gone home and all the casseroles had been eaten, he tried to keep it together, and to keep meals on the table, and a regular schedule, and a brave face for his daughter. But at night, after he tucked her in, he would go into the closet he had shared with his wife, her clothing was still hanging on her side, and he would go to the back, pulling her skirts and dresses out, move aside the box that held her big bright folded scarves, pashminas or something she had called them, to the side so he could sit with his back against the wall, and he would put his head in his hands and sob. One night he heard a whooshing sound and opened his eyes to see now six-year-old Christie settling herself in the box of scarves next to him, folding her legs under her.

She reached over took both of his big hands in hers and said, "I hear you in here every night, daddy. You don't have to worry. Mommy's in good hands."

By all means, let's work on the virtue of self-control in our lives.

But when we get to the end of our human self-control, give it over to God. "Do not worry about anything, but in everything, with prayer and supplication with thanksgiving, make your wishes known to God. And the peace of God, which surpasses all understanding will guard your hearts and yoru minds in Christ Jesus."

Six-year-old Christie is right. We don't have to worry. We are all in good hands.

Meditation Two: What Kind of Fool Are You?

Proverbs 1:4; 15:12; 17:21
1 Corinthians 1:18–31; 1 Corinthians 2:6–16

The book of Proverbs might also be called "Self-Control for Dummies." When we lack self-control, we become fools. And there are, in Proverbs, several answers to the question "What kind of fool am I?"

Imagine we are in a portrait gallery looking at portraits of each kind of fool in turn.

The Gullible Fool (*Peti*)

Let's stop first in front of the gullible fool (*peti*). One of the goals of the Proverbs collection, as we learn in the opening of the book (1:4), is to "teach shrewdness to the simple" (the *peti*).

Note the open, gullible look on his face. He doesn't know the importance of self-control to gain wisdom, so he is, in effect, just waiting for someone or something else to take control of his life. He is gullible. "The simple believe everything" (14:15). "Waywardness kills the simple (1:32). He is still teachable but somebody better get to him with some wisdom fast. (1:22; 7:7; 8:5; 9:4, 6, 16).

In the background of this portrait of the *peti* are a group of people standing around. They are the gullible fools in Paul's church at Corinth. They are sitting ducks for false teachers. Anyone who looks good and sounds good will impress them. Somebody better get to the gullible fool with wisdom fast!

The Know-It-All Fool (*Les*)

Our next stop is in front of the portrait of the *les*. Note the big mouth and the small ears. The NRSV translates this kind of fool as a scoffer. My Hebrew-English lexicon calls him a scorner (13:1–2; 14:6, 8; 15:12). He enjoys hearing himself talk. As a Greek philosopher once said with reference to his opponents, "The opposite of wisdom is not stupidity. It is knowing it all."
The *les* has become unteachable. He cannot control his own arrogance. He scorns the opinions and direction of those who are wiser. His attention is so focused on the sounds of his own voice that he cannot discipline himself to listen to anyone else.

See the lineup of good-looking, confident people in the background of this picture? These are the know-it-alls of the Corinthian church: the false teachers that wormed their way in the minute Paul left. Paul calls them the "super apostles," better looking, taller than Paul. More command presence. No callouses on their hands from tent-making. Ecstatic experiences. Special religious knowledge. They know it all.

It is a dangerous group dynamic when the *les* leads the *peti*, when the know-it-alls grab authority to teach the gullible.

The Malicious Fool (*Nabal*)

And finally we stop before the portrait of the kind of fool described by the Hebrew word *nabal*. Note the cold eyes and the cruel smirk. The nabal is far advanced in the school of folly. He cannot control his own malice. He cannot control his appetite for the misery of others. When you fail, he feels better. So much better that, while posing as your friend, he works behind the scenes to insure your downfall.

This is Paul's fear for the Corinthians. That in their gullibility they will come under the influence of know-it-alls and malicious, self-serving people who misrepresent the gospel.

Proverbs makes it all seem so clear. It promises that if we exercise self-control and make wise choices, we will be able to gain a large measure of control over our health, longevity, reputation, prosperity, and relationships. It will be obvious to everyone that we are wise. If we lack self-control and make foolish choices we will not flourish and everyone will be able to tell. If this is true, then we should easily be able to look in the mirror and tell whether we're wise or foolish. We should be able to look at the diplomas on our walls, our bank account, our cholesterol level, and our children's report cards and tell if we're wise or fools. Communities could give themselves the same test. What are real estate values here? How far or near are we to toxic waste dumps and chemical plants? What is the annual amount spent by the state on the education of each school-age child in our school districts?

Paul does not think we can discern inward wisdom by means of out-ward prosperity.

One summer during her college years, a friend of mine worked at a toy factory in Burlington, New Jersey. Her job crew was assigned to assemble tops. These were large, plastic tops that had a farm scene on a little platform at the bottom. On one side of the platform there was a cow and a sheep, and on the other side there was a cow and a goat. Her particular job was to place the little plastic farm animals on the platform, clicking them onto the knobs on the base. The animals came all lumped together in one huge plastic bag. The girl next to her had the job of digging out all the cows. Laurel's job was to dig out all the sheep and goats and separate them into two piles on the assembly line table and then snap them into place in the farm scene. As quickly and efficiently as possible.

In this passage from first Corinthians it is as if Paul took the handle of this top and started pushing on it so that the farm scene begins to spin faster and faster before our eyes. Sheep. Goat. Wise. Fool. Sheep. Goat. Wise. Fool. Geep. Shoat. Fise. Wool. Geep. Shoat. Fise. Wool.

According to Paul, it is possible for someone to be a fool within and still give the appearance of possessing wisdom by conventional standards. According to Paul, it is possible for someone to be wise within and be judged a failure in the eyes of the world. For Paul, Jesus, in his teachings, death, and resurrection, has reframed conventional definitions of wisdom and folly.

We saw in Proverbs, Job, and Ecclesiastes that being wise boils down to trusting God's Wisdom as a divine gift to which we respond with trust and trembling, the fear of the Lord.

For Paul, the source of a wise life is God's act for our salvation in the resurrection of God's Son Jesus who "became for us wisdom from God" (1 Cor 1:30). This wisdom doesn't come from observing daily life and discerning patterns of productive and destructive behavior. It comes from listening to the subversive teachings of Jesus and observing the humiliating death to which they led. We don't acquire this wisdom by exercising self-control. We acquire it, paradoxically, by relinquishing control in favor of a risky reliance on the teachings and presence of a crucified Messiah, a sacrificial sage. This wisdom goes against cultural convention. It leaves no room for the boasting rights that motivate too many of our religious practices. Living by it, we place ourselves in the hands of a God who both demands everything from us and gives everything for us. Living this way we become fools for Christ, living by the wisdom of God as revealed to us in the cross and resurrection of God's Son—which is "foolishness to those who are perishing, but to those who are being saved . . . it is the power of God" (1 Cor 1:18).

You May Be A Fool If . . .

Paul presents us with three self-checks in 1 Cor 2:6–16. Three signs that "You may be a fool if . . ."

First Sign You May Be a Fool: You Meditate on the Cross

You may be a fool if in the past month you have been meditating on the cross without meaning to. When you close your eyes do you see the outline of the cross? Have you seen its imprint in the faces of the suffering victims' families, refugee children with wide eyes like sad saucers, firefighters, rescue workers, and the young, thin shouldered boy-men crowded on trucks in dusty clothing clutching their guns?

In prayer do you ever find yourself standing before the cross offering our Lord prayers of thanks and encouragement? Do you find yourself affirming that which is far from obvious? Things like, in weakness is strength. In death there is life. Love is stronger than death.

If so, you are well on your way to being a fool by Paul's definition.

Second Sign You May Be a Fool: You Rely on the Holy Spirit

The second sign that you may be a fool is if, in the past few weeks, you have found yourself praying more than usual, for others, for wisdom, for God. That means you are coming to an even deeper sense of your need for God in your daily life. It means you are living out the first Beatitude, "Blessed are the poor in spirit." The NEB rendering is "How blest are those who know their need for God!" This is echoed in the Christian mystical tradition that tells us that our greatest perfection is to need God.[12]

And if you start recognizing your need for God more, you're going to get more disciplined about quiet times of prayer. And if you continue or begin to set aside quiet times of prayer, you are going to be listening to yourself breathe. And once you start listening to yourself breathe, you cannot help but be reminded of the Holy Spirit that animates your spirit. And it is a short step from there to your experiencing, in prayer, a growing awareness of your reliance on that Spirit.

Third Sign You May Be A Fool: You Are Motivated by Love For God/Others

And if, in a time of prayer, you should feel as if your personal anxieties are dropping away, replaced by a sense of being loved and a spontaneous love for those around you, you have placed yourself in a very dangerous position —you are about to unwrap the riskiest of gifts.

12. Soelle, *The Silent Cry,* 2.

That gift is "the mind of Christ," and it is the third sign that you may be a fool. Paul warns us that it could come to us in 1 Corinthians 2:16. "The mind of Christ" is to be so overcome with love for God and others that you are willing to risk everything, in faith that God holds your future.

Meditating on the cross instead of on trivialities is bad enough. Reliance on the Holy Spirit rather than knowing it all yourself is bad enough. But if you also have this third symptom of foolishness, then you have probably already exchanged fear for faith in God, and there may well be no turning back. You may already be what Paul calls "mature" or complete (2 Cor 2:6). You may already be a total fool . . .[13]

Congratulations!

Questions for Reflection on the Cool Spirit

1. In what area(s) of your life do you have the most trouble with self-control?

2. Have you faced a time when you realized you could not rein in your destructive impulses by your own will power alone?

3. Has there ever been at time you asked God for help and were able to make a life giving choice rather than a self-indulgent or self-destructive one?

4. In what ways have you seen people's lack of self-control hurt others?

5. In what ways have you see their exertion of the cool spirit benefit themselves and others?

6. Do you ever think your greatest struggle with self-control is with your need to be in control?

7. How do you respond to Jesus' teachings that portray a life of faith-filled willingness to risk and give over control to God?

13. Quast, *Reading the Corinthian Correspondence*, 37.

Chapter 5

Part One—The Fourth Wisdom Virtue
The Subversive Voice

"You have heard that it was said . . . but I say to you" (Matt 5:21–22)

In this chapter, we will explore the fourth wisdom virtue, the subversive voice—what it is and how to listen for it as it comes to us through the witness of biblical wisdom literature. In Chapter 5, Part Two, we will deal with how to activate the subversive voice in our own lives, how to exchange hanging back for standing up and speaking out.

The word *subvert* means to undermine the power and authority of an established system or institution. It comes from *sub* (under) and *vertere* ("to turn"). The dynamic of subversion, then, is to dig under a foundation working toward the eventual toppling of something so something else can be built from the materials that make up the rubble.

In his *Autobiography*, frontier preacher Peter Cartwright (1785—1872) tells the story of an incident in his charge in Marietta, Ohio.

> There was here in Marietta a preacher by the name of A. Sargent . . . who assumed the name of Halcyon Church, and proclaimed himself the millennial messenger. He professed to see visions, fall into trances, and to converse with angels. His followers were numerous in the town and country.
>
> On Sunday night, at our camp-meeting, Sargent got some powder, and lit a cigar, and then walked down to the bank of the

river, one hundred yards, where stood a large stump. He put his powder on the stump, and touched it with his cigar. The flash of the powder was seen by many at the camp; at least the light. When the powder flashed, down fell Sargent; there he lay a good while. In the meantime, the people found him lying there and gathered around him. At length he came to and said he had a message from God to us Methodists. He said God had come down to him in a flash of light, and he fell under the power of God, and thus received his vision.

Seeing so many gathered around him there, I took a light and went down to see what was going on. As soon as I came near the stump, I smelled the Sulphur of the powder; and stepping up to the stump, there was clearly the sign of powder, and hard by lay the cigar with which he had ignited it. He was now busy delivering his message. I stepped up to him, and asked him if an angel had appeared to him in that flash of light.

He said, "Yes."

Said I, "Sargent, did not that angel smell of brimstone?"

"Why," said he, "do you ask me such a foolish question?"

"Because," said I, "if an angel has spoken to you at all, he was from the lake that burneth with fire and brimstone!" and raising my voice, I said, "I smell Sulphur now!" I walked up to the stump, and called on the people to come and see for themselves. The people rushed up, and soon saw through the trick, and began to abuse Sargent for a vile impostor. He soon left, and we were troubled no more with him or his brimstone angels.[1]

The sage uses her subversive voice to do just what Peter Cartwright did in this scenario. She challenges human behavior and institutions—asking what assumptions are they built on, and are they in keeping with God's vision for human community?

Several of the world's great religions began with the subversive voice, the courage to speak out against unjust social systems. The prophet Muhammed incurred hostility and opposition by his insistence that Allah was not just the supreme God but the only god among the teeming competitors

1. Cartwright, *The Autobiography of Peter Cartwright*, 99–100.

of sixth-century Mecca. His challenge to that city's polytheism threatened its economy as well as its moral laxity.[2]

Buddhism has its roots in the Buddha's challenge to the priestly caste of Hinduism (*Brahmins*) in sixth-century BCE India. He objected to their fatalistic defeatism and insisted that women as well as men were capable of enlightenment.[3]

Confucius sought to subvert the brutality and social chaos of China in the sixth century BCE. His teachings commend a life shaped by compassion and integrity geared toward familial and political harmony.[4]

In most religions, the original subversive edge of the founder's voice tends to dull, and the abuses they protested have a way of reappearing after their death. Religious traditions need the periodic subversion of current practices by individuals who seek to keep them true to their founder's roots.

The Sages of Hebrew Scriptures

To use the terms *subversive* and *sage* in the same breath may seem like an oxymoron. Sages often serve to stabilize the community by instilling respect for the authority of traditional wisdom in the young. To subvert something, by contrast, means to undermine it, to disturb its equilibrium, or to over-throw it. We may judge a person who subverts tradition to have some kind of "problem with authority."

To call someone a subversive sage in biblical terms is to commend them for their respect for authority: God's. The upbeat sages of Proverbs believed they could discern divine wisdom and align their lives with it for harmony and prosperity. Two insights that show up throughout the book keep them humble about their own limited knowledge and respectful of God's transcendence. The first is the realization that human wisdom is lim-ited. The second is that God is our Sovereign God whose divine order is only partially revealed in Creation. As God says in Isaiah 55:8, "My thoughts are not your thoughts, nor are your ways my ways."

These insights are expressed in what some scholars call the "limit proverbs."

"The human mind may devise many plans, but it is the purpose of the Lord that will be established" (Prov 19:21). "All one's ways may be pure in one's own eyes, but the Lord weighs the spirit" (Prov 16:2).[5]

2. Smith, *The Illustrated World's Religions*, 151.
3. Ibid., 68–69.
4. Ibid., 119–21.
5. Perdue, "Wisdom in the Book of Job," 79–80.

These guiding insights, like two haunting strains in an otherwise major key composition, reminded the sages of their need to remain open to scenarios that did not fit their orderly equation of do good = get good.

The sages responsible for the books of Job and Ecclesiastes deserve the high compliment of being called subversive sages. These books were most likely not the work of single authors, but of schools of wisdom. They used the genres used by conventional, status quo–preserving wisdom (proverbs, admonitions, and reflections) to keep wisdom humble, to prevent it from claiming that human wisdom has all the answers. Their books are the result of their exercise of the virtue of the subversive voice: questioning the assumptions of received wisdom and the status quo it has created. So Qohelet asked himself, "If living wisely promises only positive outcomes in life, then why does everyone, wise or foolish, die?" And he coined the saying:

"The wise have eyes in their head, but fools walk in darkness. Yet I perceived that the same fate befalls all of them" (Eccl 2:14).

So Jesus perhaps asked himself, "How can religious leaders so obsessed with outward ritual cleanliness have hearts stained with apathy toward the poor?" And he coined the saying: "It is not what goes into the mouth that defiles, but what comes out" (Matt 15:11; Mark 7:15).

The Subversive Voice of the Book of Job

The book of Job is the product of a group of sages in the postexilic period asking the questions "How do we make sense of the profound suffering of our people?" and "How does it square with the received wisdom that suffering is the result of someone's foolish, unjust actions?" The book is a tapestry composed of several literary strands, each with its own unique subversive message. The first two chapters and chapter 42:7–17 are probably from the early monarchial period. They portray a traditional story of the divine testing and vindication of a righteous man. The dialogues between Job and his friends (3—31; 38:1–40:2) may have been written soon after the Babylonian invasion of 586 BCE, an event that caused a crisis of faith.[6] During the postexilic period, two additions were made: the speeches of Elihu (chapters 32—37) and the poem on the inaccessibility of Wisdom (chapter 28).[7]

From the beginning the narrative subverts the reader's confidence that God is consistent and righteous. Satan challenges the motives of a wise person for living wisely: he suggests that Job's motives for faithfulness to God are inspired by self-interest. Job serves God because God prospers him.

6. Ibid., 80.
7. Ibid., 81.

God takes the bait and allows Satan to afflict Job's family and property (Job 1:12). This portrait of a suspicious, capricious God is disturbing. Job's own monologues voice his growing suspicion that God may indeed be faithless and capricious.

Job's friends attribute his sufferings to his misdeeds and urge him to repent and confess his sins. Job refuses to attribute his misfortunes to his own sinfulness.[8] Instead, he increasingly attributes his sufferings to God. Even so, he does not abandon moral virtue and piety. Thereby he proves to Satan that he is not who Satan thought he was, someone who serves God only for what he can get out of it. As Satan misjudges Job, so Job misjudges God. Job assumes the God is the one doling out good fortune and bad fortune on the basis of human behavior. He accuses God of making a mistake in his case, since he has done nothing wrong to deserve his losses. God responds to Job out of the whirlwind in chapter 40. In effect, God is saying, "Things are not as simple as you think they are. The management of the cosmos is a matter whose complexity is far beyond your human comprehension. You are human, and I am God. Know your place."

Job acknowledges that he has overstepped. His final positive act is when he intercedes for his friends (Job 42:10).

The book of Proverbs largely assumes that people are poor because they are lazy, an elitist view that gives the comfortable an excuse to ignore the poor and even blame them for their poverty. Theologian Gustavo Gutierrez claims that Job's attitude toward poverty is closer to the prophets than to traditional wisdom represented by Proverbs. In his view, Job is an advocate for the poor and a critic of his social world.[9] Job is more than an advocate for the poor. He is poor himself, as he sits upon the ash heap of impoverished suffering (2:8). Job opens up a dimension of human experience that is absent from Proverbs: human grief. Whoever wrote the book of Job knew what it meant to vulnerable to the harshness of life, to bear the "scars of the journey."[10]

Job was written in the midst of Israel's postexilic dislocations when the question of innocent suffering was all too real. The author(s) of Job do not offer a neat solution to what theologians call the "problem of evil." The writer(s) lifts up various options for explaining innocent suffering to draw the reader into an encounter with God. Those options include:

- a built-in component of the human condition (4:1–5; 5:6–7; 7:1–6; 15:14–16; 25:4–6);

8. Ibid., 85–86.
9. Pleins, The Social Visions of the Hebrew Bible, 506.
10. Ibid, 506–7.

- the result of wrongdoing (4:6–11; 8:11–13; 11:5–6, 13–16; 15:25–35; 18; 20:15–22; 22:5–11; 27:13–23);

- the outcome of divine discipline (5:17–27; 11:7–12; 49:8–14; 42:1–6);

- the result of God's malice (7:17–21; 9:1–14; 12:12–25; 19:6–14; 30:19–31);

- the result of the exploitation of one social group by another.[11]

No one option is satisfactory. The impact on readers is to motivate us to continue to ask questions related to innocent suffering and to seek answers for our communities and for ourselves.[12] The book encourages readers to look for God in the realities of suffering, grief, and painful silence. There God will be present and will speak. God will not be met in formulas that are too tidy for the realities of life. Rather, God can be found in our struggles with grief beyond words. The subversive voice then and now speaks this good news into a do good = get good world: the presence of suffering does not mean the absence of God.

The Subversive Voice of Ecclesiastes

The subversive sages of Ecclesiastes are motivated by the same question that motivated the creation of the book of Job. "How do the upbeat promises of conventional wisdom square with our current national situation?" The book probably dates from the Persian captivity in the third century BCE. Life was precarious, and one's fortunes were dependent on the whims of a capricious, distant king who doled out plots of land to the exiles. The more God favored you, the bigger and more fertile the plot you were assigned to till. The sages' listening hearts alerted them to the pain and injustices of such circumstances. They took note of realities that traditional wisdom preferred to downplay: death, inevitable for wise and fool alike; the sufferings of the poor oppressed by the rich; our constant vulnerability to accidents and reversals of fortune; and the debilitating effects of old age. Qohelet, the name given to the author(s) of Ecclesiastes, exercised acute alertness to life around him and within him. This led him to subvert three major tenets of traditional wisdom.

11. Ibid., 508.
12. Ibid., 499–500.

Proverbs's Affirmation = "The Fear of the Lord is the beginning of knowledge." Qohelet's Subversive Version: "Fear God!"

Proverbs understands the fear of the Lord as the beginning of wisdom, the promise that God will reveal aspects of the order of life to the earnest seeker. Qohelet, by contrast, views God as distant and largely unknowable. He enjoins his students to "fear God," which for him means "Accept the fact that your human faculties are limited, and don't dishonor God by overstepping your bounds. "With many dreams come vanities and a multitude of words; but fear God" (5:7). For Qohelet, to fear God is not the first step on a journey of discovery, but a response to the fact that God is unknowable in human experience. We are to fear God because God is distant and mysterious and dispenses certain functions at certain times (3:1–8, 11). God desires awe from human beings (3:14) and such awe ranks higher for Qohelet than justice or wisdom (5:6; 7:18). For him the pinnacle of wisdom is the recognition of human limitation.

Proverbs' Affirmation: "Wisdom leads to Order and Life."

QOHELET'S SUBVERSIVE VERSION: THE PURSUIT OF WISDOM IS HEBEL (VANITY)

The sages of Proverbs saw patterns of cause and effect around them, whereby a wise life led to happy consequences (long life, good health, good reputation, and large, harmonious family). Qohelet is attentive to the scenes from his own and others' lives that disappoint those expectations. The wise age and die just like the fools (2:16–17). The righteous poor are oppressed by rich fools (4:1–3), and all our precautions cannot save us from the tragedies and sorrows of an unpredictable life (9:11–12; 10:8, 9). He calls the repeated disappointment of traditional wisdom's promises vanity, *hebel*, Hebrew for vapor (2:17). Qohelet uses the word *hebel* to describe the ephemerality of life (6:12; 7:15; 9:9). He uses the word to refer to aspects of life that are fleeting. They include joy (2:1), human accomplishments (2:11; 4:4), and youth and the prime of life (11:10).[13] This is a far cry from the sturdy order promised by Proverbs.

---

13. Mathewes-Green and Mathewes-Green, "Impact Pray-ers," 28.

Proverbs' Affirmation: "Wisdom is a Gift from God."

QOHELET'S SUBVERSIVE VERSION: "OUR PORTION (HELEQ) IS OUR GIFT FROM GOD."

The sages of Proverbs viewed wisdom as a gift from God. God has placed clues to how human beings are to live in the patterns of the created order. We can discern them and grow in the knowledge of God on the lifelong path of wisdom that guides us toward right choices with good outcomes.

Qolehet's understanding of the gift we have been given is much less comprehensive. And it is confined to each passing moment. The gift he perceives in life is what he calls our portion (*heleq*). It is a reference to a plot and can be understood literally, as the plot of land one tills, or metaphorically, as one's lot in life, with its attendant joys and sorrows. A distant, unknowable God gives us each a portion, which contains sorrows but also joys. Those joys include work, food and drink, and relationships. To focus on those blessings with gratitude in the present moment is to make the most of our portion in life (8:15; 9:7–10). It is to realize that our pleasures are all the more precious, because they are precarious. This is Qohelet's modest definition of living wisely: to live in the present moment with awe for a transcendent God, gratitude for God's gifts, and enjoyment of what is positive in our portions.

The Subversive Voice of Jesus the Sage

There are about 102 proverbial sayings in the Synoptic Gospels and over forty parables. The predominance of these wisdom genres in Jesus' Synoptic teachings strongly suggests that one important role Jesus chose for himself was that of a sage or wisdom teacher.[14]

Recent scholarship has pointed out the similarities between Jesus and the itinerant Cynic philosophers. Cynics were radical Stoics who rejected the cultural trappings of home and family. They lived wandering lives, at a subsistence level with regard to clothing, food, and shelter. Their themes of the foolishness of anxiety and dependence on social luxuries sound a common chord with some of Jesus' teachings (Matt 6:25–32; 10:7–11). However, the goal of their lifestyle and teachings was self-sufficiency, not radical reliance on the provision of God.[15]

---

14. McKenzie, *Preaching Proverbs*, 41–58.
15. Perkins, *Jesus as Teacher*, 5–6.

The Gospel of John depicts Jesus as an expression of the Word and Wisdom of God. Jesus' habitual manner of speech in the fourth Gospel is in "I am" sayings, poetic monologues more like the speeches of Woman Wisdom in Proverbs 1 and 8 than the shorter wisdom sayings of the rest of Proverbs. There are a few short sayings in John (12:24), but our focus will be on the proverbs and parables of Jesus as depicted in the Synoptic Gospels.

We have pointed out before that both proverbs and parables belong to the genre of *mashal* (plural *meshalim*).

The close kinship of proverbs and parables comes clear when we observe that several of Jesus' parables bear an uncanny resemblance to sayings from Proverbs. The parable of the chief seats (Luke 14:7–11) is closely related to Proverbs 25:6f. The parable of the friend at midnight (Luke 11:5–8) is strangely similar to Proverbs 3:28. The parable of the two foundations (Matt 7:24–27; Luke 6:47–49) is very much in the spirit of Proverbs 10:25 and 12:7.

This genre includes both proverbs and parables. *Mashal* means "to set alongside." The Greek word for *mashal* is *parabole* and carries the connotation of "to be like." Proverbs and parables share a couple of prominent traits of the *mashal* family. One is that they are memorable, employing metaphor, vivid images, and concrete language. Another is that they invite involvement, enticing listeners to evaluate their present situation in light of the insight or image they offer.

The search for the "original sayings" of Jesus, free from interpretations by the early church, is problematic at best and futile at worst. The search for teachings and themes that reflect the spirit of Jesus' message is a more modest and helpful enterprise. Of the numerous criteria scholars have suggested, four seem most fruitful to me in listening for Jesus' distinctive subversive voice. One is the criterion of "multiple attestations" or "multiple appearances." Do certain themes and sayings occur in several places? A prime example is Jesus' saying about saving life and losing life, which appears five times in the Synoptic Gospels (Matt 16:25, 10:39; Mark 8:35; Luke 9:24, 17:33). The words Jesus spoke at his Last Supper, his meeting with John the Baptist, and the theme of the kingdom of God are examples of scenarios and themes that meet this criterion of multiple appearances.

A second criterion is the criterion of coherence or consistency. Does a saying fit within the context of what we know of Jesus' mission and ministry? A third criterion is the criterion of embarrassment or contradiction. This focuses on those sayings or actions that would have created difficulty or embarrassment for the early church. Sayings related to the crucifixion, a humiliating death for their movement's inspiring leader, certainly fit this criterion.[16] A fourth criterion, closely related to the third, is the criterion of rejection and execution. It directs our attention to the historical fact that Jesus met with a violent end at the hands of Jewish and Roman officials. It asks, "What historical words and deeds of Jesus account for his trial and crucifixion as 'King of the Jews?'"[17]

To these four I would add one more which I'll call the criterion of silence. You can tell a lot about what is not important to someone by what they don't bother to talk about. When we look at Jesus' short sayings and parables, there are topics dear to the heart of traditional wisdom that he never mentions. They center on gaining control over one's future, developing habits that contribute to an orderly society, maximizing the likelihood of long life, prosperity, and preserving harmonious familial relationships.

The reason I believe he did not address those topics was because they were not relevant to those he had come to seek and to save, those silenced by the religious, political elites of his day. Working harder to better themselves was not an option for those who heard Jesus' message most eagerly. These individuals' lives were characterized by fatalism, passivity, and silence. They experienced what some sociologists calls a "dominated consciousness." Those who live within it are overwhelmed by powerful forces, overcome by an unrelenting hopelessness, relieved only by occasional and ineffectual appeals to magic or supernatural forces to alleviate their misery.[18] These were the people who had no say in their lives, who did the jobs no one else wanted to do, like tax collecting or dying cloth. They were the ones whose bodies counted for nothing except as they could be used to fulfill the desires of others. The great hierarchy of the Roman Empire thought of them as "the expendables." They were those who gradually fell through the cracks in the system into poverty and premature death. The term *expendable* comes from the analysis of anthropologist Gerhard Lenski in his classic work *Power and Privilege*.[19]

Stephen Patterson, in his analysis of the social context of Jesus' teachings, points out that the experience of being an expendable person in antiquity included three dimensions: the experience of being unclean (not clean), the experience of shame (not honor), and the experience of being regarded as sinful (not righteous).[20] Jesus did not use his subversive voice to preach traditional proverbial wisdom, to admonish these folks to work harder and

16. Meier, *A Marginal Jew*, vol. 1, 171.

17. Ibid., 177.

18. Herzog, *The Parables as Subversive Speech*, 24.

19. Lenski, *Power and Privilege*, 281–84.

20. Patterson, *The God of Jesus*, 68.

fit into society better. Rather, his sayings and parables subverted status quo values and invited expendables into the embrace of a God who offered them forgiveness, identity, and purpose. Jesus used his subversive voice to give them a voice.

Unclean, not Clean

"Blessed are the pure in heart, for they will see God" (Matthew 5:8).

Drawing on ancient Israel's connection between cleanliness and holiness (Lev 13:45–46; Deut 23:10–11; 23:13–14), unclean, in Jesus' day, was viewed as a religious category. Jesus discerned the truth that it was often a condition that resulted from poverty, disease, and race. He addresses his ministry to those who, by their very existence, were defined as unclean: lepers (Mark 14:3), Gentiles (Mark 7:24–30), and prostitutes (Luke 7:35–50). He insisted that the power to be clean lies in a pure heart (Matt 5:8), not in what goes into the mouth (Mark 7:15).[21]

Shame, not Honor

"Why do you see the speck in your neighbor's eye, but do not notice the log in your own eye? (Matt 7:3).

Honor and shame were social, economic, not purely personal or religious categories. Honor and shame were the forces that give shape to communal life. To have honor was to have a place, a role, that is recognized by one's peers and which one competently performs.[22] Jesus challenged the honor of those wishing to stone the woman caught in adultery (John 7: 53b–8:11). Just as nothing from outside can render one unclean, so one cannot be shamed from without. It does not lie within the legitimate power of one human being to shame another, to ostracize that person from divine and human company.[23] On repeated occasions, Jesus behaved "shamelessly," disregarding social and religious definitions of whom he should interact with. Examples of Jesus' "shameful" dialogue partners include Bartimaeus, a blind beggar (Mark 10:46–52), and women, who ought to have remained beneath a first-century rabbi's notice: Martha and Mary (Luke 10:38–42)

21. Ibid., 72.
22. Ibid., 74.
23. Ibid., 77.

and the Syrophoenician woman (Mark 7:27).[24] On the cross, Jesus, the one who honored those shamed by society, was himself shamed, but ultimately honored by the Father.

Sin not Righteousness

"I have come to call not the righteous but sinners" (Mark 2:17b). "Sinner" in the ancient world is not just a moral category—it is also a social one. The assumption of Jesus' day was that expendables were on the bottom rung of the social ladder because they deserved to be. "Who sinned, this man or his parents, that he was born blind?" (John 9:1–34).

Those who had no other options than to do the jobs no one else wanted to do were linked with "sinners": tax collectors, shepherds, dung collectors, tanners, peddlers, weavers, bath attendants, and gamblers with dice.[25] Jesus quotes his opponents' condemnation of the company he keeps: "Look, a glutton and a drunkard, a friend of tax collectors and sinners" (Luke 7:34b). Says Jesus of his own ministry: "I have come to call not the righteous but sinners (Mark 2:17b). Jesus is not here thinking of sinner as a moral category but a social one. He invited into his company those whose society labeled them as sinners, unclean, and shamed. Jesus by his choice of companions, at table and beyond it, honored those others considered "expendable." Jesus' short sayings and parables, alongside his ministries of healing and exorcism, proclaimed for them an alternative empire. It was the empire of God, in which the means to life are free and accessible to all by God's own gracious hand.[26]

Listening Strategies for Discerning Jesus' Subversive Voice in his Short Sayings

At times Jesus quoted sayings from the stockpile of common cultural wisdom of his day. But he used them, as we'll see, for his uncommon purposes. At other times he coined aphorisms that undercut the status quo and pointed toward an alternative way of life. Aphorisms are distinguishable from proverbs in that we know who their author was and that they often subvert traditional values.[27]

24. Ibid., 77–78.
25. Ibid., 82.
26. Ibid.
27. Williams, *Those Who Ponder Proverbs*, 78–90.

As we listen to Jesus' proverbial sayings in Matthew, Mark, and Luke, sometimes we will hear echoes of the traditional wisdom of Proverbs and the Greco-Roman world. Sometimes we will hear the sound of silence, as he refrains from dealing with conventional themes. And sometimes we will hear aphorisms that convey an edgy melody in a minor key, the sound of Jesus' subversive voice.

Listening Strategy #1: Listen for Common Proverbs that Serve Uncommon Purposes

Jesus often quotes sayings that sound like they could have come straight out of the book of Proverbs. They echo themes of the wisdom traditions of the Ancient Near East, as well as of his contemporary Greco-Roman milieu.[28]

For example:

Nothing is covered up that will not be revealed.

The sick need doctors, not the well.

No one can serve two masters.

Let the day's own trouble be sufficient for the day.

The measure you give will be the measure you get back.

Many are called but few are chosen.

A tree is known by its fruits.

One's life does not consist in the abundance of one's possessions.

A city set on a hill cannot be hid.

All that defiles comes from within.

Out of the abundance of the heart the mouth speaks.[29]

Jesus uses these traditional sayings for nontraditional purposes. He does not use them to describe life in general as they were used in his cultural context. He uses them to paint a picture of what it would mean to follow his teachings and example in the world. They become pixels in his portrait of a life which subverted current religious practices and attitudes.

When Jesus says that what is hidden now will be revealed, it was to allay his disciples' fear of the enemies of the gospel (Matt 10:26). When he reminds his listeners that the sick need doctors, not the well, he is defending

28. Perdue, "The Wisdom Sayings of Jesus," 6–7.

29. Carlston, "Proverbs, Maxims, and the Historical Jesus," 98.

his choice of table companions to the scribes (Mark 2:17). When he reminds listeners in Mark 4:23–25 that "the measure you give will be the measure you get," he is not just making a general observation like "What goes around comes around." He is alerting listeners to pay attention to and internalize his teachings. In Matthew and Luke the saying warns hearers that they will be judged by the same standard with which they judge others (Matt 7:2; Luke 6:37–38).

When Jesus points out that "many are called but few are chosen," he is expressing the fact that while everyone is invited to God's banquet, not everybody's response is rightly motivated (Matt 22:14).

When Jesus tells us, "Don't worry about tomorrow, for tomorrow will bring troubles of its own," he is not just making the point that the future is unknown (as in Prov 27:1). He is encouraging us to take the risk of having faith in a God who both demands all and provides all.

When he exposes hypocrisy with talk of log and speck (Matt 7:5–7), he is warning that we will be judged by the standards of our own hypocrisy. The blessedness he describes is not a matter of good health and good fortune. It is a merciful attitude toward others based on our admission of our own weaknesses and our affirmation of God's mercy to everyone.

Common human wisdom pointed out that life is more than just possessions (Prov 11:28). But it also viewed material prosperity as a positive condition that often resulted from wise living (Prov 3:15). Jesus' teachings reveal a radical suspicion of the corrupting influence of wealth. "Be on your guard against all kinds of greed; for one's life does not consist in the abundance of possessions" (Luke 12:15). This saying is followed by the parable of the Rich Fool. That parable ends with the warning that it will not go well with those who "store up treasures for themselves but are not rich toward God" (Luke 12:21).

The parable of the Dishonest Steward in Luke ends with this proverb: "You cannot serve both God and wealth" (Luke 16:13; see also Matt 5:14). Greed destroys community and distracts followers from God.

Common wisdom acknowledged that a tree is known by its fruits. Jesus uses the proverb to warn against false prophets (Matt 7:20) and to encourage hearers to build their lives on the foundation of his teachings (Luke 6:43).

Common wisdom knew full well that "a city set on a hill cannot be hid." Jesus used this sayings to call his followers to let their light shine in the world so their good works will glorify God.

Common wisdom knew that one's character was the wellspring of one's speech and that, therefore, what defiles comes from within. Jesus used this insight to challenge a myopic focus on ritual purity among the religious elite (Matt 15:10–11).

Jesus clearly respected the commonsense proverbs of traditional wisdom and their general insights about daily life. He borrowed them whenever he could and harnessed them in service of his own subversive message. He used them to commend his vision of the kingdom of God and to challenge current practices.

Listening Strategy #2: Listen for the Sound of Silence

We have seen how Jesus did not deal with a number of themes that were central to traditional wisdom. Jesus' wisdom is characterized by an absence of the Golden Mean, the sense of balance and restraint that is characteristic of so much of the wisdom tradition.[30]

His wisdom sayings lack any admonitions to seek wisdom, a feature basic to the wisdom tradition as a whole (Prov 1;7; Job 38). He does not commend wisdom as being more precious than jewels (Prov 3:15; 8:11). He does not commend the wisdom of foresight. He does not talk about the rewards of wisdom. He does not promise that cultivating wisdom will help us to make sense of life.[31]

He includes no character-building proverbs, sayings that insist that hard work is the road to excellence. He does not dwell on the folly of anger, with the exception of Matthew 5:22, nor on the importance of trustworthiness. He does not talk much about proper speech, one of the major themes of the book of Proverbs.[32] He has much more to say about listening than he does about speaking.

He does not talk about avoiding evil companions and fools, a major theme in Proverbs. In fact, he was constantly criticized for the company he kept. He is silent on the subject of the dangers of alcohol, a commonplace theme in the wisdom of the ancient world.[33] Jesus says little about family relationships, marriage, and parenthood. He has absolutely no conventional "wisdom" about women. Proverbs and Sirach are full of sayings that portray women as a negative influence and as inferior to men. Says New Testament scholar Charles Carlston: "Jesus' countercultural stance on this matter is as refreshing as it is certain."[34]

30. Carlston, "Proverbs, Maxims, and the Historical Jesus," 98.
31. Ibid., 92.
32. Ibid., 93.
33. Ibid., 97.
34. Ibid.

Listening Strategy #3: Listen for that which Puzzles and Provokes: Equations You Can't Solve, Advice You Can't Follow, and Questions You Can't Answer

Equations you can't solve: (Paradox) The Equation of Opposites

Antithetical Sayings in Proverbs
Jesus' Antithetical Sayings = Paradoxes
Beatitudes in the Hebrew Scriptures
Jesus' "Beatitudes

Traditional wisdom offers formulas that tell us how to act if we want positive results. They are a sort of wisdom equation: wise actions = positive outcomes. Jesus offers equations that don't add up by conventional standards. Traditional wisdom portrays actions, situations, and conditions it labels "blessed" or "fortunate" (beatitudes). So does Jesus, but his depictions of poverty, hunger, and persecution don't strike us as blessed states.

Antithetical Sayings in Proverbs: The Opposites Game

In chapters 25—29 of Proverbs there are a number of sayings that make analogies between two phenomena. For example, "A word fitly spoken is like apples of gold in a setting of silver" (Prov 25:11).

An equally prominent form is the oppositional proverb in which the second line contrasts with or opposes the first.[35] This is the primary form of the proverbs in chapters 10—15 of the book of Proverbs. "A wise son makes a glad father, but a foolish son is a sorrow to his mother" (10:1; see also 10:31 and 11:17). Such proverbs show the antithesis between two different types of people or two different ways of life. They make clear-cut contrasts between wisdom and folly, good and evil, rich and poor, success and failure. They present cut and dried choices of good over evil. Jesus himself at times used this form: "The good man out of his good treasure brings forth good, and the evil man out of his evil treasure brings forth evil" (Matt 12:35; Luke 6:45).[36]

---

35. Another, equally common form is the comparative proverb, which makes analogies between two phenomena. For example, "A word fitly spoken is like apples of gold in a setting of silver" (Prov 25:11). Comparative proverbs abound in Proverbs 25 through 29.

36. Perdue, "The Wisdom Sayings of Jesus," 9.

The kind of antithesis that provides the background for Jesus' Synoptic paradoxes is the antithesis that expresses a reversal of one's situation in the future based on one's behavior, good or bad, in the present. "A person's pride will bring humiliation, but one who is lowly in spirit will obtain honor" (Prov 29:23).

"He that exalts himself shall be humbled," in commonsense wisdom is a warning against what the Greeks called *hybris*, a stepping out of place, what my father used to call "getting too big for your britches." Similar warnings appear in wisdom sayings from Israel's Ancient Near Eastern neighbors.[37] Their message is, if you get above your place in life, the results are disaster. "Everyone who exalts himself will be humbled, and he who humbles himself will be exalted" (Luke 14:11; 18:14; Matt 23:12).

"Many are first that will be last, and the last will be first" (Mark 10:31; Matt 19:30; 20:16; Luke 13:30)

Jesus' Version of Antithetical Sayings: Paradoxical Sayings

When an antithesis or oppositional saying is sharpened and intensified to the point that it equates opposites in the present moment, it becomes paradoxical. It does not refer to future consequences, but to a present reality.

It provokes the listener into figuring out in what situations in his or her life the equated opposites are, or could be, a reality. This kind of form is absent from Proverbs, but occurs in Ecclesiastes (1:18; 7:1b; 7:4).

"In much wisdom is much vexation" (Eccl 1:18a).

"The heart of the wise is in the house of mourning; but the heart of fools is in the house of mirth" (Eccl 7:4).

Rather than commend balanced foresight, these provocative paradoxical statements go to extremes in making their point. Robert Tannehill calls these paradoxical proverbs "antithetical aphorisms."[38]

"Those who want to save their life will lose it, and those who lose their life will save it" (Luke 17:33; Mark 8:35; John 12:25). This dynamic is what New Testament scholar William Beardslee calls "the distinctive intensification of proverbial wisdom in the Synoptic tradition." The paradox negates the project of seeking security as the purpose of life, insisting that life is conferred through this paradoxical route.[39] It provokes the listener/reader to reflect on situations in his own life in which self-centered living has

---

37. Beardslee, "Uses of the Proverb," 67.

38. Tannehill, *The Sword of His Mouth*, 88.

39. Beardslee, "Uses of the Proverb," 67–68.

meant loss of self and those in which making sacrifices for the sake of God's kingdom has brought gain of integrity and benefit to others.

Other examples of paradoxes are "To those who have will more be given, but to those who have not, even what they have will be taken away" (Luke 8:18; 12:48b; Matt 13:12; Mark 4:25).

"Whoever would be great among you must be your servant, and whoever would be first among you must be slave of all" (Mark 10:43–44; Luke 22:26; Matt 20:26–27).

"What is prized by humans is an abomination in the sight of God" (Luke 16:15b).

"It is not what goes into the mouth that defiles a person, but it is what comes out of the mouth that defiles" (Matt 15:11; Mark 7:15).

Conventional wisdom sayings pair good behavior with good results and foolish behavior with disastrous results. Jesus' paradoxical proverbs pair what is viewed as good by conventional wisdom with disastrous results. These include cautious, self-protective living (saving one's life), wealth and position in the community viewed as a witness to one's wise living, and ritual cleanliness in table fellowship. Jesus' paradoxical proverbs pair what is viewed negatively by conventional wisdom with positive outcomes. These include risky, sacrificial living that makes no provision for future security, disregard for reputation and material well-being, and making relationships with social rejects a priority over religious obligations.

By their pairing of opposites they disorient us to our habitual goals of seeking order and harmony. They subvert conventional wisdom's notions of wisdom and folly and subvert our quest for the orderly life.[40] Humility and willingness to risk all for love of neighbor take the place of careful, moderate living and a good reputation in the community.

Beatitudes in the Hebrew Scriptures

Occurring almost exclusively in the Psalms and wisdom literature, beatitudes or "blessed are those who" sayings are declarations of well-being to those who engage in life-enhancing behavior. Such behaviors include studying and obeying Torah (Ps 1; Prov 29:18), caring for the poor (Ps 41:2; Prov 14:21), trusting in God (Ps 112:1; 128:1; Prov 16:20), fearing God (Prov 28:14), finding wisdom (Prov 3:13), and listening to wisdom (Prov 8:33f). The state of blessing largely refers to blessings that lie in store for individuals in the future. But there is also present benefit. Comforted and strengthened

40. See my treatment of Jesus' subversive sayings in McKenzie, *Preaching Proverbs,* 75–76.

by that future assurance, one can engage in wise behavior that benefits self and others and be surrounded by a sphere of well-being (Ps 41:2–4).[41]

Jesus' Paradoxical Beatitudes

Jesus' beatitudes or pronouncements of blessing are paradoxical, pairing attitudes and circumstances we think of as undesirable with positive consequences. They are clustered in Luke's Great Sermon and Matthew's Sermon on the Mount, but they also appear elsewhere in the Gospels as well (Matt 11;6; 13:16; 16:17; 24:46).[42] Luke's version of the beatitudes in his Great Sermon proclaim a state of blessedness for the "poor," the "sad," the "hungry," and the "hated," categories of people hardly considered blessed by conventional wisdom. Matthew takes the edge off Jesus' critique of the wealthy and well fed by adding "poor in spirit" and "hunger and thirst for righteousness." He implies that the wealthy can be blessed if they rely on God and seek God's righteousness.[43] Matthew turns the message toward the spiritual, eschatological, and the ethical, but the beatitudes also refer to the physical state of those who are poor, hungry, thirsty, and persecuted.[44]

The beatitudes in Matthew 5:3–12 are not meant to burden readers/hearers with impossible moral standards. Instead, they aim to bring solace. They paint a picture of the good things of the life to come to comfort those who are suffering in this world because of their commitment to Jesus.[45] It seems clear that the beatitudes come out of Jesus' own experience of persecution because of his involvement with the "expendables," the term used by the Romans to refer to those on the social margins.

Matthew scholar Dale Allison points out that the beatitudes were meant to startle hearers. Simple observation of the world as it is informs us that the rich, not the poor, are blessed; that those who are happy, not those who mourn, are blessed; that those who have power, not the meek, are blessed; that those who are filled, not the hungry and thirsty, are blessed; and that those who are well treated, not those who are persecuted, are blessed. The beatitudes have things backward. To take them seriously is to subvert and call into question our ordinary values, who we look up to and who we look down on.[46]

41. Perdue, "The Wisdom Sayings of Jesus," 17.

42 Allison, *The Sermon on the Mount*, 41.

43 Perdue, "The Wisdom Sayings of Jesus," 18.

44. Bonino, ed., *Faces of Jesus in Latin American Christologies*, 110–11.

45. Allison, *The Sermon on the Mount*, 44.

46. Ibid, 43.

Advice you can't follow: (Hyperbole) Extreme and Impractical Admonitions

Admonitions in Proverbs

Jesus' Admonitions = Focal Instances

Admonitions in Proverbs

Traditional wisdom offers us good advice, admonitions (what to do) and prohibitions (what not to do). Jesus offers us unlikely scenarios in which he commends extreme behavior like turning the other cheek and cutting off our own hand.

Some proverbs makes a statement of fact that the listener can then apply if she discerns a situation(s) in her life that seems like an apt fit. "A soft answer turns away wrath, but a harsh word stirs up anger" (Prov 15:1). "Like clouds and wind without rain, so is one who boasts of a gift never given" (Prov 25:14). Admonitions are more directive. They offer explicit advice to the listener that they are to pursue a particular action. "Answer fools according to their folly, or they will be wise in their own eyes" (Prov 26:5). "Drink water from your own cistern, flowing water from your own well (Prov 5:15).

The opposite of the admonition, the prohibition, seeks to dissuade its hearers from a particular course of action.[47] "Do not say, " I will repay evil; wait for the Lord, and he will help you (Prov 20:22; 27:1; 24:17–18; 24:28–29; 24:1). "Do not boast about tomorrow, for you do not know what a day may bring" (Prov 27:1). Admonitions and prohibitions are plentiful in Proverbs 22:1—24:34.

With both positive and negative commands, the listener must decide which are most applicable to specific situations in his or her own life. Where in our lives do we need to be reminded to avoid crooked speech (4:24), to honor the Lord with our substance (3:9), to be faithful to our spouses (5:15), or to plan ahead (24:27)? Where do we need to be reminded not to envy the wicked (24:1), to be a witness against one's neighbor without cause (24:28), to turn gleeful cartwheels when our enemies fall (24:17), or to boast about tomorrow (27:1)? The work of setting sayings in context falls on the shoulders of the listener. Conventional wisdom counts on the listener fearing the Lord and approaching life with a listening heart. Such a one, who, while remaining humble, has gained a measure of wisdom, is best equipped

---

47. It is still up to the listener, with both positive and negative imperatives, to decide which situations in their lives fit the advice given. This is made clear in Proverbs 26:4–5, in which two seemingly opposite admonitions are juxtaposed.

to know what life situations call for particular nuggets of proverbial advice. It takes wisdom to use wisdom.[48]

Jesus' Version of Admonitions: Focal Instances

Jesus does use some straightforward admonitions and prohibitions in his teachings. These include Mark 7:27 = Matthew 15:26; Mark 12:17 = Matthew 22:21 = Luke 20:25; Luke 12:15; Matthew 7: 6; 5:16.

Jesus' subversive version of admonitions employs hyperbole or exaggeration and come across as extreme and impractical. This is nowhere more obvious than when we look at what New Testament scholar Robert Tannehill has called "focal instances." These sayings portray a specific scene and make a command relative to it. They are specific and extreme. They employ vivid metaphorical scenes and hyperbole. Literary critic Frank Kermode has dubbed this strategy of hyperbole a "rhetoric of excess."[49]

Focal instances deal with the following subjects: temptations to sin (Matt 18:8,9 = Mark 9:42–48), judging others (Matt 7:3–5 = Luke 6:41–42), inward motives and outward behavior (Matt 5:21–26; 5:27–30), retaliation (Matt 5:39–42), private piety and public opinion (Matt 6:1–7), family ties (Luke 12:52–53 = Matt 10:34–36), and the call of God's kingdom (Matt 8:21–22 = Luke 9:57–62). They are not meant as general, literal regulations, though there are those who generalize "turn the other" cheek into a blanket ethical approach to violent aggression. But surely we are not actually to cut off our own foot, tear out our own eye, pull logs out of our eyes, stand still while someone slaps us twice, walk two miles with no covering, antagonize members of our own family, and skip our own father's funeral!

Focal instances function more like proverbs, prodding us to name situations in our daily lives in which they challenge our deeply entrenched attitudes and habitual behaviors. They paint a vivid pictorial scene. They combine it with a "rhetoric of excess," which dramatically contrasts the extreme teaching they advocate with conventional human behavior. They induce a new way of looking at a whole field of human behavior. We have to decide how and where they apply to our daily lives.

48. Examples of straightforward admonitions and prohibitions in Jesus' teachings include Mark 7:27 =Matt 15:26; Mark 12:17 = Luke 20:25; Luke 12:15; Matt 7:6, 5:16.

49. See Williams, "Paraenesis, Excess, and Ethics," 174ff.

Questions you can't answer: (Impossible Questions)

Rhetorical Questions in Proverbs
Jesus' Impossible Questions

Rhetorical Questions in Proverbs

There are plenty of rhetorical questions in Proverbs. They beg an obvious answer and are a useful didactic tool. Several deal with sexual temptation and fidelity. "Should your streams be scattered abroad, streams of water in the streets?" (5:16). "Can fire be carried in the bosom without burning one's clothes? Or can one walk on hot coals without scorching the feet?" (6:27–28).

Some are more general. "Does not wisdom call, and does not understanding raise her voice?" (8:1).

Jesus' teachings include some rhetorical questions. They beg an obvious answer just as those in Proverbs do.

"Are grapes gathered from thorns, or figs from thistles? (Matt 7:16 = Luke 6:44).

Others questions involve whether it is preferable to give stones or bread to hungry children, whether one should bind the strong man before robbing him blind, and whether it is usual practice to place lamps under bushels (Matt 7:9; Matt 12:29 = Luke 11:21f = Mark 3:27; Luke 11;11–12; Matt 7:10; Mark 4:21 = Matt 5:15 = Luke 11:33).

Jesus' Version of Rhetorical Question: Impossible Questions

In the settings of Ecclesiastes and Job a form called the "impossible question" surfaces. This is a subversive form in which the answers are not so clear. These questions point to the limits of human wisdom and knowledge and the inscrutability of God.

"How can the wise die just like fools?" (Eccl 2:16).

"What do mortals get from all the toil and strain with which they toil under the sun?" (Eccl 2:22).

"Where is the way to the dwelling of light, and where is the place of darkness?" (Job 38:19).

Several impossible questions appear in the teachings of Jesus in the Synoptic Gospels.

"Which of you by being anxious can add one cubit to his span of life?"
(Matt 6:27 = Luke 12:25).

"What does it profit a man to gain the whole world and forfeit his life?"
(Mark 8:36 = Matt 16:26 = Luke 9:25).

"Salt is good; but if the salt has lost its saltiness, how can you season it?"
(Mark 9:50 = Matt 5:13 = Luke 14:34).[50]

Jesus' distinctive subversive voice comes through in the way he coins
sayings that conform to traditional wisdom forms like beatitudes and proverbs, not to resolve the conflicts of life, but to heighten them. The Synoptic
sayings that seem most characteristic of his subversive voice take a wisdom
insight and concentrate and intensify it. They do this most often by means of
paradox, hyperbole, and impossible questions. He uses these strategies not
to preserve the status quo, but to subvert it, to push the hearer to question
her own and society's assumptions and values.[51]

Listening for Jesus' Subversive Voice in his Parables

Listening Strategy #1 Listen for Commonplace Stories with an Uncommon Twist

We turn now to discerning Jesus' subversive voice in his parables. There
are over forty parables attributed to Jesus in the Synoptic Gospels. Parables
are a genre tailor-made for a teacher who wanted to challenge conventional
notions of wise and foolish, virtuous and sinful, chosen and outcast. While
they are largely absent from Old Testament wisdom literature, the prophets
do occasionally use them. They are comparisons (similes) that have been
fleshed out into brief narratives (2 Sam 12:1–3; Ezek 17:3–10; Isa 5:1–6).[52]

Throughout the long history of parables scholarship, they have been
read in many ways. They have been read as allegories, moral example stories, or stories that can be boiled down to one point. So, for example, the
Good Samaritan boils down to the lesson, "Be kind to people when they are
in trouble." Or the parable of the Ten Bridesmaids boils down to the lesson,
"Plan ahead so you don't run out of resources." This kind of reading can
suppress the subversive voice of Jesus' parables. To hear that voice we need
to keep in mind that his parables are metaphors. The dynamic of metaphor
is that we place something familiar to us next to something less familiar and

50. McKenzie, *Preaching Proverbs*, 78.

51. Meier, *A Marginal Jew*, vol. 2, 4–6.

52. Drury, *The Parables in the Gospels*.

allow the sparks of meaning to fly back and forth between them. Differences and similarities spark in the space between the familiar and the unfamiliar. Parables scholar Robert Funk understands the subversive dynamic of metaphor as the juxtaposition of two things that impact the imagination and create a vision of reality that could not be conveyed by conceptual explanations.[53]

Many of Jesus' parables begin with the words "The kingdom of God is like . . ." Jesus then offers a brief narrative set in the context of first-century village life. The reader/listener is to set the narrative and the mysterious entity of the kingdom of God side by side in her mind. The kingdom of God, a reality that is already present in Jesus' ministry, but not yet fully revealed, is something listeners didn't fully understand or even recognize. The scenario contains familiar details, but has a strange twist, an aspect or outcome not in keeping with the way things work in the world, then or now. A wealthy person invites the poor and homeless to his wedding banquet (Luke 14:16–24; Matt 22:1–14). A gardener takes time to fertilize an apparently dead tree (Luke 13:6–9). We are to place the strange twist in the story next to the mysterious reality of the kingdom of God and allow the sparks of meaning to leap between them.[54]

More than four decades ago C. H. Dodd defined a parable as "a metaphor or simile drawn from nature or common life, arresting the hearer by its vividness or strangeness, and leaving the mind in sufficient doubt about its precise application to tease it into active thought."[55] Clearly, parables have subversive potential. For they are realistic, yet strange, paradoxical, challenging, and open-ended.

Realistic and Yet Strange

Parables start off looking like commonplace stories set in familiar scenes from everyday life, but by the end of the story, something uncommon has happened. It's as if we recognize the stage settings as true to life, but there is something off in the action or dialogue.[56] There is an extraordinary harvest from carelessly strewn seeds (Mark 4:8), or workers receive equal pay no matter how many hours they worked (Matt 20:8). A formal dinner party ends up packed with street people (Matt 22:1–14; Luke 14:16–24). A

---

53. Donahue, *The Gospel in Parable*, 8.

54. Patterson, *The God of Jesus*, 121.

55. Dodd, *The Parables of the Kingdom*, 5.

56. For a list of the "top ten" strange twists in Jesus' parables, see Buttrick, *Speaking Parables*, 17.

shepherd leaves ninety-nine sheep unprotected to go after one stray (Luke 15:4–6; Matt 18:12–13). A fool builds his house in the middle of a sandy arroyo (Matt 7:24–27; Luke 6:47–49). A gardener begs time to fertilize an absolutely dead tree (Luke 13:6–9). A boss congratulates a manager for marking down the boss's own collectible invoices (Luke 16:1–8a). A Near Eastern father throws dignity to the winds and runs down the road to meet his undeserving son (Luke 15:11–32). The meaning of the parable begins to emerge at the point at which its realism begins to break down.[57]

All the parables, in one way or another, serve the message that the kingdom of God is not only future, but present, powerful, and active. Because of God's working in the world, the world is in a process of transformation.[58]

Paradoxical and Challenging

We have seen paradox at work in Jesus' short sayings is in the equation of opposites. The same dynamic is present in parables in the strange twist we have spoken of. There is often an equation of something we think of as odd or negative with something positive, something, in fact, that points to an aspect of God's presence and power in the world. A sign of corruption (leaven) is put forth as a simile for the kingdom of God (Matt 13:33; Luke 13:20). Someone looked down on and despised is the one who acts as the neighbor (Luke 10:30–35). A wily steward's dubious business practices are commended to those who would enter the kingdom of God (Luke 16:18a). A shepherd is portrayed as "good," who leaves ninety-nine sheep to go look for one (Matt 18:12–13; Luke 15:4–6). A Pharisee, looked up to by the community comes off looking less righteous than a tax collector, looked down on by that same community (Luke 18:10–14a).

The paradoxical equation draws us in, puzzled and thoughtful. We ask ourselves, if this is how the kingdom of God looks, what assumptions of ours need to change? Our notions of who is in and who is out? Our conviction that we have to earn everything we get in this life? Our belief that prosperity is a sign of righteousness and divine favor? Our habit of keeping score and holding grudges? Parables subvert our assumptions about rights and duties, sin and virtue. Thereby they open us to the advent of God's kingdom as gift. How would daily life look different if we gave up our preconceptions and accepted the gift? Parables are not good advice but good news, a vision of reality present but also yet to come.

57. Donahue, *The Gospel in Parable*, 15.
58. Ibid., 10.

New Testament scholar John Dominic Crossan interprets this paradoxical language as an extension of the prohibition of images of God in biblical thought. God cannot be captured by a verbal image any more than by physical representations. Only when we stand before the limits of knowledge and language and the transcendence of God are we able to accept the inbreaking of God's kingdom as a gift. For Crossan, the most fundamental message of Jesus' parables is that we must be open to having our tidy vision of reality shattered, so that God's alternative vision for human life can gain an entrance.[59] That sounds like subversion!

Open Ended

The parable is a question waiting for an answer, an invitation waiting for a response. Like a proverb, it fulfills its function as we appropriate it and then set in the context of situations in our own lives. Like the proverb, the parable respects the free will of the listener and leaves it up to his or her wisdom to make applications.

Listening Strategy #2 Listen for Jesus' Subversive Voice in His Answers to the Question "What is the Kingdom of God Like?"

A clue to the parables' subversive purposes comes to us in the fact that they all are answers to the questions "What is the kingdom of God like?" In the Synoptic Gospels Jesus describes his activity as the *basileia* of God. The term occurs over 100 times in the Synoptic Gospels. We most commonly translate this term in English as "kingdom." When the word shows up in a nonbiblical text from the ancient world it is usually translated "empire." Jesus chose a very risky, political concept as the central metaphor for his ministry, for in his world there was only one empire, and that was Rome.[60]

Every time Jesus uses the term "the basileia of God" he is implying the injustice of the ruling elite. What ruling elites do in every age is set up social, political, and economic constructions of reality that justify their right to power, wealth, and privilege while simultaneously rationalizing the subsistence existence of the masses.[61] This dominant group controls education, both formally and informally and codifies a "wisdom" that, in effect, attributes the social status quo to a divinely ordained cosmology.

59. Ibid., 15–16. Donahue is drawing on Crossan, *Cliffs of Fall* and *In Parables*.
60. Patterson, *The God of Jesus*, 60–61.
61. Herzog, *The Parables as Subversive Speech*, 28.

We remember that this was an ever-present danger for Old Testament wisdom. When an educated, relatively prosperous group makes sense of their world, they are always tempted toward a rigid theory of retribution that attributes their own status to righteousness and the less auspicious situations of others to sin. Despite the sages' best efforts, a rigid theory of retribution was alive and well in Jesus' day. It served the social, economic purposes of both Jewish religious elite and Roman occupiers. What were presented by the religious elite as theological categories (clean or unclean; honorable or shameful; sinful or righteous) were, in reality, categories that had everything to do with maintaining the privileged status of those in economic, political, and religious power.[62]

Jesus' parables offer four responses to the question "What is the kingdom of God like?" They point to the kingdom's subversive impact on status quo-preserving attitudes, actions, and entities. The first subversive theme is that the kingdom of God is not under our control. A second is that it shows up when and where we least expect it. A third is that it disrupts business as usual. A fourth is that it is a kingdom of forgiveness and justice. In my book *The Parables for Today,* I offer a full discussion of these questions and the parables that respond to them in each of the Synoptic Gospels. Here I can only point toward a few parables that illustrate each question in the hopes that the reader will explore them further.

The Kingdom of God Is Not under Our Control.

When I think of the theme that the kingdom of God is not under our control, the seed parables from Mark come to mind: the parable of the Sower (4:3–8), the Seed Growing Secretly (4:26–29), and the Mustard Seed (4:30–32).

Mark wrote toward the end of the reign of the Emperor Nero (54–68 CE) when Christians in Rome were suffering terrible persecutions. A seed was a marvelous metaphor for a congregation that felt out of control, at the mercy of the Roman Empire. Jesus' own ministry could be likened to a vulnerable seed growing secretly: its power hidden on the cross, glimpsed in the resurrection, now growing steadily in the world. All that despite the appearance of failure and domination by the Roman Empire. And the same could be said for the church ministering in Jesus' name.

The images presented in the seed parables of Mark 4 are realistic, yet strange. Miraculous harvests like the one the parable describes don't happen in such adverse conditions. The mustard bush, a scruffy shrub, seems like an

62. Ibid.

odd choice as a metaphor for God's kingdom, when Jesus could have chosen to compare it to a magnificent cedar.

Seeds are not under our control. Neither is the kingdom of God. Which is good news and bad news for conventional wisdom. It means we cannot plan all the unpredictability and pain out of our futures. It means that God's gracious influence in the world is steadily growing out of sight at its own time and rate of growth, whatever the world may say or do. Says New Testament scholar John R. Donahue, these parables cause us to "look beyond what we see to what we hope for."[63]

The Kingdom of God Shows up When We Least Expect It.

Much of conventional wisdom is devoted to factoring out the unpredictability of life by means of moderate, restrained living. This was not the takeaway from Jesus' sayings and parables. Hence another theme in which we hear his subversive voice in the parables is that the kingdom of God shows up when we least expect it. It would be a good idea, then, to be paying attention! Two parables come to mind around this theme. One is the parable of the Faithful and the Unfaithful Slaves (Matt 24:45–51) which depicts a master returning sooner than expected and finding that while the cat was away, the mice did play. A second parable is the one that follows it, the parable of the Ten Bridesmaids (Matt 25:1–12). In this case, the bridegroom is delayed in coming, and the bridesmaids have not made provision for the long haul. Whether the return is sooner or later than we expected, the theme is "Be ready, for you do not know the day or the hour . . ." (Matt 25:13).

The Kingdom of God Shows up Through Whom We Least Expect It.

The kingdom of God not only shows up when we least expect it, but through whomever God chooses for it to show up. In the parable of the Judgment (Matthew 25:31–46) the poor, the naked, the imprisoned, and the hungry are where we encounter the kingdom of God. In relating to them we are offered the opportunity to enter into the kingdom by our gift of empathy and assistance.

The kingdom of God shows up in the character of the Samaritan (Luke 10:25–37), whose designation as "good" would have been an oxymoron to devout Jews of Jesus' day. The kingdom of God shows up in the parable of the Rich Man and Lazarus, a parable that overturns the notion that wealth is

63. Donahue, *The Gospel in Parable*, 47.

a sign of righteousness and poverty a sign of sin. The opportunity to participate in the kingdom of God, which is built on love of neighbor, was available
to the rich man every day, but he stepped over Lazarus on his way to and
from his mansion. Indeed the kingdom does show up through whom we
least expect it.

The Kingdom of God Disrupts Business as Usual

A third theme through which we hear Jesus' subversive voice in his parables
is that the kingdom of God disrupts business as usual. Two parables that
come to mind related to this subversive theme are the Rich Farmer (Luke
12:16–20) and the Workers in the Vineyard (Matt 20:1–15). In the parable
of the Rich Farmer, God disrupts the farmer's life's work, accumulating
wealth for his enjoyment, with the message of his imminent death. There is
some common ground here with Proverbs and Ecclesiastes. Proverbs says,
"Do not wear yourself out to get rich. Be wise enough to desist" (Prov 23:4).
Ecclesiastes points out that rich and poor alike die, and that sometimes our
hard-earned wealth goes to those who did nothing to contribute to it. But
there is no time left for the rich farmer to take Proverbs' advice. And the
negative consequence of his actions is far worse than seeing the undeserving
get his wealth. Someone else will get what he prepared for himself and he
will get what is coming to him.

The Workers in the Vineyard disrupts business as usual with its strange
twist of portraying everyone as receiving the same wages, no matter how
long they worked in the vineyard. It subverts our habitual conviction that
you only get what you deserve and have worked for. It injects a disruptive
element of grace into the picture. We realize that our response to the owner's
decision would probably depend on where we were in the line (Matt 20:1–
16). The religious elite, who felt they had been righteous workers all along,
resented Jesus' offering of a place in the kingdom to those they viewed as
sinful latecomers.

The Kingdom of God is a Reign of Forgiveness and Judgment

Jesus' ministry was not just about undermining and subverting. In undermining the religious and political "empires," Jesus projected a positive vision
of the empire or kingdom of God. In this kingdom we exchange retaliation
for forgiveness, rigid ritual purity rules for inclusion of all at God's table,
narrow definition of neighbor for radical love of all God's children. In this
kingdom suffering, misfortune, and disability are not signs of God's disfavor

but occasions for God's merciful presence. In this kingdom, all can be clean, honored, and righteous through the forgiveness of God who purifies the inner life, honors the identity of each child God has created and calls us all to a righteousness that begins with our acknowledgment of our need for God. In this kingdom, all who reject and oppose God's work in the world will one day feel the weight of God's justice.

There were those in Jesus' day who felt that their position and prosperity were signs that they were beyond judgment. There were those in his day who felt that their poverty and shame were signs that they were beyond forgiveness. Jesus' parables subvert both misconceptions by holding together twin realities about the kingdom of God. The kingdom of God is a kingdom of justice, but also of mercy. The kingdom of God is a kingdom of mercy, but also of justice.

The kingdom of God is a kingdom of justice, but also of mercy. The parable of the Prodigal Son(s) conveys the unconditional quality of divine love for those who reject and abandon a relationship with God, whether by leaving carelessly or staying resentfully. Many other parables convey the gracious, forgiving love of God the Father. They include the Feast in Luke (14:16–24), the Vineyard Laborers, (Matthew 20:1–15), the Friend at Midnight (Luke 11:5–8), the Barren Fig Tree (Luke 13:6–9), and the Lost and Found parables of Luke chapter 15 (lost sheep, lost coin, lost sons).

The kingdom of God is a kingdom of mercy, but also of justice. Numerous parables convey the theme that we need to respond to divine forgiveness and be prepared to face the returning Son. We will be judged by whether or not we respond to the gracious initiative of God and show mercy and compassion to one another. Relevant parables include the Tenants (Mark 12:1–8; Matt 21:33–39, Luke 20:9–15a), the Returning Master (Mark 13:34–36; Luke 12:35–38), the House Builders (Matt 7:24–27; Luke 6:47–49), the Feast in Matthew (Matt 22:1–14), the Talents/Pounds (Matt 25:14–28; Luke 19:12–24), the Judgment (Matt 25:31–46) and the Unmerciful Servant (Matt 18:23–34).

The emphasis on divine forgiveness subverts the judgmental attitude of those in the religious elite who would blame the poor and the sick for their conditions and exclude them from the table of God. It subverts the self-loathing of those who have been taught that they have no one to blame but themselves. God cares for and sees value in everyone in society, rich and poor, healthy and ill, freshly bathed and coated in filth, educated and illiterate. The emphasis on divine judgment, even for those society judges to be righteous by their wealth and position, subverts self-congratulation.

In his short sayings and parables Jesus, inspired by the example of Ecclesiastes and Job, uses his subversive voice to challenge the status quo and to give voice to those who have been silenced in his political, religious setting. Cultivating that subversive voice in our everyday lives will be the topic of our final chapter.

Chapter 5

Part Two—Speak Out!
Activating the Subversive Voice

In Part One of Chapter 5, we practiced listening for the subversive voice of God as it comes to us through Proverbs, Ecclesiastes, Job, and the sayings and parables of the Synoptic Jesus. In this chapter we will practice activating our own subversive voices to speak out in everyday situations.

Some years ago a friend told me this story and gave me permission to share it.

> I was working for the city, earning good money. I had been made head of the Missionary Society and was making talks all over town about raising youth in the right way. Then my teenage daughter became pregnant at age sixteen. This was a girl who had had lots of attention, music and dance lessons, plenty of opportunities. She was bright and beautiful. I thought I would die, I was so hurt. I knew the ladies would whisper behind their hands: "Who is she to give us advice? She can't even control her own home!" I was thirty-six years old, not ready to be a grand-mother. At church in Sunday School, they took her off the piano stool, even though they had no one else to play.
>
> As I was crying in my room one night, saying to God, "How could she do this to me?" God spoke directly to me "What about your child?" So I went down the hall to her room and sat on the edge of her bed and hugged her and said, "We're going to get through this together." When the baby was born I raised her like my own until she was six so my daughter could focus on

finishing her education. I carried her on my hip, this gorgeous
little baby, to all my church activities. You can't whisper about a
beautiful baby reaching out for you. It melted their hearts. From
that experience, I learned to confront the wrong where I see it,
even in myself.

I began the Introduction to this study with the image of our having
bought the wrong things and bringing them back to the customer service
desk for an exchange. When it comes to the virtue of the subversive voice,
that means an exchange of timid conventionality for persistent, strategic
courage. Speaking out to undermine oppressive conventional wisdom is
what is meant by the "subversive voice." It requires that one transition from
being a "bystander" to being an "upstander," one who speaks out to subvert
systems of injustice and intolerance. That sounds dramatic, and sometimes
it is. But sometimes, it's just a matter of walking down the hall and hugging
your child and then witnessing to the world that love is stronger than petty
human judgments.

Activating the Subversive Voice: Practicing the Other Three Virtues

If our subversive voice is weak, it is because we are out of practice in the
other three virtues from which it grows. The subversive voice requires the
other three wisdom virtues to function: the awestruck attitude (the fear of
the Lord), the listening heart, and the cool spirit. The more we practice the
other virtues, the stronger the subversive voice becomes.

There is an old saying that "You are always entering into a storm, in a
storm, or coming out of a storm." It's true. And there are all sorts of questions we ask ourselves in such situations. When we are facing a challenge,
entering into a storm, we ask "Why am I dreading this so much? How can I
best handle this situation?"

When we are coming out of a challenging time in our lives we ask
ourselves any number of questions. "How could I have handled that better?
How can I avoid getting into this sort of situation again? How can I apply the
positive things I did and said to future situations?"

Since working on this book, I have developed a new spiritual practice
in relation to my own storms. I call it the "wisdom checklist." I scroll down
the four virtues in my mind and ask—Where is each virtue in the mix? Is
one or more of them missing? Have I forgotten to trust God in this situation?
Am I so focused on my fears and needs that I've factored out those of others? Am I forgetting that, with God's help, I can rein in my self-destructive

thoughts and habits? Am I lapsing into timid silence in a situation that calls for speaking up? Many times, the uneasiness and lack of direction I feel is because at least one of the four wisdom virtues is taking a vacation day.

I picture myself standing at the customer service desk clinging to the four items that are the opposite of the four wisdom virtues, items I should never have bought in the first place: self-sufficiency, self-preoccupation, self-indulgence, and self-preservation. And I picture myself handing them over, one by one, exchanging them for the four wisdom virtues that feed and guide my soul.

I open my heart and hands to the "awestruck attitude" (the fear of the Lord) we talked about in chapter 2. This first wisdom virtue reminds me of my own limited wisdom and the need to respect divine transcendence. It opens my mind to perspectives beyond my own life experience. I am receptive to the "listening heart" we looked at in Chapter 3. This second wisdom virtue supplies me with the compassion for the sorrows and struggles of others that replaces a tendency to judge and dismiss them. I receive the cool spirit, the third wisdom virtue that we examined in Chapter 4. Armed with it, I access the self-discipline needed to choose my words and my battles. And having received all three of these wisdom virtues, I am ready to welcome the fourth: the subversive voice, the habit of consistent challenge of false assumptions and unjust situations. I am willing to take on the daily practice of the awestruck attitude, the listening heart, and the cool spirit which must be present and accounted for if the subversive voice is to gain in wisdom and power.

Activating the Subversive Voice: Asking Questions of Biblical Texts

To activate our subversive voices, we follow the example of the subversive sages of Scripture. We question received religious traditions and cultural values, what passes for wisdom, both in biblical texts and in contemporary life. Our focus here will be primarily on proverbs and parables, with a brief word about narrative texts.

Questioning Proverbs and Aphorisms

Here is a method for posing questions to biblical and contemporary proverbs about the values hidden in them to unleash the subversive voice in our everyday lives.

Our questioning of proverbs and aphorisms is based on two features of the genre: Proverbs as Flashlights, not Floodlights

The first is that proverbs are ethical flashlights, not floodlights. They are nuggets of wisdom meant to be used in certain situations, but that make no claims to be applicable to every situation in life. This is why there are diametrically opposed proverbs. "Look before you leap." "He who hesitates is lost."

> "Do not answer fools according to their folly, or you will be a fool yourself" (Prov 26:4).

> "Answer fools according to their folly, or they will be wise in their own eyes" (Prov 26:5).

While the sayings appear to contradict one another, they are simply offering different strategies for different situations, and we have to decide which is better in our particular context.

Proverbs as Building Blocks of a Worldview

The second is that proverbs are the building blocks of a worldview. Some stabilize the status quo, emphasizing cautious moderation, hard work, prosperity, personal security, and social stability. Some subvert it in favor of all-in leaps of faith and living for others.

Here are some questions we can pose to biblical proverbs and aphorisms to activate our subversive voices.

1. Does this saying confirm or subvert conventional wisdom?

"A soft answer turns away wrath" (Prov 15:1) affirms the conventional value of wise speaking to maintain social harmony. It is not a blanket strategy for all conflictual situations, since there are times when harsh, direct speech is called for.

"Blessed are you when people revile you and persecute you and utter all kinds of evil against you falsely on my account" (Matt 5:11) subverts the conventional value placed on a good reputation. It is not a command to seek out situations of suffering at the hands of others. It is a testimony to the fact that, in some situations, the disapproval and ridicule of others is a sign, not of failure, but of faithful discipleship.

"The highway of the upright avoids evil; those who guard their way preserve their lives" (Prove 16:7) affirms the conventional values of caution and moderation as ways of minimizing one's exposure to the chaotic aspects of life. It might be wise word in some situations, but is not a universal truth to live by, according to Jesus.

He offers this alternative option: "Those who try to make their life secure will lose it, but those who lose their life will keep it" (Luke 17:33). This saying subverts self-protection as a comprehensive life goal in favor of the risk and sacrifice that attend the life of discipleship.

  2. Can you envision a situation that would benefit by the advice provided by a particular proverb?

For example, let's take Proverbs 15:11. A parent might let it guide her to speak mildly to a teenager who is not at his or her best first thing in the morning (Prov 15:1).

Can you think of a situation for which this proverb would be inadequate? That same parent could decide it is not an adequate response at a town meeting in a discussion of the vast inequity in books, supplies, and education between two elementary schools in adjoining towns in her county.

Activating the Subversive Voice: Asking Questions of Contemporary Cultural Proverbs

The subversive voice not only questions received religious traditions, but also challenges secular slogans and sayings. Benjamin Franklin published brief educational booklets annually from 1733 to 1758 under the name of Richard Saunders. They were filled with sayings he largely borrowed from other sources and rephrased to make them more memorable. Next to the Bible, *Poor Richard's Almanac* was the most frequent reading material in the colonies. "He that goes a borrowing goes a sorrowing." "Laziness travels so slowly that poverty soon overtakes it." "The sleeping fox catches no poultry." And, of course, the ever popular, "Early to bed, early to rise, makes a man healthy, wealthy, and wise." These sayings embody a pragmatic worldview conducive to capitalistic accomplishment that continues to influence contemporary American wisdom. It boils down to the conviction that hard work and moderation lead to a life of material prosperity.

The subversive sage recognizes that proverbs, though short, are not always sweet. They are certainly not as innocent as they might appear. They are what proverbs scholar Alan Dundes calls "building blocks of a worldview" that support common cultural convictions.

Four such convictions in contemporary American life are visual empiricism, pluralism, the notion that everything can be measured in terms of its monetary worth, and the conviction of unlimited good and unfettered progress.[1]

The subversive voice questions the adequacy of these convictions, guided by the biblical witness, her theological tradition and her own experience of God.

The sage engages in a "dueling proverbs" dynamic in which biblical proverbs can be called upon to subvert contemporary proverbs.

"Seeing is believing." "What you see is what you get." ("Faith is the assurance of things hoped for, the conviction of things not seen"—Hebrews 11:1).

"Different strokes for different folks." ("And if a house is divided against itself, that house will not be able to stand"—Mark 3:25).

"Money talks." "Money makes the world go around." "The one who has the most toys when he dies wins" ("What will it profit them to gain the whole world and forfeit their life?—Mark 8:36; Matt 16:26).

"You get what you pay for." "Time is money." "Everyone has his price." "Do not wear yourself out to get rich. Be wise enough to desist" (Prov 23:4).

"There is more where that came from." "The sky is the limit."[2]

The sage can call on contemporary proverbs that are compatible with our biblical faith to reinforce its teachings. For example, Paul McCartney's famous song title, "Money Can't Buy Me Love," and common wisdom sayings like "Appearances are deceiving" and "What goes around comes around."

Activating the Subversive Voice: Asking Questions of Parables

We have seen that parables in Jesus' hands, have a built-in subversive intent. They are realistic, yet strange, paradoxical, challenging to the status quo and open-ended. They invite the reader/listener's response. The subversive sage asks the following questions of a parable to activate its subversive voice in life today.

What is realistic about this parable?

What is strange?

What is paradoxical?

What is challenging?

What is open ended?

1. Dundes, "Folk Ideas as Units of Worldview," 109–10.
2. McKenzie, *Preaching Proverbs*, 79–81.

What is threatening to the religious, economic, and political system of the text's context, of our context?

Strange Twist: What is the strange twist or barb of this parable? What seems to not be in keeping with life as you have observed it? What doesn't fit in with the way the world runs, the way people habitually act?

Conflict: Is there conflict in the setting in which the parable appears? If so, what is it? What caused it? Remember that conflict can occur both in and behind a biblical text.

Power: Who has power and who doesn't?

Challenge: How does this parable challenge some of our ways of looking at the world? How might it challenge the ways we usually look at and handle certain situations?

Comfort: In all of its strangeness, how might it be comforting, freeing, saving, good news in the daily situations we find ourselves in?

Situations and People: Does it speak to something that is going on in your community? How would the passage speak to the various situations people you know are going through? Think about variables like gender, race, economics, occupation, sexual orientation, and generation. Think about specific people you know.

A Personal Word: Does the text speak to something that is going on right now in your own life?

What does this parable tell us about the mysterious reality Jesus calls the "kingdom of God"? A creative approach to unleash a parable's subversive voice is to rewrite the parable—and then to ask yourself why you made the changes you did. Sometimes we will find ourselves making changes that bring the parable more in line with the way things are in our world, but not always. Suppose you wanted the father to put the prodigal son to work in the kitchen, rather than run out to welcome him and throw a party. Maybe you wanted the parable of the Feast to end on a happy note in Matthew 22:1–14, as it does in Luke 14:16–24. Maybe your shepherd doesn't go after the lost sheep but lets him be a lesson to any of the others who feel like wandering off (Luke 15:4–6).

Consider crafting a contemporary version of a parable. Quite a few theologians, philosophers, and novelists have used parables to nudge readers to question their assumptions and life experiences. Set the parable in a contemporary setting and see what happens! This is a good way to unleash the subversive voice in contemporary situations.

Activating the Subversive Voice: Asking Questions of Narrative Texts

The intention of a narrative text is to draw the reader in to identify with a character and to undergo a transformation along with that character. If we always identify with the character who represents the status quo, there won't be much room for transformation. An effective strategy to unleash the subversive voice in reading a narrative biblical text is to identify with those in the text usually ignored by society.

I recently attended an event at which British novelist Jo Baker read from her novel *Longbourn*. It's a retelling of the classic Jane Austen novel *Pride and Prejudice* from the perspective of the servants. One of the main characters is the young housemaid Sarah. Early in the morning, standing at the washtub with reddened, chapped hands, Sarah thinks to herself: If Elizabeth Bennet had the washing of her own petticoats, she'd most likely be a sight more careful with them.[3] We activate the subversive voice in interpreting biblical narratives by asking them two questions:

1. Who is not being listened to in the text?

2. How does their perspective subvert (undermine, threaten, challenge) the status quo?

    Of the time and context of the text?

    Of our time and context?

Some additional strategies and questions to sharpen the subversive voice are:

- List all the characters and groups in the text.

- To whom are you listening or paying attention as you approach this text? Whom are you ignoring or discounting? What does the focus of your attention say about what is important to you? About what you seek to protect? What does it say about what is too painful for you to see, hear, and acknowledge in life around you or within you?

- How, in your judgment, would various groups of people in your community answer the last two sets of questions?

- To whom do people in the text seem to easily listen? Who seems to be the power-wielder?

- Rank your list of characters as to who is more powerful (listened to more easily) and who is less powerful.

3. Baker, *Longbourn*, 5.

- Ask, what is the person or group that seems to wield least power trying to say or do?

- How is this related to what you perceive to be the work of God or the gospel through this text?

- How would your life, your family, and your community's life be different if you (we) heeded the lesson of one you (we) seldom listen to?

These questions are most directly applicable to narrative texts that deal with the interaction between individuals and groups of people.

For example, we could apply these questions to characters in cameo roles in biblical texts, like the servant girl who challenges Peter and exposes his cowardice in all four gospels (Mark 14:66–70; Matt 26:69–72; Luke 22:54; John 18:15). Though apparently powerless, she is a catalyst that moves Peter to recognize the depth of his betrayal of Jesus.

These questions could also apply to non-narrative texts, because there is always a story behind the text. We could pose these subversive questions to psalms, apocalyptic texts, epistles, genealogies. Who are the enemies referred to in a psalm? What power do they have? To whom does the psalmist pay primary attention in his/her plight? Who are the groups in conflict in Paul's First Letter to the Corinthians? Who has power and who doesn't? Where are similar power dynamics at work in our community today? What alternative vision of community does Paul offer?

Activating the Subversive Voice in Everyday Life: Biblical Themes that Question Our Questions

The virtue of the subversive voice becomes most uncomfortable when we have to turn its truth on ourselves, opening the cellar door of our souls and listening to the rats scurrying around. These are deeply held convictions or assumptions that are undercut by biblical wisdom. The subversive voice forces us to be honest with ourselves, undermines shallow faith on the way to deeper understanding. There is discomfort in the process, but it is the only way forward.

What's in this for me?

"What's in this for me?" is a question we are by no means the first to ask. Peter asks it of Jesus in Matthew 19:27. "Lord, we have left everything and followed you. What then will we have?"

Satan accuses Job of serving God for hope of reward in Job 1:9.

There may come a time in our lives when we realize that our motivation for kindness and service are self-serving, to gain reward or to avoid punishment. The book of Job subverts our pretension and points out our shallow motivations. It pushes us to ask how we can purify our motives so that we love God for God's own sake and not for hope of gaining heaven or avoiding hell.

Legend recounts the following dream by sixteenth-century Spanish mystic St. Teresa of Avila. She was walking down the street of a town and saw coming toward her a prophetess carrying a torch in one hand and a bucket of water in the other. "Why do you carry these things?" she asked the prophetess. The prophetess answers, "With this torch I will burn down the halls of heaven and with this bucket of water I will douse the flames of hell. Then people will worship God, not for hope of heaven or fear of hell, but for God's sake alone."[4]

Whose fault is this anyway?

"Is it for your piety that God reproves you?" (Eliphaz's challenge to Job in Job 22:4).

Being human, we like to explain things. When suffering strikes, we blame ourselves, God, or someone else. Anyone or anything is preferable to admitting that tragedy strikes the innocent. As a young man who attended a workshop I once led on biblical wisdom said, "Human beings would rather feel guilty than out of control." Job subverts the blame game and nudges us to not attribute our suffering to our own sin or divine malice.

Why can't we figure this out?

Traditional wisdom promises that we can figure out quite a bit about God and about how human beings should live to be in line with God's will. There is some truth there, but every now and then we reach the edges of our human wisdom and have to face the painful fact that, as Paul says, we "see in a glass but darkly" this side of the grave (1 Cor 13:12).

The book of Job subverts our pretensions to comprehensive wisdom with this eloquent question: "Where is wisdom to be found and where is the place of understanding?" (Job 28: 20). Chapter 28 ends with the affirmation,

---

4. Stookey, *Baptism*, 36.

couched as God's words to humankind, "Truly, the fear of the Lord, that is wisdom: and to depart from evil is understanding" (28:28).

We don't know all the answers about God and God's management of a complex and unwieldy universe. God is mysterious and transcendent. Job subverts all human hubris, assuring us that when human wisdom can take us no further, we rest secure in the fear of the Lord—we tremble, trust, and take directions from God, not ourselves. What a relief!

Why isn't life fair?

There comes a point when we realize, by observing others' lives, that things aren't always fair. That's disillusioning, but it's nothing like the blow we feel when we realize that our life isn't fair. Job subverts the assumption that we were ever promised it would be. The message is akin to the refrain of Lynn Anderson's 1970 hit song, "Rose Garden": "I beg your pardon. I never promised you a rose garden."

Deep down we feel that moderate, wise living should be rewarded, and when misfortune comes to us and our loved ones, we feel betrayed. But God never made this absolute promise. The book of Job subverts that assumption as God speaks to Job out of the whirlwind: "Who is this that darkens counsel by words without knowledge?" (Job 38:3). Life may not be fair, but God is faithful and promises to be present in good fortune and bad. Are we courageous enough to live without our "rose garden illusion" and face life confidently, assured of God's presence in adversities of which God is not the cause?

Doesn't the presence of suffering means the absence of God? (Job 38—42)

In times of suffering our knee-jerk reaction is often to assume that it is a sign that God has abandoned us. It was quite a shock for Job when, in the midst of his complaining, God showed up out of the whirlwind, subverting his abandonment assumptions, demanding that he "gird up his loins" and hear things from God's side. As readers of the book, we are as surprised as Job. We weren't expecting a show of divine transcendence, power, and mystery. We weren't expecting a reminder that God has a lot more on the divine mind than us and our circle of suffering. Nor were we expecting the rigorous assurance that God is most present in times of suffering, that nothing can separate us from the presence of God in such times. We were hoping for an answer to the "why" question. Instead we receive the answer to a more modest, more important question: Is God present with us in times of suffering? And the answer is yes. The presence of suffering does not mean the absence of God.

What's the point?

Many people think that the book of Ecclesiastes reinforces a sense of futility about life. What's the point? On a closer look, though, the book subverts such a sense of futility by its recommendation that we enjoy work, relationships, and food and drink.

There is no getting around certain hard facts of life if you are a reader of the book of Ecclesiastes.

We all die, wise and fool alike. "How can the wise die just like fools?" (2:16).

We cannot see into what, if anything, lies beyond this life. "Who knows whether the human spirit goes upward and the spirit of animals goes downward to the earth?" (3:21).

This life is fleeting. These "facts of life" subvert some of our habitual priorities and preoccupations.

We are obsessed with possessions and status that cannot follow us beyond this life and are quickly forgotten. "Who knows what is good for mortals while they live the few days of their vain life, which they pass like a shadow?" (6:12).

We are buffeted by anxieties about the future that distract us from the real, though fleeting, joys of the present moment. "What do mortals get from all the toil and strain with which they toil under the sun?" (2:22).

Ecclesiastes subverts our question, "What's the point?" For the sage, that is the wrong question, because we can never know the answer. The better question is, "How do we live today, recognizing that our human wisdom is limited and that life is tough and short?" He subverts naïve optimism. But he also subverts blanket pessimism, absolute faith in futility. There is pleasure to be found in each present moment. The way to live wisely is to savor it, giving thanks in work, play, friendship, love, and meal fellowship, to the mysterious, distant God who is the giver of them all.

Isn't there something more?

There come times in our lives when we begin to think that maybe Jesus' strange equations add up to a more fulfilling life than one shaped by our obsession with security and self-preservation. All of the musings that follow are meant to be read through both a personal lens as well as the lens of a faith community, cultural group, or nation.

What happens when the subversive voice creates such moments of decision in our lives?

We latch onto Jesus' subversive aphorism that is at the heart of his teachings and ministry "Those who want to save their life will lose it, and those who lose their life will save it" (Luke 17:33; Mark 8:35; John 12:25). Or, as I call it, "Finders weepers, losers keepers."

We latch onto Jesus' strange definitions of what it means to be fortunate or blessed, and are open to seeking God's will in attitudes and actions viewed as unproductive by our social setting: inward devotion over outward recognition (blessed are the pure in heart), meekness and humility over self-assertion ("Blessed are the meek," Matt 5:5), lament over the plight of others rather than focus on one's own advancement ("Blessed are they who mourn," Matt 5:4), disregard for reputation, and material prosperity ("Blessed are you when people revile you and persecute you and utter all kinds of evil against you falsely on my account," Matt 5:11).

When do such moments occur?

When are fed up with our own hypocrisy: taking specks out of others' eyes and stumbling around with logs in our own; when we realize we have allowed every relationship in our lives to take precedence over our relationship with God; when we find ourselves doing the very thing we just judged another for doing; when we are sick of being anxious and realize it has gotten us nowhere; when we are counting our stuff and wondering where, in the midst of it all, we can find our life again.

When a glimmer of a fresh reality breaks into our field of vision. And we recognize in it . . .

The presence of God that is not under our control, invisible, but growing secretly out of sight like tiny seeds taking root underground.

A kingdom of God for which we suspect we are not ready, but begin to believe is both already present and arriving at any moment.

A kingdom of God that embodies both the mercy and the justice of God for every person and every community.

A kingdom of God we glimpse in the most unlikely people.

The Subversive Voice in Action: Inspiring Examples!

What follows are some examples of people brave enough to activate their subversive voices. They are meant to encourage us to look for opportunities to activate our own and to follow it up with action, letting the chips fall where they may.

Aspiring woman preachers in the Methodist movement in England in the 1770s faced consequences when they dared to speak. Zechariah Taft, an early historian of Methodist women preachers, wrote this account of Madame Perrott, one of the first women preachers on the Isle of Jersey. "Madame Perrott, preached the word of life to all who would hear, in private houses, both in town and country; and while thus engaged she was sometimes pelted with mud, and otherwise very roughly and cruelly treated."[5]

John Wesley came to recognize the preaching and teaching of women as an "extraordinary call" through which God was bringing renewed life to the Church of England.

To another woman preacher, Miss Martha Chapman, Wesley offered this stringent encouragement: "If you speak only faintly and indirectly, none will be offended and none profited. But if you speak out, although some will probably be angry, yet others will soon find the power of God unto salvation."[6]

Wesley was firmly convinced that "Whatever religion can be concealed is not Christianity."[7]

Theologian Ada Maria Isasi-Diaz (1943–2012) summed up her vision of the subversive sage when she described her lifelong vocation of helping to shape a theology that would speak from and to the lives of Hispanic women, a traditionally silenced social group. "When in doubt, I act; for if I do not, possibilities will never unfold. Risk is part of life. So I do not attempt to avoid it. I am afraid but not paralyzed . . . . My goal, my hope, is the creation of the community and its common good: that is what the 'reign of God' is all about. The common good is always being understood afresh and cannot fall under ideological control. Therefore, leadership belongs to the community, and to hold those who exercise it accountable is both the right and obligation of the community."[8]

This kind of bold sense of purpose is what energizes each of us to activate our subversive voices to challenge assumptions, sometimes our own, that exclude and silence members of the community.

Several years ago I interviewed pastors from various denominations in multiple contexts around the US. I was interested in how they understood

5. Taft, *Biographical Sketches of the Lives and Public Ministry of Various Holy Women*, 1:171.

6. Chilcote, *John Wesley and the Women Preachers of Early Methodism*, 148.

7. Wesley, *Sermons*, 269.

8. Isasi-Diaz, "Apuntes for a Hispanic Women's Theology of Liberation," 26.

their vocations as sages, wisdom teachers, especially with regard to their preaching ministries. Their responses are applicable to all of us in our various walks of life. Said one of the pastors I interviewed, who served a conservative United Methodist church in a small town in Central Texas: "I give voice to people who would never have spoken without me. I take the heat for change to take place. I have paid for it several times over. It can be like walking through a minefield blindfolded."[9]

In this regard, the following saying by the bold social reformer and evangelist Catherine Mumford Booth, who, with her husband William Booth, founded the Salvation Army in eighteenth- century England, is comforting: "The waters are rising, but so am I. I am not going under, but over."[10]

A fortysomething Baptist pastor from a medium sized church in university town near Washington, DC told me: "I think preachers need to be fearless in speaking what they believe to be the truth. Whether you are talking about what you think is sin or what you think is good news or whether you're talking about your own faults or you're talking about faults you perceive in others, you've got to stand up and tell the truth. There is great energy in that. There could be great hubris in that also, so the second thing is you've got to be correctable. If you're not, you become unbearable and insufferable and foolish."

If you're not fearless, you end up playing it safe and saying nothing that touches anybody at all. I've listened to preaching like that all my life. I think sermons are like kites. The preacher may construct a beautiful kite, a well-constructed kite. But if you throw it in the air, does it take off? The preacher has something to do with that, and God has something to do with it, and the congregation has something to do with it. And fearlessness has something to do with it. At some point, you've just got to throw it. And if it falls flat, then there you are. But if the wind, if the Spirit takes it then, you've got something."

This same pastor shared this: "My people have showed me what discipleship in the world is like or could be like. In the late '70s, early '80s there was a farmer in the rural church I was serving. He became convinced that he and the church had a responsibility to do something to help Indochinese refugees in this country. He 'blamed it' on my preaching! As a result of his efforts this rural community resettled twenty-two refugees, got them homes and jobs, taught them English. They were Laotians and they were welcomed in this rural, all-white Kansas town."[11]

9. McKenzie, *Hear and Be Wise,* 171.

10. Ibid.

11. Ibid., *Hear and Be Wise,* 172–73.

The activation of the subversive voice moves us into a new gear, shifting us from bystander to upstander. The word *upstander*, coined by diplomat Samantha Power, was popularized in the curriculum of the "Facing History and Ourselves Movement," a non-profit organization in the United States, founded in 1976. The group develops educational material on prejudices and injustice in American and European society, with a focus on Nazi Germany and the Holocaust. Two New Jersey high school students now in college from the program, Sarah Decker and Monica Mahal, were working on an anti-bullying project. They noticed that the word *upstander* was not to be found in *The Oxford English Dictionary*. Annoyed that two newly added words were *twerk* and *selfie*, the students went on a mission to get *upstander* into the mix. They felt it sent a bad message that the word *bystander* was in the dictionary, but *upstander* was not. After circulating a petition, in September 2016 they achieved their goal. *Upstander* is now an official entry in *The Oxford English Dictionary*.

An upstander is an individual who sees wrong and acts. Anyone can become an upstander. Anti-bullying programs advocate that people engage in "positive bystander intervention." Upstanders don't feel this is strong enough language to describe someone who takes a stand against an act of injustice or intolerance. That person is not a "positive bystander," they are an upstander. Advocates of the word and the concept believe the word itself has the ability to empower students to make an active change in their schools, in an effort to build communities that support difference and unify against intolerance.

In every era there have been those who spoke boldly in opposition to unjust systems. Martin Luther, in opposing the abuses of the established church, is reported to have said, "Here I stand, I can do no other." Martin Luther King Jr., opposing the abuses of racism in the US, wrote from a Birmingham jail cell, "Injustice anywhere is a threat to justice everywhere." Susan B. Anthony, advocating for women's right to vote, famously said "Men, their rights, and nothing more; women, their rights, and nothing less." Archbishop Oscar Romero spoke out against poverty, social injustice, assassinations and torture in El Salvador, activating his subversive voice, encouraging others to do the same. "Each one of you needs to be God's microphones." He paid the price with his life, murdered while saying mass in March of 1980.[12] All these faithful people exercised their subversive voices on behalf of the silenced in their times and places. But they went a step further and took action.

---

12. Clarke, *Oscar Romero*.

Whole books are filled with examples of subversive sages, those who have spoken out for the rights of those who face discrimination for their sexual orientation, religion, disability, gender, race, and/or age. I encourage readers of this book, as part of your exercise of your subversive voice, to heighten your attentiveness to examples of this virtue in history and contemporary life. Be encouraged and energized by their stories in your own witness, and share them with others. The examples I've chosen may seem bigger than life, but they are composed of small, daily decisions to cultivate faith, compassion, and disciplined determination on behalf of God's kingdom of justice and mercy for all.

In every time of history, speaking out is a matter of life and death, both for the subversive sage and for those on whose behalf he/she speaks. I've chosen two examples of the subversive voice from the era of Nazi Germany that illustrate the power of a community's voice as well as that of a few impassioned individuals.

From December 1940 to September 1944, the inhabitants of the French village of Le Chambon-sur-Lignon (population 5,000) in south central France and the villages on the surrounding plateau (population 24,000) provided refuge for an estimated 5,000 people. This number included an estimated 3,000–3,500 Jews who were fleeing from the Vichy authorities and the Germans.

Led by Pastor André Trocmé of the Reformed Church of France, his wife Magda, and his assistant, Pastor Edouard Theis, the residents of these villages offered shelter in private homes, in hotels, on farms, and in schools. They forged identification and ration cards for the refugees, and in some cases guided them across the border to neutral Switzerland.

The people of the village of Le Chambon were nurtured by their subversive sage, Pastor André Trocmé. He was sent to their remote town in south central France where the church thought his pacifist leanings would cause the least trouble. In his preaching he spoke out against discrimination as the Nazis were gaining power in neighboring Germany and urged his Protestant Hugenot congregation to hide Jewish refugees from the Holocaust. He urged them to do the will of God, not the will of men.[13]

In the words of Elizabeth Koenig-Kaufman, a former child refugee in Le Chambon,

> Nobody asked who was Jewish and who was not. Nobody asked where you were from. Nobody asked who your father was or if you could pay. They just accepted each of us, taking us in with

13. Haille, *Lest Innocent Blood Be Shed,* xiii–xxi.

warmth, sheltering children, often without their parents—children who cried in the night from nightmares. [14]

Three young German students, siblings Sophie and Hans Scholl and their friend Christoph Probst, were key leaders in what they called the White Rose, a student resistance movement in Munich in Nazi Germany. Raised by their parents to boldly stand up for their beliefs, and influenced by Catholic social teachings, they were horrified by what they had learned of Hitler's crimes in Russia, the mass shootings of Jews and the burning of villages. With the help of professors and volunteers, they published pamphlets and distributed them to motivate others to join their opposition efforts.

On a winter day in 1943 they threw stacks of pamphlets into the stairwell at Munich's Ludwig Maximillian University. A janitor at the university reported them to the Gestapo, the Hitler's secret police.

Twenty-four hours later, they were under arrest and, within days Sophie Scholl, her brother Hans, and their friend Christoph Probst were all beheaded for treason.

In the People's Court before the notorious Judge Roland Freisler on February 21, 1943, Scholl was recorded as saying "Somebody, after all, had to make a start. What we wrote and said is also believed by many others. They just do not dare express themselves as we did."[15]

Else Gebel shared Sophie Scholl's cell and recorded her last words before being taken away to be executed. "It is such a splendid sunny day, and I have to go . . . . What does my death matter if by our acts thousands are warned and alerted?"[16]

Prison officials emphasized the courage with which she walked to her execution. Her last words were *"Die Sonne scheint noch"*—"The sun still shines." Her brother Hans, just before the blade fell, cried out *"Es lebe die Freiheit!"*—"Long live freedom![17]

What would motivate three young students to such bravery? The clue lies in the final words of their fourth pamphlet. "We are your bad conscience. We will not be silent. The White Rose will not leave you in peace!"[18]

---

14. *The Holocaust Encyclopedia*, https://www.ushmm.org/wlc/en/article.php?ModuleId=10007518.

15. Sophie Scholl revolt & resistance, www.HolocaustResearchProject.org.

16. Burns, "Sophie Scholl and the White Rose," http://www.raoulwallenberg.net/holocaust/articles-20/sophie-scholl-white-rose/.

17. The Holocaust Education and Archive Research Team, "Sophie Scholl," http://www.holocaustresearchproject.org/revolt/scholl.html.

18. White Rose Leaflets, www.holocaustresearchproject.org/revolt/wrleaflets.html.

The movie *The Help,* based on the novel by Kathryn Stockett, is the story of Skeeter, played by actress Emma Stone, a white socialite who returns home to Jackson, Mississippi in 1962. Inspired by the injustices done to two women she admires, Minny and Abileen, black maids in the homes of her white friends, Skeeter records their story in their words about what it was really like to work as a black maid in the white homes of the South. Her mother, played by actress Allison Janney, shows tight-lipped disapproval for Skeeter's unconventional interests and disinterest in attracting a husband. In one poignant scene, she finally realizes the importance of the work her daughter is doing and says to her, sadly, yet proudly, "Courage sometimes skips a generation. Thank you for bringing it back to our family."

Sometimes courage does skip a generation, but it doesn't have to skip mine or yours, or those of our children and grandchildren. Not when we allow our subversive voice to be activated by the cultivation of its three collaborator virtues: the awestruck attitude, the listening heart, and the cool spirit.

Meditation on Activating the Subversive Voice

"A Different Drummer"

Psalm 1
Job 28:12–28
Matthew 5:38–48

Almost everybody I've ever talked to about their call to discipleship at one point in the story says, "Why me? Why would God choose me?" God's answer is the same he gave to Solomon "No one like you has ever been before, and no one like you will ever arise again."

There is a lot that's unique about you—but our present focus is on on just one thing: your subversive voice. That is, your willingness to speak an unpopular, often unconventional word. The subversive voice is the fourth pillar of the wise character.

Jesus' words were seen as presumptuous. Many resented them. So today, when we speak our conscience, dare to subvert prevailing views, we will be criticized. It takes courage to raise your voice.

But if you fear the Lord and listen with your heart, you'll start saying "Now wait a minute! What is wrong with this picture?" Not everyone will agree with your position or applaud you for your conscience. But you will be able to say, "I let my voice be heard."

A pastor in North Texas was invited to participate in a funeral of a young man who had been killed in a one-car accident while driving just a little too fast on a rain slick back road one night. The young man was just twenty-four years old. His young wife had grown up in my friend's church. The young man had been a member of the Baptist church in town. At the funeral, the Baptist preacher got up and said, "Friends, we don't know why, but it was John's time. God needed John in heaven, and who are we to question the Lord Almighty? John is in a better place and we thank God for that."

My friend got up to speak. "I know that some people find comfort in a notion of God needing people in heaven and taking them as members of the heavenly choir or flowers in a heavenly bouquet, but I have to tell you, friends, I don't find that vision of God very comforting. I believe John died in a tragic accident on a wet country road. I believe God welcomes him in love, but that God grieves with you and me today."

He was surprised by how many members of both churches thanked him around town that week with words like "I was so glad to hear a minister say that. I've never believed God doled out tragedies like that. Thank you!"

A Bolivian pastor now serving a small Hispanic Methodist congregation in South Texas made this comment:

> My people's lives are filled with the reality of suffering, and they interpret suffering as God's punishment. I need to preach that it is not a punishment. Poor, marginal people in a Spanish setting believe that suffering is predetermined and deserved. "I am not good enough to please God," they say. Suffering is our own fault. I must challenge this false belief.

Tony Freeman is the pastor of a Metropolitan Christian Church in San Diego. The MCC is a church that welcomes gay, lesbian, transgender, and bisexual individuals to its worship and ministry. Pastor Freeman is clear that his congregation has a ministry to the community, not just itself. In a downscale section of town, the church serves soup, provides clothes for, prays for, and tutors children at the Homeless High School.

He heard that a United Methodist Church nearby was holding a seminar to help gays and lesbians transform themselves and take up heterosexual lifestyles. He had lunch with the pastor and told him he planned to be there on the premises in his clerical collar, when people arrived, as a peaceful witness. "I have to be there. My conscience won't let me stay away." So when participants arrived, he and five other local gay clergy were there, standing silently, prayerfully, in clergy garb, near the entrance.

In 1993 my dad ran for the State Senate in Pennsylvania where I grew up. He was a Democrat running in a heavily Republican district against a familiar incumbent. My husband and I attended a kickoff dinner for the campaign. My husband had an interesting conversation with a young woman who turned out to be my dad's campaign director. Not knowing Murry was a family member, she confided in him: "The candidate is well-meaning, but naïve. He refuses to do negative campaigning and he refuses to kowtow. He actually thinks it's all about the issues. He'll never win that way!" Sure enough, he didn't! I guess she was right.

Don't feel too bad, Dad. Jesus was not a very good politician either. "Good" politicians placate those who have power over them, from whom they want favors. They speak harshly to underlings, those who can't do anything for them. Somehow, Jesus got this whole principle backwards.

Jesus spoke his mind, often harshly, but not impulsively. His words strike me as quite strategic. The product of prior profound prayer and keen thought.

Sooner or later everyone who answers God's call to discipleship asks the question, "Why did God call me?" I believe our righteous anger and our spirit of lament is a big part of the reason God has called us into service. Every calling comes with a temptation. Ours is a lifelong temptation to become status quo preservers rather than subversive witnesses to God's good news in Jesus Christ in and for the world.

A young preaching student of mine called me the Saturday morning before Easter. "Dr. McKenzie, " he began, "I hate to bother you at home, but I did something really strange at the church where I'm interning, and I have to talk to somebody about it!" I sat down and said, "All right, David, what did you do?" He said, "I did something I've been fantasizing about for years!" And he told me his story.

"I was assigned to play Pontius Pilate in the reenactment of the passion. Everything was going along fine, I hadn't blown any of my lines, but when we go to the part where I was supposed to give Jesus over to be crucified, as the members of the Searchers parenting class who were playing the part of the crowd were chanting, 'Crucify him! Crucify him!' I heard myself yelling 'No! Not this year! Everybody, be quiet! Settle down. Sit down. You heard me.'

"Martha, the director, sitting on the front row, glared at me and started chewing through her bottom lip. The rabid crowd obediently sat down and arranged their itchy burlap robes over their knees, looking at each other as if I had completely lost it this time.

"The other intern, Rick, who was playing Jesus, who had, up until now, been a good friend of mine, was looking at me as if he intended to do me serious harm later, and he was asking me with his eyes: 'Where are we going with this?'

"'Now,' I said to the congregation, putting my arm around Jesus' shoulders, 'You obviously haven't been listening to this man closely enough or you would know that he is good and that his teachings bring life. I don't know what has kept you from listening, but I'm going to give you one more chance. I gestured to Jesus. 'Speak, good teacher, of the way of truth and this time we will listen.'

"I moved to sit down. Jesus, grabbed my burlap sleeve tightly, 'No, you tell us, Pontius Pilate, what is truth? Tell us, which of my teachings is most memorable to you?' Then he sat down, arms folded across his chest, smiling expectantly.

"Martha, the director, had her head in her hands. The seventh-grade Sunday school boys were leaning forward with their elbows on their knees, actually listening. The congregation as a whole had stopped rattling their phlegm and their candy wrappers.

"I thought to myself, Well, I'd come this far, I delved into my memory bank and began to speak, 'You have heard it was said, an eye for an eye and a tooth for a tooth. But I say to you, if anyone strikes you on the right cheek, turn the other also; and if anyone wants to sue you and take your coat, give your cloak as well; and if anyone forces you to go one mile, go also the second mile. You have heard it said Love your neighbor and hate your enemy, but I say to you 'Love your enemies and pray for those who persecute you, so that you may be children of your Father in heaven.' Those who have ears to hear, let them hear!'

"After the service we were supposed to greet people at the back. I made a move to slip out, but I felt a small, vise-like hand, digging into my arm. 'Oh, no you don't!' Martha hissed. 'You're going to stand here and face the music with me!' She turned as the first person came through the line.

'Martha, terrific skit! You are so creative! It really made us listen up!'

'Martha, really great. Where do you get your ideas?'

'Martha, even my kids listened this year!'

"Finally the last person had gone through the line. Martha turned to me, her eyes narrowing: 'OK, David, lucky for you, you're off the hook this time. But promise me you'll never pull anything like this again!'

"'Oh, David,' I said to him over the phone, 'I hope you didn't make that promise. In fact, don't every make that promise, David!'"

Why would I give him that particular piece of advice? Because . . .

Because each of us, in all our uniqueness, has been called to serve God, upheld by the four pillars of wisdom: the bended knee, the listening heart, the cool spirit, and the subversive voice.

Because the words God spoke to Solomon centuries ago, God still speaks to each of us: "No one like you has been before you and no one like you shall arise after you" (1 Kgs 3:13).

Final Word

Some journeys end in the same place where they began. When we return to where we began, we are, not only older, but also wiser. I could think of no better ending for this journey than the place where it began. So let's take our places at the divine customer service desk. It is time to present our items for return. It's time to push the four items we would like to return across the counter toward God: self-sufficiency, self-absorption, self-indulgence, and self-protection. We watch God take them from us and slide across the counter toward us four life-restoring alternatives. They are the four virtues of the wise life: the fear of the Lord that is the beginning of wisdom (the awestruck attitude); the listening heart that fuels a lifetime of compassion; the cool spirit, which replaces unchecked appetites with disciplined determination; and the subversive voice, by which we move from the shadows as bystanders into the full light of day, as upstanders, unafraid to speak out and stand up for those who have been silenced.

And now it is time to walk out into a sunlit world, lighter, freer, relieved of a burden. It is time to walk the path of wisdom, which is paved with faith, compassion, discipline and moral courage.

It is time to follow the advice of the sages of Israel.

> Trust in the Lord with all your heart
> And do not rely on your own insights
> In all your ways acknowledge God
> And God will make straight your paths (Prov 3:5–6).

Questions for Reflection on The Subversive Voice

1. Which of the four virtues comes most easily to you? Which one is most challenging and why?

2. Who is someone, in contemporary life or history, whose subversive voice you admire and respect?

3. What, if anything, hinders you from exercising your subversive voice?

4. Can you think of a time when you have kept silent and wished you had spoken?

5. Can you think of a time when you have spoken up and paid for it?

6. Can you think of a time when you have spoken up and been glad that you did?

7. Is there a topic on which you would like to be more vocal/active?

Bibliography

Allison, Dale C. *The Sermon on the Mount: Inspiring the Moral Imagination.* New York: Crossroad, 1999.

Armstrong, Karen. *The History of God: The 4,000-Year Quest of Judaism, Christianity and Islam.* New York: Ballantine, 1993.

Bader-Saye, Scott. *Following Jesus in a Culture of Fear.* Grand Rapids: Brazos, 2007.

Baker, Jo. *Longbourn.* London: Black Swan, 2014.

Beardslee, William. "Uses of the Proverb in the Synoptic Gospels." *Interpretation* 24 (1970) 61–73.

Bland, Dave. *Proverbs and the Formation of Character.* Eugene, OR: Cascade, 2015.

Beasley-Topliffe, Keith, ed. *The Dictionary of Christian Spiritual Formation.* Nashville: Upper Room, 2003.

Bergant, Dianne. *Israel's Wisdom Literature: A Liberation Critical Reading.* Minneapolis: Fortress, 2000.

Bishop, Harold. "Misleading 'Sprinkle, Eat, and Lose Weight' Claims Result in $26M Refund." http://health.wolterskluerlb.com/2014/12/misleading-sprinkle-eat-and-lose-weight-claims-result-in-26m-refund/.

Blekinsopp, Joseph. *Sage, Priest, Prophet: Religious and Intellectual Leadership in Ancient Israel.* Louisville: Westminster John Knox, 1995.

Bonino, José Miguez, ed. *Faces of Jesus in Latin American Christologies.* Maryknoll, NY: Orbis, 1984.

Brown, William P. *Character in Crisis: A Fresh Approach to the Wisdom Literature of the Old Testament.* Grand Rapids: Eerdmans, 1996.

Brussat, Frederic, and Mary Ann Brussat. *Spiritual Literacy: Reading the Sacred in Everyday Life.* New York: Charles Scribner's Sons, 1996.

Burns, Margie. "Sophie Scholl and the White Rose." http://www.raoulwallenberg.net/holocaust/articles-20/sophie-scholl-white-rose/.

Buttrick, David. *Speaking Parables: A Homiletic Guide.* Louisville: Westminster John Knox, 2000.

Camp, Claudia V. *Wisdom and the Feminine in the Book of Proverbs.* Decatur, GA: Almond, 1985.

Carlston, Charles E. "Proverbs, Maxims, and the Historical Jesus." *Journal of Biblical Literature* 99 (March 1980) 667–70.

Cartwright, Peter. *The Autobiography of Peter Cartwright.* Nashville: Abingdon, 1984.

Chilcote, Paul. *John Wesley and the Women Preachers of Early Methodism.* London: Scarecrow, 1991.

Clarke, Kevin. *Oscar Romero: Love Must Win Out*. Collegeville, MN: Liturgical, 2014.

Clifford, Richard J. *The Wisdom Literature, The Interpreting Biblical Texts Series*. Nashville: Abingdon, 2011.

Collins, John. "Proverbial Wisdom and the Yahwist Vision." *Semeia* 40 (1980) 1–17.

Crenshaw, James Lee. *Old Testament Wisdom: An Introduction*. Louisville: Westminster John Knox, 2010.

Crossan, John Dominic. *Cliffs of Fall: Paradox and Polyvalence in the Parables of Jesus*. New York: Seabury, 1980.

————. *In Parables: The Challenge of the Historical Jesus*. New York: Harper and Row, 1973.

Davis, Ellen E. *Proverbs, Ecclesiastes, and the Song of Songs*. Louisville: Westminster John Knox, 2000.

De Graaf, John, David Wann, and Thomas Naylor. *Affluenza: The All-Consuming Epidemic*. San Francisco: Berrett-Koehler, 2005.

Dodd, C. H. *The Parables of the Kingdom*. 2d rev. ed. New York: Charles Scribner's Sons, 1961.

Donahue, John R. *The Gospel in Parable: Metaphor, Narrative, and Theology in the Synoptic Gospels*. Philadelphia: Fortress, 1988.

Doyle, Arthur Conan. *The Hound of the Baskervilles*. In *The Complete Illustrated Sherlock Holmes*, 486–525. New York: Barnes and Noble, 1990.

Drury, John. *The Parables in the Gospels: History and Allegory*. New York: Crossroad, 1985.

Dundes, Alan. "Folk Ideas as Units of Worldview." In *Essays in Folkloristics*, 93–103. Kailash Puri Meerut: Ved Prakash Vatuk, 1978.

Dyer, Wayne W. *Wisdom of the Ages: 60 Days to Enlightenment*. New York: HarperCollins, 1998.

Eaton, John. *The Contemplative Face of Old Testament Wisdom in the Context of World Religions*. Philadelphia: Trinity, 1989.

CBS. *Face the Nation*. August 14, 2016, hosted by John Dickerson.

Farmer, Kathleen. "The Wisdom Books: Job, Proverbs, Ecclesiastes." In *The Hebrew Bible Today: An Introduction to Critical Issues*, edited by Steven L. McKenzie and M. Patrick Graham, 129–53. Philadelphia: Westminster John Knox, 1998.

Fox, Michael V. *Qohelet and His Contradictions*. Sheffield: Almond, 1989.

Gaustad, Edwin S., ed. *Memoirs of the Spirit: American Religious Autobiography from Jonathan Edwards to Maya Angelou*. Grand Rapids: Eerdmans, 1999.

Gibran, Kahlil. *The Prophet*. New York: Alfred A. Knopf, 2014.

Goldin, Judah. *The Living Talmud: "The Wisdom of the Fathers" and Its Classical Commentaries*. New York: New American Library, 1979.

Gottlieb, Claire. "The Words of the Exceedingly Wise: Proverbs 30–31." In *The Biblical Canon in Comparative Perspective: Scripture in Context IV*, edited by K. Lawson Younger Jr., William W. Hallo, and Bernard F. Batto, 277–98. Lewiston: Edwin Mellen, 1991.

Gutierrez, Gustavo. *On Job: God-Talk and the Suffering of the Innocent*. Maryknoll, NY: Orbis, 1987.

Haille, Philip P. *Lest Innocent Blood Be Shed: The Story of Le Chambon and How Goodness Happened There*. New York: Harper and Row, 1994.

Herzog, William R. *The Parables as Subversive Speech: Jesus as Pedagogue of the Oppressed*. Louisville: Westminster John Knox, 1994.

"History of the Hall." Carnegiehall.org. https://www.carnegiehall.org/History/History-FAQ.

Holmer, Paul. *Making Christian Sense*. Philadelphia: Westminster, 1984.

The Holocaust Education and Archive Research Team. "Sophie Scholl." http://www.holocaustresearchproject.org/revolt/scholl.html.

The Holocaust Encyclopedia. https://www.ushmm.org/wlc/en/article.php?ModuleId=10007518.

Isasi-Diaz, Ada Maria. "Apuntes for a Hispanic Women's Theology of Liberation." In *Voces: Voices from the Hispanic Church,* edited by Justo L. Gonzalez, 24–31. Nashville: Abingdon, 1992.

Jarboe, Betty M. *Wesley Quotations: excerpts from the writings of John Wesley and other family members*. Metuchen, NJ: Scarecrow, 1990.

Johnston, Robert M., and Harvey K. McArthur. *They Also Taught in Parables: Rabbinic Parables from the First Centuries of the Christian Era*. Eugene, OR: Wipf and Stock, 2014.

Josephson, Michael. *Making Ethical Decisions: The Basic Primer on Using the Six Pillars of Character to Make Better Decisions and a Better Life*. Marina Del Rey, CA: Josephson Institute of Ethics, 2002.

Lang, Bernhard. *Wisdom and the Book of Proverbs: An Israelite Goddess Redefined*. New York: Pilgrim, 1986.

Lenski, Gerhard. *Power and Privilege*. New York: McGraw Hill, 1966.

Lewis, C. S. *The Lion, the Witch and the Wardrobe*. New York: HarperCollins, 2008.

MacArthur, Harvey K., and Robert M. Johnston. *They Also Taught in Parables: Rabbinic Parables from the First Centuries of the Christian Era*. Grand Rapids: Academie, 1991.

Manser, Martin H. *The Westminster Collection of Christian Quotations*. Louisville: Westminster John Knox, 2001.

Mathewes-Green, Gregory, and Frederica Mathewes-Green. "Impact Pray-ers: Five Men Who Still Define Orthodox Spirituality." *Christian History* 54.2 (1997) 28.

McCreesh, Thomas P. "Wisdom as Wife: Proverbs 31:10–31." *Revue Biblique* (1985) 25–46.

McKenzie, Alyce M. "The Appeal of Wisdom," A Lectionary Study of texts from Song of Solomon and Proverbs. *Quarterly Review,* September 24 (2000) 216–23.

————. *Hear and Be Wise: Becoming a Teacher and Preacher of Wisdom*. Nashville: Abingdon, 2004.

————. *Novel Preaching: Tips from Top Writers on Crafting Creative Sermons*. Louisville: Westminster John Knox, 2010.

————. *Preaching Biblical Wisdom in a Self-Help Society*. Nashville: Abingdon, 2002.

————. *Preaching Proverbs: Wisdom for the Pulpit*. Philadelphia: Westminster John Knox, 1996.

McMeel, Andrews. *Keep Calm and Carry On*. Kansas City, MO: Andrews McMeel, 2009.

Meier, John. *A Marginal Jew: Rethinking the Historical Jesus,* vols. 1 and 2. New York: Doubleday, 1994.

Melchert, Charles F. *Wise Teaching: Biblical Wisdom and Educational Ministry*. Harrisburg, PA: Trinity, 1998.

Moberly, R. W. L. "Solomon and Job: Divine Wisdom in Human Life." In *Where Shall Wisdom Be Found? Wisdom in the Bible, the Church and the Contemporary World*, edited by Stephen C. Barton, 3–17. Edinburgh: T & T Clark, 1999.

Muehl, William. *All the Damned Angels*. Philadelphia: Fortress, 1971.

Murphy, Roland E. *The Tree of Life: An Exploration of Biblical Wisdom Literature*. New York: Doubleday, 1990.

_____. "Wisdom Theses." In *Wisdom and Knowledge*, edited by John Armenti, 191–220. Villanova, PA: Villanova University Press, 1976.

Nouwen, Henri J. M. *In the Name of Jesus: Reflections on Christian Leadership*. New York: Crossroad, 1996.

Oesterley, W. O. E. *The Book of Proverbs*. London: Methuen, 1929.

Oestreicher, Amy. "What's a Detourist?" https://www.amyoes.com/whats-a-detourist/.

Patterson, Stephen J. *The God of Jesus: The Historical Jesus and the Search for Meaning*. Harrisburg, PA: Trinity, 1998.

Pemberton, Glenn D. "It's a Fool's Life: The Deformation of Character in Proverbs." *Restoration Quarterly*, 50.4 (2008) 213–24.

Perdue, Leo G. "Wisdom in the Book of Job." In *In Search of Wisdom: Essays in Memory of John G. Gammie*, edited by Leo G. Perdue, Bernard Brandon Scott, and William Johnson Wiseman, 73–98. Louisville: Westminster John Knox, 1993.

_____. "The Wisdom Sayings of Jesus." *Forum* 2 (1986) 3–35.

Perkins, Pheme. *Jesus as Teacher*. New York: Cambridge University Press, 1990.

Pleins, J. David. *The Social Visions of the Hebrew Bible: A Theological Introduction*. Louisville: Westminster John Knox, 2000.

Quast, Kevin. *Reading the Corinthian Correspondence: An Introduction*. New York: Paulist, 1994.

Rad, Gerhard von. *Wisdom in Israel*. Nashville: Abingdon, 1972.

A Reader's Hebrew–English Lexicon of the Old Testament. Grand Rapids: Zondervan, 1989.

Scholl, Inge. *The White Rose: Munich 1942–43*. Hanover, NH: Wesleyan University Press, 1983.

Shapiro, Rami M. *Wisdom of the Jewish Sages: A Modern Reading of Pirke Avot*. New York: Bell Tower, 1993.

Sinnott, Alice M. "Job: Cosmic Devastation and Social Turmoil." In *The Earth Story in Wisdom Traditions*, The Earth Bible, vol. 3, edited by Norman C. Habel and Shirley Wurst, 78–91. Cleveland: Pilgrim, 2001.

Smith, Huston. *The Illustrated World's Religions: A Guide to Our Wisdom Traditions*. New York: HarperOne, 1995.

Soelle, Dorothee. *The Silent Cry: Mysticism and Resistance*. Minneapolis: Augsburg Fortress, 2001.

Stookey, Laurence Hull. *Baptism, Christ's Act in Church*. Nashville: Abingdon, 1986.

Taft, Zechariah. *Biographical Sketches of the Lives and Public Ministry of Various Holy Women, Whose Eminent Usefulness and Successful Labours in the Church of Christ, Have Entitled Them to be Enrolled Among the Great Benefactors of Mankind*. vol. 1. London: Published for the author, and sold in London by Mr. Kershaw, 1825.

Tannehill, Robert C. *The Sword of His Mouth: Forceful and Imaginative Language in Synoptic Sayings*. Philadelphia: Fortress, 1975.

Thompson, Marjorie. *Soul Feast: An Invitation to the Christian Spiritual Life*. Louisville, Kentucky: Westminster John Knox, 1995.

Taylor, Barbara Brown. *The Preaching Life.* Boston: Cowley, 1993.

Thurman, Howard. *Deep is the Hunger: Meditations for Apostles of Sensitiveness* Richmond, Indiana: Friends United, 1990.

Toombs, Lawrence E. "The Theology and Ethics of the Book of Proverbs." *Consensus* 14 (1988) 2:7–24.

Trimble, Joseph, and Celia B. Fisher, eds. *The Handbook of Ethical Research with Ethnocultural Populations and Communities.* Thousand Oaks, CA: Sage, 2006.

Troeger, Thomas H. *Creating Fresh Images for Preaching: New Rungs for Jacob's Ladder.* Valley Forge, PA: Judson, 1982.

Vance, J.D. *Hillbilly Elegy: A Memoir of a Family and Culture in Crisis.* New York: HarperCollins, 2016.

Wall, Steve, and Harvey Arden. *Wisdomkeepers: Meetings with Native American Spiritual Elders.* Hillsboro, OR: Beyond Words, 1990.

Wesley, John. *Sermons on Several Occasions.* London: Forgotten, 2015.

_____. *The Works of John Wesley Volume XIII: Letters and Writings.* The Ages Digital Library Collections, 29.

Weiderkehr, Macrina. *A Tree Full of Angels: Seeing the Holy in the Ordinary.* San Francisco: HarperSanFrancisco, 1990.

Williams, James G. "Paraenesis, Excess, and Ethics: Matthew's Rhetoric in the Sermon on the Mount." *Semeia* 50 (1990) 163–87.

_____. *Those Who Ponder Proverbs: Aphoristic Thinking and Biblical Literature.* Sheffield: Almond, 1981.